About Island Press

Island Press, a nonprofit organization, publishes, markets, and distributes the most advanced thinking on the conservation of our natural resources—books about soil, land, water, forests, wildlife, and hazardous and toxic wastes. These books are practical tools used by public officials, business and industry leaders, natural-resource managers, and concerned citizens working to solve both local and global resource problems.

Founded in 1978, Island Press reorganized in 1984 to meet the increasing demand for substantive books on all resource-related issues. Island Press publishes and distributes under its own imprint and offers these services to other nonprofit organizations.

Support for Island Press is provided by the Geraldine R. Dodge Foundation, the Energy Foundation, the Charles Engelhard Foundation, the Ford Foundation, the Glen Eagles Foundation, the George Gund Foundation, the William and Flora Hewlett Foundation, the John D. and Catherine T. MacArthur Foundation, the Andrew W. Mellon Foundation, the Joyce Mertz-Gilmore Foundation, the New-Land Foundation, the J. N. Pew, Jr., Charitable Trust, Alida Rockefeller, the Rockefeller Brothers Fund, the Rockefeller Foundation, the Tides Foundation, and individual donors.

For the Wild Places

For the Wild Places: Profiles in Conservation

Janet Trowbridge Bohlen

Foreword by Al Gore

ISLAND PRESS
Washington, D.C. · Covelo, California

Library of Congress Cataloging-in-Publication Data

Bohlen, Janet Trowbridge.

For the wild places : profiles in conservation / Janet Trowbridge Bohlen : foreword by Albert Gore, Jr.

p. cm.

Includes bibliographical references and index.

ISBN 1-55963-125-2 (acid-free paper).

1. Conservationists—Biography. 2. Biological diversity conservation. 3. Habitat conservation. 4. Endangered species.

I. Title.

QH26.B63 1993

333.95'16'0922—dc20

[B] 92-38118

CIP

Printed on recycled, acid-free paper

Manufactured in the United States of America

10 9 8 7 6 5 4 3 2 1

To our first grandchild,

Turner Kolbe Bohlen,

whose future it is

But those with the opportunity and
vision to make a difference are rare.
Their appearance, no matter how brief,
is a gift we must appreciate, for they
give us reason to hope.

Alston Chase
Playing God in Yellowstone

Contents

Foreword

As this extraordinary century closes, we are witnessing the stunning end of the political, economic, and military structures that have defined our view of the world since 1945. Now, nations around the globe boldly aspire to American-style democracy and a free market economy.

But even as we seek greater economic and political harmony among the countries of the world, we cannot ignore the fact that the natural systems which support life itself are groaning under the weight of more than 5 billion human beings striving to do all they can for their families. As populations grow and natural systems are degraded further, these stresses will mount.

It isn't hard to see where we're headed. We simply can't realize our aspirations for social and economic progress unless we also make great strides in our ability to manage and replenish the natural resources of the planet. To do so, we must harness the creative force and incredible power of science, technology, and private enterprise and draw upon the strengths that have made our nation the greatest source of technological progress the world has ever known.

For most of this century, American universities and research institutions have turned out the world's finest scientists and engineers. And by offering creative genius unparalleled opportunities to explore ideas and to realize dreams, America has become the adopted home of countless other researchers and technicians from every corner of the world. For the last half-century, much of that talent has been devoted to producing the weapons of war. Now it's time to invest this energy in the effort to increase economic prosperity while sustaining the environment.

By profiling five scientists and their inspirational stories from the front lines of environment and development challenges around the world, Janet Bohlen has spotlighted the types of efforts that, when multiplied many times over, will help us to forge a path toward sustainable development.

I hope in particular that this book is read by young people, and that it will help inspire them to learn how to use and manage *nature's* wealth creatively. I hope that it inspires them to stay in school and to stick with the science and math courses that will prepare them for the sophisticated world that lies ahead—a world in which possessing knowledge of technology and the natural environment is a moral responsibility, as well as a gateway to new careers and a source of personal satisfaction. In that way, they will become part of the solution to the environmental challenges that are shaping the world we inhabit, and the one they will inherit.

Al Gore

For the Wild Places

PROLOGUE

Genesis

Thirty years ago I stood on a hillside overlooking Murchison Falls in Uganda, East Africa, and experienced an indefinable rush, a starburst of self-awareness that led long afterward to the writing of this book. At the end of the rainy season the land was strikingly green, the sky brilliant and without a cloud. Beside the river trees grew tall, yet the understory was dense. We—my husband and I—were on a track made perhaps by animals seeking water, perhaps by humans, for humans had been a part of this landscape for thousands of years. Below us mist rose from beneath the crashing torrent of the falls. The turbulent current coiled away to relative tranquility a few hundred yards downstream. There ten or so hippopotamuses rose and fell in the wash, whooshing as they came up for air, opening their massive jaws to reveal pink piebald gullets. On a sandbar across the way ten- and twelve-foot crocodiles lay comatose. Occasionally one would raise its primeval head and slide sideways into the water. Baboons clambered along a cliff. Hunting herons and large storks stood poised in backwaters or immobile on fallen twisted tree trunks grayed by wind and water. We dropped down to the water's edge to examine tracks in the sand. Elephants, a large cat or two, and a number of ungulates—hooved animals—had visited this spot earlier in the day. Here in the gorge a wind blew. The roar of the falls drowned out all sound. The mist damped my hair.

I remember welcoming my own insignificance amid all this thunderous life, a sudden visceral response to my existence as a mere speck in an endless landscape that did not need me and would not miss me when I died. I felt a strange joy in the humility this thought evoked. Then, as we struggled up the steep trail back toward the lodge and lunch, the age-old thought occurred to me that of all life on earth, insofar as one could tell, only humans were ethical beings. Ours was the only species to consider the rightness or wrongness of its actions. It followed that we had some degree of responsibility toward the whole of life. If we cared at all for its continuance, we would have to treat it gently, nurture it, and share its bounty with future generations. What a tremendous burden! Would humans make the right choices? That our sheer numbers and political posturing affected world events went without saying. But could we as single individuals make a difference?

Uganda has since experienced war and devastation from which its wildlife and wild places have yet to recover, and I have not been back. But that brief exposure to its natural wonders changed the course of my professional life. Shortly after returning to the United States, I went to work for the African Wildlife Leadership Foundation (now known as the African Wildlife Foundation). My career in conservation had begun. After a short break to begin a family, I joined World Wildlife Fund–U.S. (WWF) as its communications director. I grew increasingly curious about the people I met there—young men and women for the most part, blue-jeaned and casual, just "in from the field" where they had been "doing science," the science of nature conservation. What made them tick? Why did they so enjoy the rigorous, sometimes dangerous life in the rain forest, on the tundra, in the mountains, at the edge of the sea or on it? Why did they stick to their work, underpaid, wet, hungry, often lonely, often ill? I hazard it was something more than a search for scientific truth.

I remember two in particular: one a blond biologist who camped out for months at a time on a remote Mexican beach, fighting for the life of every baby sea turtle hatched there, holding off *bandidos* who would otherwise steal turtle eggs for urban restaurants and kill adult turtles for their shells, the other a man with incurable river blindness, contracted when he spent two years inventorying biota to help delineate a future West African park boundary. Appearing suddenly in my urban asphalt world, usually just passing through, they were the Indiana Joneses, the unheralded frontline soldiers, of the conservation movement.

Was their training and their science and all their time and effort really making a difference? Would the end product be worth all their tenacity and sacrifice? As I sat behind my desk at WWF and wrote newsletters and fund-raising appeals and annual reports, these questions haunted me. I became disenchanted with my backseat role and longed, like the adventure-seeking Walter Mitty, to become engaged. This book is the next best thing.

Given present rates of rain forest and other habitat destruction around the world, latest estimates indicate that a quarter of the world's remaining species, more than two million, may be lost in the next thirty to fifty years.[1] According to Harvard's eminent biologist E. O. Wilson and others, "deforestation condemns at least one species of bird, mammal or plant to extinction daily," not counting invertebrates. "Time after time, creatures thought useless or harmful are found to play crucial roles in natural systems. Predators driven to extinction no longer keep populations of rodents or insects in check; earthworms or termites killed by pesticides no longer aerate soils; mangroves cut for firewood no longer protect coastlines from erosion. Diversity is of fundamental importance to all ecosystems and all economies."[2]

In response to this biological cataclysm, concerned scientists have developed a new strategy they call conservation biology, in part to describe what the men and women who visited my office in the 1970s and early 1980s were already doing to stem this tide, in part to direct their own efforts. Strictly defined, conservation biology is research ultimately directed toward solving the swift erosion of biological diversity.

What, then, is biological diversity, or biodiversity as it is sometimes called? A common definition holds that it is the entire array of animal and plant life that makes up the complicated, interactive communities of species within ecosystems. These can be rich in terms of numbers, or impoverished. Areas with the greatest concentration of different species are said to be high in biological diversity. Most conservation biologists argue these places—tropical forests, for example—are where they should concentrate their efforts. However, an area with fewer species more widely dispersed is not necessarily less valuable; many ecosystems with fewer species are as productive as many species-rich systems. Thus the continued well-being of a savannah or an arctic tundra may be as important in the long run for biodiversity as that of the Amazon rain forest. That is, these ecosystems have roles just as vitally important to maintaining nature's balance. Ecosystems are broad, overlapping geographic areas that are often given artificial boundaries by scientists: forests, lakes, deserts, plains, rivers, swamps, oceans. One ecological approach lumps various isolated but actually overlapping ecosystems under one umbrella—a watershed, for example, whose components are rainfall, hillside, lake, river, and ocean. This "landscape" thinking looks at the spatial patterns of land use by all users, not just humans, and at the distribution of developed and undeveloped patches and how they relate to one another over time.

Ecologists also measure biodiversity in terms of multiple habitat or ecosystem types. In fact, biodiversity can be observed at many levels—boxes within boxes, as one ecologist friend is wont to say. Thus genetics, species, communities of species, ecosystems, and landscapes are simply different measurable levels of community organization within which diversity is definable.

Why should we as humans care about biodiversity? Setting aside for a moment philosophical arguments about the intrinsic worth of species, that is, about species being valuable solely because they exist, we care because "ecosystems, species, and genes are the basic elements of life that support humanity and the biosphere, which supports all life. As species disappear, humanity loses critical food, medicines, and industrial products. . . . As genetic diversity erodes, our capacity to maintain and improve agricultural, forest and livestock productivity decreases, and we reduce our ability to adapt food production to future climate and environmental conditions."[3] And not to be overlooked are art, music, and poetry, important byproducts of biodiversity that enrich human cultures everywhere. Our worry about species loss is largely anthropocentric and pragmatic, although there is an increasing number of people who weigh the inherent right to existence of other species, even inanimate objects such as rocks. Wherever one stands in these debates, few would question that the quality of future human life depends on whether we can keep the soup of life simmering on the stove without letting it boil away.

Primarily because of increasing human activity, the global rate and scale of biological change today is unprecedented. The world's population hovers at the 5.3 billion mark, but it is destined to triple to 15 billion long before the end of the next century. What will this mean in terms of environmental destruction, human misery, and the gap between rich and poor societies? What will it mean for global peace and security?[4]

Peter Berle, president of the National Audubon Society, writes, "Today nature is defined by human activity. . . . We determine, not always consciously, what lives and what dies. Under these circumstances, how should we be defining nature? How should we define our relationship to it? What values should be brought to bear? How much of nature and what natural resources do we wish to leave for our children? Who decides, and how do they do it? How do we cope with the fact that our capacity to destroy is so much greater than our understanding that even the most reasoned course can produce unpredictable results? How can the beauty and sense of awe that nature inspires be preserved in an economic system that cannot price these values?"[5] In 1933 Aldo Leopold wrote, "The hope of the future lies not in curbing the influence of human occupancy—it is already too late for that—but in creating a better understanding of the extent of that influence and a new ethic for its governance."[6] When I came across these words a year or so ago, I knew I wanted to find out who out there is trying to meet his challenge. I decided to start at what I call the bottom of the conservation food chain, that is, where conservation action all begins, with science. Can good science help maintain biological diversity and ecological processes while mitigating the effects of modern human behavior?

Conservation biologists say their job is to provide "the intellectual and technological tools that will anticipate, prevent, minimize and/or repair ecological damage."[7] By this is meant damage to nature so profound that it alters the biological makeup of a location, an ecosystem, or a landscape too quickly for the natural processes of growth and change to continue unimpeded. To be a conservation biologist, then, is to play a role of great potential power and responsibility, for applied conservation biology almost inevitably leads to human management or manipulation of species and/or ecosystems. This is not a popular idea with those wildlife conservationists who believe a laissez-faire approach is best. I often wonder, Where does science stop and conservation begin? Is there always a hard line between the two, or is it sometimes blurred?

And so I begin this book, searching for answers to these endless questions. To satisfy my thirst for firsthand knowledge, I chose to go into the field myself, to seek out and profile five scientists with hands-on experience in conservation biology. I believed instinctively that the answers might lie in who they were, how they came to be scientists, and how they used their training to tackle conservation issues, but I had no proof. In all fields of human endeavor, certain achievers stand out. I have on file countless names of wildlife biologists and ecologists nominated by colleagues and friends. Tom Lovejoy, William Conway of the New York Zoological Society, and Michael Soulé, founder-president of the Society for Conservation Biology and now a professor at the University of California at Santa Cruz, were particularly helpful. I asked acquaintances for names of people working in different kinds of ecosystems, with different sets of problems, in different parts of the world. (Happily, only one turned me down, for an understandable reason: A *gringo* working in Latin America, he told me he did not wish to raise his head "above the canopy." He meant he was no better nor worse at his job than his native-born colleagues, and did not wish to be singled out.) I purposely did not choose well-known scientists, looking instead for the unsung whose work however does seem to be making a difference in conservation. If there are enough people like them out there with as large a capacity to dream and take risks as they, we will not be too late.

"There's so little wildlife in this business. It's all people," anthropologist Richard Leakey, head of the Kenya Wildlife Service, once told Jonah Western, one of the people I visit in this book. Indeed, this is where I start on my quest—with people, five individuals who have spent their lives looking at single species, communities of species, ecosystems, and broad landscapes, sometimes manipulating them to conserve wildlife and natural processes. These are their stories as told to me. I am no scientist; any errors in explanation are mine, not theirs, although I have done my best to avoid them. If scientists find some of the views expressed here controversial, so much the better; that is the stuff of democratic dialogue, and I would like to hear from them. And if by writing this I manage to nudge the ethic Aldo Leopold talked about into further circulation, it will have been worth the effort.

Special thanks to my five new friends, Pat Wright, Jonah Western, George Archibald, Luis Diego Gómez, and Rick Steiner, whose sharing of knowledge and devotion of valuable time to me have made this book possible. Thanks also to their many friends and associates who helped me gain further insight. Thanks to my editor, Barbara Dean at Island Press, who kept the faith and guided me out of many dark areas into light, and to our son, Curtis Bohlen, who helped me countless times with corrections and definitions, conveying many aspects of his own environmental wisdom as he did so. Last but not least, I am grateful to my husband, Curtis "Buff" Bohlen, who has lived through it all, including the long absences, and to our daughters Nina and Julie, who are always there.

CHAPTER 1

Patricia Chapple Wright: The Creation of a Park

BLOOD AND FIRE

My Air France jumbo jet settles slowly through intermittent, wind-strewn clouds to land at Antananarivo, Madagascar's capital. Below, the Betsiboka River flows blood-red in the morning light, swollen by early autumn rains. It is April 1991, springtime in the northern hemisphere and the opposite season here. Hundreds of connected, terraced rice paddies gleam to the horizon. Scattered toylike villages that seem bucolic to the untutored eye are in fact the sites of extreme poverty. Most Malagasy—as the people of Madagascar call themselves—are subsistence farmers. Per capita income is under $225 a year.[1] As forests here are cleared for agriculture ochre-tinted soil erodes into waterways and cascades over granite cliffs. Once-white water is churned into a muddy froth. Near the coast soil-laden rivers coil past carefully diked rice paddies and thatched-roof villages before mixing with Indian Ocean currents and fanning out into ever-paling shades of pink.

Madagascar does not only bleed. It burns. More than 80 percent of its forests have disappeared since humans came to this minicontinent 1,500 years ago and began slash-and-burn farming, the process of clearing woods by fire and then planting crops. The productivity of Madagascar's soil is limited. After two years or so the farmer must abandon his plot to burn, clear, and plant another. The only alternative to replanting exhausted plots is to reinvade the forest. Some 579 to 1,158 square miles of forestland are set fire every year. With current population growth at more than 3 percent per year human numbers will more than double from 11.2 million today to 28 million by 2015, unless the birth rate can be slowed. The nation's continuing ability to provide fuel and food for its people will be sorely tried. Madagascar is already one of the ten poorest countries in the world.[2]

In the highlands, eroding slopes are etched by canyonlike depressions. Mudslides are common, roads pock-marked, detours a way of life. Everywhere terraced rice paddies step their way up mountainsides in inverted Vs, gradually occupying steeper inclines until a person can no longer stand upright to work the land. On the high plateau, as central Madagascar is called, almost no endemic or indigenous plants are left. They have been replaced by corn, coffee, rice, and bananas, eucalyptus, pine, and acacia trees. Here and there a few stands of native trees surround family burial tombs. The Malagasy believe ancestral spirits are at peace only in a forest.

Along Madagascar's east coast a kind of grass called *alang alang* has taken over. Unpalatable to livestock, *alang alang* is an exotic (nonnative) grass imported from Southeast Asia, perhaps with the first settlers. It can only be controlled by shade but there are few trees left to do the job. With deforestation comes not only erosion of the poor soil and *alang alang* but dehydration. Many once permanent streams now flow only seasonally. The people know the cause is forest loss but their options are few.

I am on my way to meet Patricia Chapple Wright, an associate professor of anthropology at Duke University (now in the department of anthropology at State University of New York at Stony Brook). Pat is a primatologist in her mid-forties whose discoveries in 1986 in

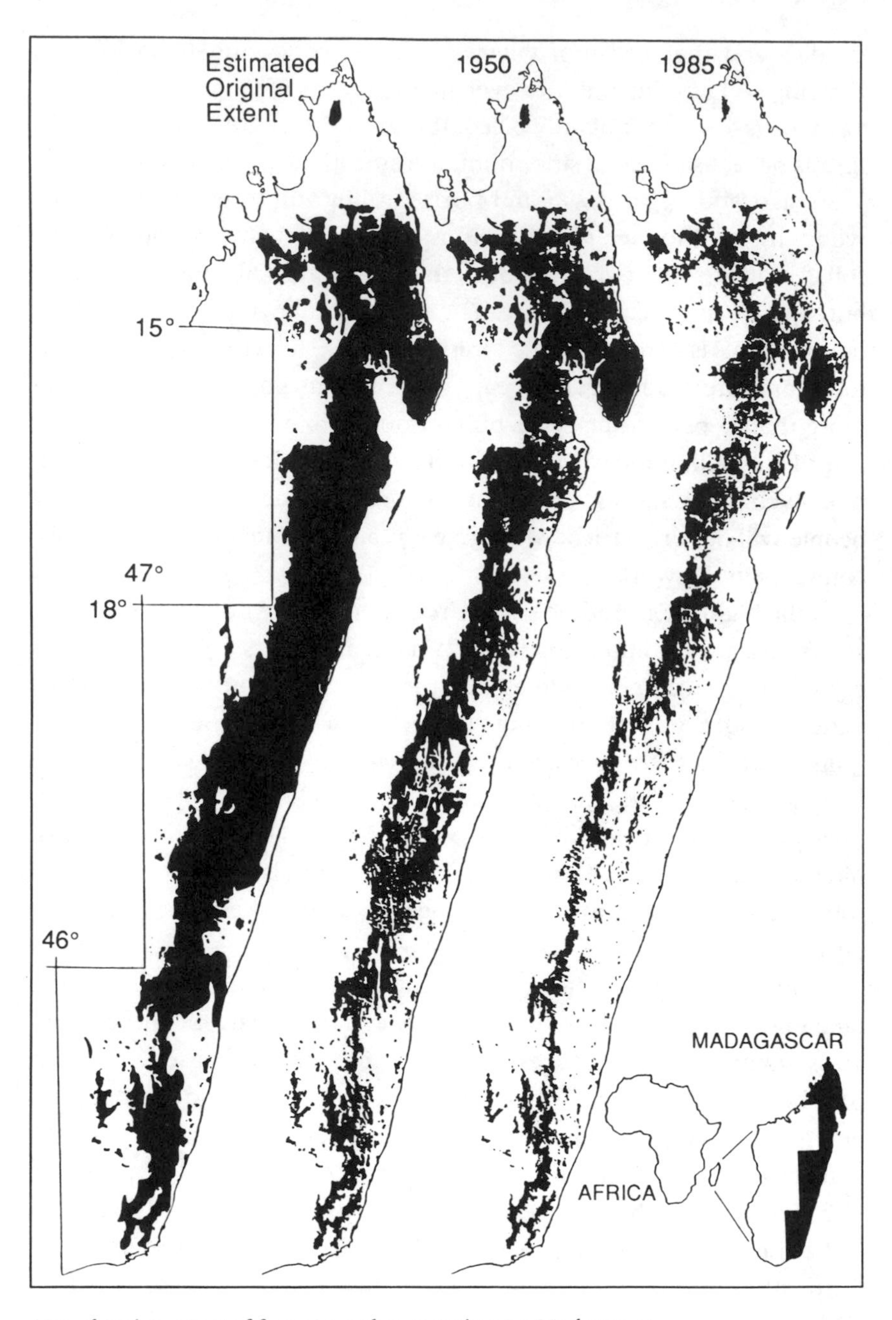

Map showing extent of forest-cover loss over time on Madagascar

(Map by Dr. Glen Martin Green, Center for Earth and Planetary Studies, Smithsonian Institution, Washington, D.C.)

Madagascar of an animal thought to be extinct and of another until-then not known to science catapulted her into the scientific equivalent of Hollywood notoriety. And into conservation work. In fact she is on this crowded flight, in another row, returning from a lecture tour of the United States. In the ensuing weeks I will follow her to Ranomafana, site of Madagascar's newest national park 250 miles southeast of Tana, as the capital is sometimes called.

"Pat is Ranomafana's mother," a Ministry of Water and Forests official, Ratsiriarson, tells me early the next morning when we meet by chance outside his office. "If that's so," Pat shoots back, "then you're its father." Ratsiriarson is one of a handful of people, Malagasy and Americans, who with Pat "walked the boundaries" for the new park four years ago. Walking boundaries is a euphemism for slogging through streams, and clawing up cliffs through tangled vines and bamboo thickets, for coping with rain and mud and leeches. Seven expeditions each lasting about a week were undertaken to identify where the park should be. Pat's initial motive was to protect the habitat of the extremely rare animals she had found there. "All we had were rough regional maps from 1960," Pat says. "We didn't have time to do thorough biology, but we tried to avoid villages. We didn't want to alienate the people."

The Water and Forests Ministry drew the final boundaries. The park is roughly 175 square miles. At elevations from 1,300 to 4,500 feet, the park ranges from lowland rain forest to cloud forest and high-plateau chaparral. In the one-third that has never been cut towering palms, giant ferns, bamboo, twisted vines, orchids, and mosses fill the slopes with an abundance of textures and gradients of green to thrill the latent artist in a visitor. The rest has been logged or planted at one time or another in the last fifty to one hundred years. Several small streams and one large river, the Namorona, tumble over boulders and cascade down cliffs in magnificent displays of clear white water.

Madagascar's government is firmly committed to the principle that nature conservation of any sort must be accompanied by economic and social benefits. Surrounding the park is a 580-square-mile buffer zone approximating a doughnut where human activity including reforestation, *tavy* (hillside farming), fish farming, and vegetable gardening will be continued, developed, or improved. There are over a hundred small communities within the zone ranging in size from ten to six hundred people. Most are reached only by footpaths, but the largest, Ranomafana (Hot Springs), is bisected by a paved if potholed highway. "Nowhere else in Madagascar can you drive *right through* a rain forest," Pat says. (Pat often speaks in italics, I will find.)

Park headquarters and a small nature museum have been opened in Ranomafana. The town boasts a huge but aging hot springs swimming pool set close beside the river. Nearby there are public baths and showers costing less than ten cents to use. Researchers who spend weeks in the forest bathing only in the river head for these baths promptly whenever they hit town. Most guests at the one European-style hotel in town, Station Thermale, use the pool in early morning before breakfasting on a wide veranda overlooking town.

"When you tell about how the park began," Pat says to me, "be sure to show I am only part of a much larger continuum. A lot else has been going on in Madagascar in conservation for a very long time. Many other people have been involved." Primatologists Russell Mittermeier and Elwyn Simons encouraged her from the start. She is also grateful to Patrick Daniels, a colleague who walked the park's boundaries and helped develop the early plans; graduate student Claire Kremen, now with the Xerxes Society; Duke University graduate Paul Ferraro, who helped write and rewrite a request for a grant from the U.S. Agency for International Development (AID); and Benjamin Adriamihaja, the national (Malagasy) coordinator for Ranomafana. All these people have certain traits in common. In the words of one researcher who has worked closely with Pat, they are all "can-do people and unflappable. Pat needs a practical other half while she pursues her dreams."

The most important person in Pat's life is her daughter, Amanda, eighteen when I meet her. Raised in rain forests from the age of three, tagging (or dragged) along to her mother's research sites, Amanda "is so at home in the forest she seems born of it," says a British graduate student who has worked in Ranomafana. Now she is spending her last year of high school in Madagascar and her time with Pat is limited.

Madagascar is the fourth largest island in the world, stretching some 1,000 miles north to south and 280 miles east to west. Separated from mainland Africa more than 150 million years ago by tectonic plate motion, it became wholly isolated about 40 million years ago when the Mozambique Channel became too wide for life forms to raft over on logs or other debris from the mainland. As a result of this "splendid isolation," most animals and plants on Madagascar are found nowhere else on earth.[3] Eighty percent of its eight to ten thousand plants and 90 percent of its reptiles and amphibians (mostly frogs) are unique, as are nearly all of its mammals and half of its birds. There are no poisonous snakes, although there are several varieties of boa constrictors whose cousins inhabit South America. There are more kinds of orchids and palm trees here than in all of Africa.[4] The rosy periwinkle, a highly endangered plant unique to Madagascar, is the source of a now-famous drug used to treat childhood leukemia. What other medicinal or industrial properties does the unusual plant and animal life of Madagascar hold? Knowledge of its incredible genetic diversity is still limited. The island is a researcher's paradise, its unique biota the primary focus of foreign conservation efforts.

All of Madagascar's thirty species of primates are lemurs, a name that derives from the Latin word for ghost. Lemurs, or prosimians, evolved before monkeys and apes. They range in size from the two-ounce mouse lemur to the twenty-pound indri. Today they face almost no predators save man and very little competition. Twenty-eight of the thirty known lemur species are endemic. Ten are considered endangered (in imminent danger of extinction) by the International Union for the Conservation of Nature (IUCN); fifteen others are listed as in trouble.[5] It was lemurs that brought Pat to Madagascar for the first time in 1984, lemurs that captured headlines and brought her fame.

An eighteenth-century visitor, Jean-Philbert Commerson, described Madagascar as "the naturalist's promised land," but is it still? As forests shrink extinction of the island's marvelous life forms accelerates. Since humans came to the island at least fourteen species of lemurs, all larger than those alive today, have disappeared. So has a ten-foot-tall elephant bird, a pygmy hippopotamus, and huge tortoises, to name only a few. Some were hunted to extinction while others simply disappeared, perhaps as a result of habitat loss. In response to this problem, in 1927 Madagascar created ten nature reserves for scientific study. There are now eleven of these, plus twenty-three special reserves protecting specific species and three national parks, including Ranomafana, where limited tourism is allowed and local villagers continue to exploit certain traditional products.

Scientists note that as Madagascar's forests become more isolated and smaller the continued decline of many species—both plant and animal—has to be assumed, although this assumption "is in part a measure of ignorance."[6] Meanwhile, Madagascar has been identified as one of seven countries in the world that together contain perhaps 50 to 60 percent of all known species. Among them, Madagascar has the greatest number of unique species in the greatest danger of imminent extinction. The word "megadiversity" has been coined to describe such wildlife *bouillabaisses*, where many conservationists believe they should focus their efforts.[7]

Why protect biological diversity at all? Pat's feeling, I glean over several days, is that irreparable ecological damage is occurring because humans now dominate the planet. Damage from desertification, siltation, and pollution, for example, endangers human health and quality of life and even threatens to alter climate. Large-scale extinctions are occurring, including unknown species which, like the rosy periwinkle, might provide a cure for cancer or for AIDS, humanity's most recent scourge. Protecting biological diversity is both a question "of insurance and investment . . . necessary to sustain and improve agricultural, forestry and fisheries production, to keep open future options, as a buffer against harmful environmental change, and as the raw material for much scientific and industrial innovation—and a matter of moral principle."[8]

How can Madagascar help its people prosper and at the same time protect its wondrous array of wildlife? Before the 1980s a collision between the needs of local people and the desires of (mostly foreign) wildlife conservationists to preserve relatively pristine areas appeared inevitable. Then in 1986 Russell Mittermeier, president of Conservation International, drafted a national conservation plan that called for surveys of natural areas, the establishment of central data banks, a biological inventory, the training of professionals, and the development of conservation awareness, tourism, and captive breeding of endangered species. The ambitious result is a fifteen-year national environmental action plan drawn up by the Malagasy government with help from the World Bank, World Wildlife Fund (WWF), and a number of other groups. The plan recognizes the interdependence of conservation and human survival and calls for the integration of conservation and development on a broad scale, with an emphasis on alleviating human poverty. For the first five years beginning in 1990 $140 million has been budgeted, to be obtained largely from outside sources: the World Bank, the European Community, AID, and other governmental and nongovernmental sources. The plan's rationale is that the protection of biological diversity, of remaining albeit fragmented forests and watersheds, benefits local people indirectly but must also benefit them directly, in social and economic terms. On Madagascar, conservation and human survival are inextricably linked in the minds of both local officialdom and foreign aid givers.

HERBY THE OWL MONKEY: PET OWNERSHIP TO PHD

"In one year I have gone from zero to thirty-six employees," says Pat as she dumps the contents of suitcases and duffel bags onto the floor of the airy house-cum-office she has just rented opposite Madagascar's national zoo in Tsimbazaza, a hillside section of Antananarivo. "Management has overtaken science in my life."

After three years of formal proposal writing and rewriting Pat received her AID money, a three-year, $3.3 million grant beginning in October 1990 to create Ranomafana National Park. Pat is beginning to spend it. The red-tiled stucco house has two small offices on the first floor. A large living room steps up to a dining area and kitchen where coffee perks and a purring refrigerator holds bottled water and colas. The stereo is soft but constant: Neil Young, Bob Dylan, Joni Mitchell. Upstairs there are three bedrooms, one Pat's, one Amanda's, the third for technical advisors and consultants to the park. In the last I find left-behind sleeping bags, knapsacks, water bottles, shampoo, rain gear. There is also a stack of science fiction, a Gerald Durrell novel, two scientific papers, a 25-watt bulb to read by, and a sink.

Downstairs Pat digs into her bags. Out come two computers, a laser printer, two hundred T-shirts ("Ranomafana–Lemur City" and "RNP–Land of Lemurs"), film, computer paper, a toilet seat, jeans and a shirt from The Gap for Amanda, a toy lamb. Several people sit in the living room waiting to talk to Pat and leafing through magazines she has brought from Paris: *Elle, Audubon* (with a story in it that mentions Pat), *The New Yorker.* Pat stops unpacking long enough to chat with each and to pay salaries to two administrative assistants, the accountant, and the watchman. She doles out wads of outsized Malagasy francs from a large black leather shoulderbag she carries with her everywhere, snug against her hip. It is a Mary Poppins satchel filled with money, medicine, Band-Aids, official permits, keys, notebooks, chocolate. In fact Pat is a little like Mary Poppins, a blend of charisma, high-voltage action, and dreams.

Suddenly Pat and Benjamin Adriamihaja, the project's national coordinator, disappear for a meeting somewhere. They return after an hour to collect me; together we head into the chaotic maze of downtown Tana to pick out badly needed office shelves and a desk. With the delivery of these items assured within the hour, we thread our way across town through snarled traffic to begin negotiations to obtain three motorcycles for park staff at Ranomafana. Quick stops at a bakery and fruit stand follow. We make it home in time for Pat to oversee the unloading of the new furniture.

Nigel Asquith, a research student from Oxford who happens to be at the house when we return, helps. "She needs to learn to delegate more," he says with grudging admiration as he hefts a shelf. "She may appear scatterbrained, but she gets lots done and she really motivates people. Her goal may have been initially to save lemurs, but now for Pat conservation has become people. Not all researchers can handle that transition."

"I hate to miss anything," says Pat. "I wish I could clone myself." She disappears into the next room to talk to a contractor about wiring.

Pat is in overall charge of the Ranomafana project, a joint effort of Duke University's Center for Tropical Conservation and the triuniversity World Environment Center, which includes Duke, the University of North Carolina (UNC), and North Carolina State (NCS). Under the AID grant Duke provides research and consultation on biodiversity and park management. NCS is developing new forestry and agricultural techniques as options to slow the destructive slash-and-burn practice. UNC has fielded public-health experts to study endemic parasites and human health, especially sanitation. Under the grant there is a Malagasy counterpart for every expatriate technical advisor.

In 1991 Pat was granted tenure at Duke University and at the State

University of New York at Stony Brook. She opted for Duke, where she has spent the last seven years helping to build the Primate Center and the Center for Tropical Conservation including devoting a great deal of time to Madagascar. Pat says with a grin, "I was told, 'You can't do conservation and get tenure. That's juggling conservation with science, and it won't work.' But I got tenure." She has still managed to publish more than thirty-eight scientific papers since receiving her PhD while teaching and working with graduate students.

I ask, "If a tenured professor can't easily be a conservationist, how can a teacher-researcher who wants to get ahead also be a conservation biologist?"

"A conservation biologist is someone who already has tenure," she says, grinning more widely. Then, more seriously, "Conservation is politics. Conservation is about power. Science is science. It's hard, but you *can* do both. If you have tenure it's just that much easier. In conservation we can't afford to muck around. There isn't time. You have to be convinced what you're studying is worth saving or you'll just be studying fossils. I don't want to do that. I like to get things started."

The next day we pile into a four-wheel-drive Toyota to go to Ranomafana, 250 miles and eleven hours away. It is raining hard. At one point we detour a washout, adding an extra hour and a half to the trip. Our driver maneuvers from pothole to pothole without mishap, but the ride is not smooth. The windshield wipers mesmerize me on this long ride, as does Pat.

"I was *born* a biologist," she says, tossing her shoulder-length hair somewhat defiantly and glancing sideways at me from under eyelids that have a faintly oriental cast. "I once told Gerry Durrell it was all his fault. As a child I read all his books. I also read Albert Payson Terhune, all his books about Lad, the collie. My mother was a Phi Beta Kappa in chemistry. My father was a Canadian bush pilot, part owner of an airfield. They were very much in love when they married, and still are. I was the oldest of six children. We lived near Buffalo, New York. I *hated* the cold.

"When I was about ten my father's partner ran off with the airfield's proceeds. I remember the shock of sudden poverty. I remember my mother's tears and her resentment at being tied down to so much housework. But I also remember her ambitions for us, her children, and I remember wonderful long treks in the Canadian wilderness with my father.''

Pat went to Hood College in western Maryland on a full scholarship, majoring in biology and graduating in 1966. Her first job was as an immunologist in a New England laboratory, not because it was her best offer but because the man she was soon to marry, Jim Wright, was nearby, a senior majoring in fine arts at Brown University. By twenty-one she was married, living in a brownstone walk-up in New York City and working for the Department of Social Services in Brooklyn while Jim attended graduate school. ''Four years working in the housing project, Bedford Stuyvesant, taught me a lot about people,'' Pat recalls. ''People deceive and stretch the truth, for example, and I had to learn to accept that. I think I learned then how to play bureaucracies, too, and how to interview. But I was responsible for a hundred families.'' The work was tiring. Guessing that President Johnson's Great Society era was soon to end and welfare programs would be affected, she began to think she might be more effective elsewhere.

At about this time Pat and Jim ''bought a pet monkey for forty dollars, an owl monkey we named Herby. The first day he hid in the bed springs and we thought we'd lost him. But as soon as the sun set he came out. Herby, a nocturnal species of primate, was ready to socialize—at night. Two years later he would have temper tantrums whenever we went out. Jim and I decided he needed the company of his own species, but we couldn't find another owl monkey anywhere in the United States.''

Taking a leave of absence from her job and Herby with her, Pat traveled with Jim to Colombia. ''Wildlife trafficking was still horrendous in the early 1970s. We easily found a female and paid only two dollars for her.'' With both monkeys in tow they traveled to Ecuador and Peru and a year later to Costa Rica. Amanda was born back in New York in 1973. Pat quit her job to become a full-time mother. A month later the pet monkeys also had a female infant.

''Suddenly I saw Herby was doing all the parenting,'' Pat said. ''How can this be? I wondered. How did this kind of behavior evolve? Herby's doing all the work in his family, and I'm doing all the work in mine. I started to haunt the New York Public Library. I wrote primatologist Jane Goodall and mammalogist George Schaller, and wildlife behaviorist

John Eisenberg of the Smithsonian and asked how I could find out more about these animals. Jane never answered my letter—maybe it got lost. But Schaller and Eisenberg said, 'You've got to get a PhD.' I didn't have money to get a PhD, but I still wanted to find out more about these animals.'' (Pat had stumbled upon an aspect of primatology that had never been closely studied. Subsequent research by others has revealed similar parenting participation, if not leadership, on the part of some male primates.)

Pat, Jim, and Amanda, age three, traveled to Peru in 1976 to look for wild owl monkeys. ''Nearly all the forests were cut where I first wanted to study. I finally found an uncut forest and went out alone at night to look. These forests have fer-de-lances, South America's most dangerous snake. And jaguars. Wild pigs. I was terrified. My flashlight batteries began to fail. The noise of some large animal or animals thrashing through the brush sent me racing up a tree. The tree had two-inch thorns along its trunk. Whatever it was thundered past below me in the dark. I spent the rest of the night picking thorns out of my hands and knees.

''At dawn I looked up. Directly overhead was an owl monkey. You can't imagine the elation.''

Two months later Pat returned to New York. Her first paper, ''Home Range, Activity Pattern and Agonistic Encounters of a Group of Night Monkeys (*Aotus trivirgatus*) in Peru,'' was published a year later, the first study ever done by any scientist on owl monkeys in the wild. Professor Warren Kinzey of the City University of New York urged her to go to graduate school. ''No one will take you seriously unless you do,'' he said. Kinzey later became head of the committee at City University that reviewed and approved her PhD thesis.

The week she decided to take Kinzey's advice her husband Jim left. To this day Pat is not sure what caused the breakup. ''We had been married ten years. I was devastated. To my horror I learned everything in the apartment was in his name—telephone, electricity, everything. All utilities were cut off. Amanda and I were hungry but I wasn't going to give up.''

Pat's doctoral thesis was on the costs and benefits of nocturnal life for wild owl monkeys. With Amanda she traveled to Manu National Park in Peru, to a research and camp site managed by John Terborgh, then associated with Princeton, now director of Duke's Center for Tropical Conservation. "It took us ten days by canoe to reach the study site," Pat recalls. "There was a lot of white water. We tipped over—Amanda was in the other boat, then suddenly on the far shore surrounded by Piro Indians, a local tribe. I thought I'd never see her again. After boats were righted and wet gear and people sorted out, we went on. We spent a year there. When money ran out John [Terborgh] and Charlie Janson, another researcher at Manu, saw Amanda and I got fed until I had collected enough data. I'll always be grateful."

Pat learned in Manu that the small monkeys she was studying were nocturnal primarily because there was less predation at night than in the daytime, when Harpy eagles and other raptors were active. At night, the monkeys moved about quite freely.

Before she could get her PhD, Pat had to prove her theory by studying the same species at a site where there were no daytime predators but instead large owls, which are nocturnal. Grants from the National Science Foundation and the Wenner Foundation allowed her to spend several months in the Chaco Forest of Paraguay. Here the same species behaved quite differently from the monkeys at Manu. "At Manu they entered and exited their nest at dawn and dusk like clockwork, always avoiding daylight. Here they stayed *very* quiet at night, because of the owls, and spent one to three hours actively foraging in broad daylight."

In 1985 Pat got her PhD and was offered the job at the Duke University Primate Center. The year before she had visited Madagascar for the first time while attending an international primate meeting in Nairobi. On a whim she flew to Madagascar. "I was very disappointed. The poverty was awful, the roads, the deforestation, and the effects of socialism all sad and depressing." Since then, she says, an official shift away from communism has opened Madagascar to Western financing and consumer goods. "There was no soap to be had, anywhere, back then. Now you can find soap even in the smallest towns. That's just symptomatic of the changes for the better going on. . . .

"Then one day [back in the States] I ran into Russ Mittermeier. Russ had control of a small WWF fund which he could use at his own discretion for primate conservation. He said, 'You've got to get into conservation. Go back to Madagascar and study an endangered species.' " In 1986 he gave Pat enough money to put together a small expedition to survey primates.

With graduate students Patrick Daniel, David Myers, and Deborah Overdorff, Pat began exploring remnant forests of Madagascar where an unusual species, the greater bamboo lemur, might have once roamed. This animal had not been seen since the early 1970s and was possibly extinct. Eventually Pat and her colleagues came to Ranomafana.

I met Patrick Daniels just before Pat and I left for Ranomafana. He had just come back from an exploratory trip in the north. His feet were badly swollen and covered with a violent red rash of unknown origin. He was wearing thong sandals and limping badly but seemed to shrug off this inconvenience with stoicism, almost machismo. Foreigners who work in Madagascar are inclined to make light of such unexplained conditions. After all, much of Madagascar's biota (including disease organisms) remain unidentified. Patrick tells me what happened next: "Up to the moment we dropped down over the escarpment at Ranomafana, we'd seen only small patches of forest. Suddenly here was an incredibly beautiful forest on both sides. We drove slowly and pulled off the road just above the village of Ambatolahy. We ran up this wonderfully steep trail. We knew from that first moment we had a special site. Here was *real* rain forest."

Pat and her colleagues began to see signs of bamboo lemurs everywhere, droppings and chunks of half-eaten bamboo on the trail. They saw quite a few of the relatively common small gray bamboo lemurs and got glimpses of something much larger, the greater bamboo lemur.

Then on June 17, 1986, Pat "walked into the forest and saw a different animal. Deborah Overdorff was just behind me. It was smaller than the greater bamboo lemur was supposed to be and somewhat reddish. I was glad Deborah was there because she could verify to me I wasn't dreaming." The lemur turned out to be the one never before described, a newly discovered species. Because of the golden tint of its facial hairs it has been named *Hapalemur aureus*, the golden bamboo lemur.[9] *Hapalemur aureus* was the first new primate to be discovered in over ten years. The news hit front pages everywhere. It was, said one writer, "the zoological equivalent of a supernova."[10]

"I still wasn't really 'into' conservation," Pat continues. "This was science." We have stopped at a small restaurant, or *hotelly*, for salad, rice, and chicken in a thin broth. She stabs at a tomato with her fork. "Then they began logging the forest just as we finished the study. I saw red! The forest you see now is not what we saw then. It's been partially logged. Even so, it's the best in Madagascar, and we still have some virgin forest. Lemurs need virgin forest (although they adapt to some degree to secondary growth). There are twelve species of primates at Ranomafana, more than in any other area. Three of these are bamboo lemurs. And two of those are found *only* here.

"When I got back to Tana I went straight to the Water and Forests Ministry to ask for a park to protect the lemurs. I was still just thinking science. They gave me a list of twenty-five things needed to help local people improve their lot. Among them were new schools, improved health services, and technical advice to farmers. 'There's more to it than just lemurs, Patricia,' Philemon Randrianajoina, the director, said. 'If you help us get these benefits for the people, we will help you create a park.'

"That's when conservation happened to me," Pat continues. "Back in the 1970s when I was in Peru I cursed developers and agriculturalists for opening up roads to the interior. Back then developers thought conservationists wanted to save animals without thinking about people. Until the 1980s they were mostly right. Now conservationists work closely with many of the same people. Philemon helped me realize conservation could only happen if local human needs were met."

At one-thirty in the morning we pull into Ranomafana. Because of the rain the hotel is full. A British tour group has elected to sleep indoors rather than tent. We wake the watchman at park headquarters; he unlocks a back room where there are mattresses. Others who have convoyed with us in a second Toyota bunk down in the cars and in a nearby storeroom.

VOICE OF THE VILLAGERS

Slowly I wake to the smell of cooking fires and to village sounds. A cock crows, a dog barks, a door slams nearby. I hear the splintering of kindling and a child's brief wail. Outside, people stroll in twos and threes toward the hot springs pool, trailing small gray towels. They cross the Namorona River by a wide foot bridge to reach the pool. In the distance mist-shrouded mountains rise steeply from the valley floor. Creamy datura and ginger and colorful impatiens and poppies flower along the path. I follow and soak for half an hour before heading to the hotel for breakfast.

Pat joins me. She introduces an octogenarian of military bearing, dressed in freshly pressed khakis and a plaid shirt, panama hat set squarely on his head. This is Roi Phillipe, king of Anpitomita, a village fifteen miles away. There are no roads to his village; Roi Phillipe has walked the entire way to meet us. Of the Tanala tribe, he served with the French in Europe in World War II and returned to fight against them in the Malagasy rebellion of 1947, which was sparked right here. Eight hundred guerrillas served under him during the uprising. He was wounded and condemned to death. "I laughed," he tells us. "I told them,

HOLLY YOUNG HUTH

Patricia Wright with Malagasy villagers

'I will die in my country for my country.' " When the French conceded defeat and withdrew, Roi Phillipe was released from prison before the death penalty could be carried out. Now he has written a book about these events "so that future generations will not forget." Pat agrees to have the book translated and to sell copies at the park museum. Roi Phillipe will use the income for his people.

"I hope you will succeed in saving the forest," he tells Pat. "God put the forest there for the villagers, but they get no money from it. We don't have many good fields left, so we have to cut the forest, although we know the soil won't last. There are too many people in the valleys, so we have to go up into the forest. In the beginning the soil is very good. Then it is washed by the rain and ruined. Now we need safe water, but as the forest is lost, the clear water goes." Pat tells me it takes fifteen years for regeneration of forest on such exhausted soil to begin, 200 to recreate a reasonable facsimile of the original forest.

"The biggest change in my life has been the coming of electricity," Roi Phillipe continues. "Now there is the park. I hope the young people will participate to learn how to manage it. We need a road to my village for civilization to come to us. That is the first thing." Roi Phillipe moves into the white-hot sunshine for me to snap his picture. He takes off his glasses for this, and squares his shoulders. Then he leaves to walk the fifteen miles back home.

The next morning after swimming I meet Lon Kightlinger and his wife Mynna Bodo Kightlinger at breakfast. The Kightlingers have spent thirteen years in Madagascar as health-service missionaries. Pat has told me, "We have to build trust. We want to save the forest. The people want a better life. So we say, 'If you agree not to cut the forest, we will help you improve conditions.' You work with each village committee, especially with the village president—an elected officer—and the village 'king,' its most venerable elder." Lon and Mynna are among the first participants in the Ranomafana project to do so. They speak fluent Malagasy.

Madagascar achieved independence from France in 1960, but "since the 1947 uprising we are the first outsiders to show up here," says Pat. "Building trust takes time."

Lon tells me that "Pat has won the battle of the ministries in Tana. Now the local people must be convinced of our good intentions. The people are scared about the park. Are they going to be allowed to keep their cattle there? They also need fuel wood. Where will they get it? What else can they do but slash and burn when the soil they are using is exhausted and they have nowhere else to go? If they can make the land they have now more productive, they won't be driven to clear the forest."

Soil experts who have come and gone before my visit have told Pat chemical fertilizers will help restore the land. French forestry experts say the people should plant fast-growing exotic eucalyptus trees for fuel. I ask, "Won't these practices back-lash?" Chemically dependent soil can become uneconomical; its runoff can contaminate water. As for trees, the need for firewood far outstrips supply. No one has ready answers to these problems.

"We're working with health first because it's their priority," Mynna says. Mynna and Lon are conducting the first health survey in the region, investigating conditions in twenty-six villages near the park in order to generate base-line data on which the success or failure of future health-care strategies can be measured. Their team includes six Malagasy, five nurses and a doctor. Focusing on children under nine years old, they have found that 82 percent have at least one intestinal worm, 50 percent have malaria, and 30 percent have running sores on their bodies. The children are generally healthy until they are about five months old, when they quit nursing. "It's downhill from then on," says Lon. A sixth of the children are underweight, 10 percent undernourished. What little protein they get comes from wild crayfish caught in forest rivers. The people nearer the forest seem healthier than those removed from it.

Ambatolahy is a village five miles from Ranomafana, just off the main road. It is near the entrance to the park in what scientists call high humid cloud forest. All seven of the park guides Pat has hired to lead tourists into the park come from this town. There are thirty households—small thatched mud-brick houses, single-room dwellings about eight by fourteen feet. The dirt floors are sometimes covered with straw mats. On the average six people live in each. Villagers defecate anywhere, anytime, and drink and wash from a stream that runs through rice paddies above the village and then tumbles through rapids past the houses into a culvert under the road. Lon and Mynna found only a third of the mothers knew that unsanitary preparation of food might contribute to disease. About one-quarter used infusions made from forest plants to get rid of parasites and to control malaria symptoms.

The men average four years of schooling, the women three. Eighty percent of the children have had no schooling whatsoever. Pat, with AID funding, has promised that the first of several planned primary schools will be built at Ambatolahy. The foundation has been dug. Bricks are on order. After improved health, education is the villagers' highest priority. (More remote villagers put the building of access roads and bridges higher on their list. Their children universally want a soccer ball.)

The idea of family planning has only just come to Madagascar. Most women give birth to twelve children of whom roughly half live to adulthood. Long-held customs slow family-planning progress: A large family is still needed for labor-intensive subsistence farming, and as in so many Third World societies, numerous children are insurance against old age.

Later that day Pat and Ranomafana's national coordinator, Benjamin Adriamihaja, invite me to join them to call upon Ambatolahy's elders. Poverty is the absence of color here: Children blend into the dusty background of packed earthen paths, their faded, mended clothes the same color as their skin, somewhere between coffee and beige. One six-year-old pounds coffee in a pestle made from a tree trunk. Nearby another plays with a truck carved from sugarcane. Only the occasional flash of gap-toothed grins and sparkling eyes brightens their demeanor. In my notebook I sketch pictures of several, together with their razor-backed dogs. They run off with these tiny scraps of paper, giggling, to show their friends.

Rice is drying on rush mats outside the "president's" house. Together with about twelve villagers we squeeze inside. The president, Edouard Nala, introduces us to his wife and two-week-old baby huddled on a pallet in a corner. Two other children lean against Mrs. Nala's knee, their eyes big with our coming. An old Raleigh bicycle leans against one wall, a precious radio nearby. Over it a wall hanging proclaims in the local language, "Go with the flow."

Pat's intention is to tell the villagers about plans for the park's inaugural celebration, scheduled for late May, and to enlist their support. A large carved stone will be erected at the park entrance a mile from Ambatolahy, she tells them. The stone will be dedicated to the ancestor spirits who live in the forest. A cow will be sacrificed, its blood spilled on the rock. Rum will be passed around. Government officials from Tana, the U.S. ambassador, and other VIPs will be coming for the day. After speeches a parade will march the six miles into Ranomafana proper where a feast, music, and dancing will conclude the day. Much needs to be done: park bridges and trails improved so that visitors can see the park interior for themselves, parking areas cleared, signs made. A women's cooperative is already hard at work embroidering items for sale. (Pat bought them two sewing machines, one manual, the other electric, to speed the process.)

"We will help," says Edouard. "But we are upset about the park. We are upset because it was created from the top, by the government. We have written the Ministry [of Water and Forests] about our problems. First, it is now forbidden for our cows to go into the park, yet we need to hide them there from rustlers."

"I agree this is a problem," Pat says. "I will talk again with ministry officials." Later she will explain to me that cattle have little ecological impact on the forest. They follow human trails and are not there in sufficient numbers to destroy vegetation.

"Also, the forest is our resource," Edouard continues, implacable. "We collect honey there and fronds from the pandanus plant from which we make our mats." The villagers also use the trunks of giant tree ferns to make flower pots to sell along the road, and cut and polish coils of strangler fig vines, which are sold as table and lamp stands. For villages near the highway these are important market crops from the forest. Harvesting must be carefully managed in the future, or alternatives found.

Pat tells the gathering that boxes for apiculture are already being constructed in Tana. Someone will come soon, she says, to teach the villagers how to raise bees domestically. As for the pandanus fronds, she has no immediate answer. "That's what the forest is all about. It's not just a park with a border, it's there to help the village too. We understand the value of the forest to you, but don't expect instant solutions to everything." Later she suggests the pandanus might be cultivated outside the forest rather than harvested within it.

Edouard complains that there are too many babies and not enough land. He gestures uphill behind the house where terraced rice paddies and small plots for other crops creep inexorably up the mountain. "Besides, we hear rumors that tourists pay big money for permits in Tana, but we don't see any of that." This is true. As a tourist I had paid twenty dollars for permission to enter Ranomafana National Park.

Pat promises to talk to the ministry about that, too. "I agree some of the money from tourism should be spent locally."

"What about jobs for our young people?"

"Our seven guides all come from this village," Pat replies, "but we will be hiring more people for other jobs soon." Under the AID plan only seventy-six jobs will be available in the park, but perhaps entrepreneurial service job opportunities in roadside villages will increase as tourism grows. There is a lot of hope resting on tourism.

"I feel better after our talks," Edouard says.

"You see," says Benjamin, as we walk back to our car, "how they trust her?" Ambatolahy's trust puts a heavy burden on Pat and other project leaders. What if things don't work out? What happens when the AID project money dries up three years hence?

Building this degree of local acceptance is an uneven, ongoing process. Later an official from another village flags down our Toyota to say to Pat, "We must have a meeting to rediscuss the boundary of the park. Here it has been drawn through our *tavy* patches. The people are not happy."

Pat replies, "We want to keep the headwaters of the Namorona clean. Both soil erosion and sewage from your village affect that." The officials in Tana know the villagers are suspicious of them, and they know they can't accomplish anything without the support of the countryside. No one wants trouble. The solution will probably be a compromise.

"Until we actually deliver," Pat tells me, "AID's Ranomafana project has little credibility. At first the money was slow to come. Now we have the money and can move ahead but we still have to solve the problem of trust—between us and them, between villages and Tana, among the villagers themselves."

Quite often local people are afraid to exercise authority because of internal village rivalries. Rising above one's peers is not always considered wise or safe, so locals are inclined to move cautiously in any new endeavor. "This does not translate well back at AID in Washington,"

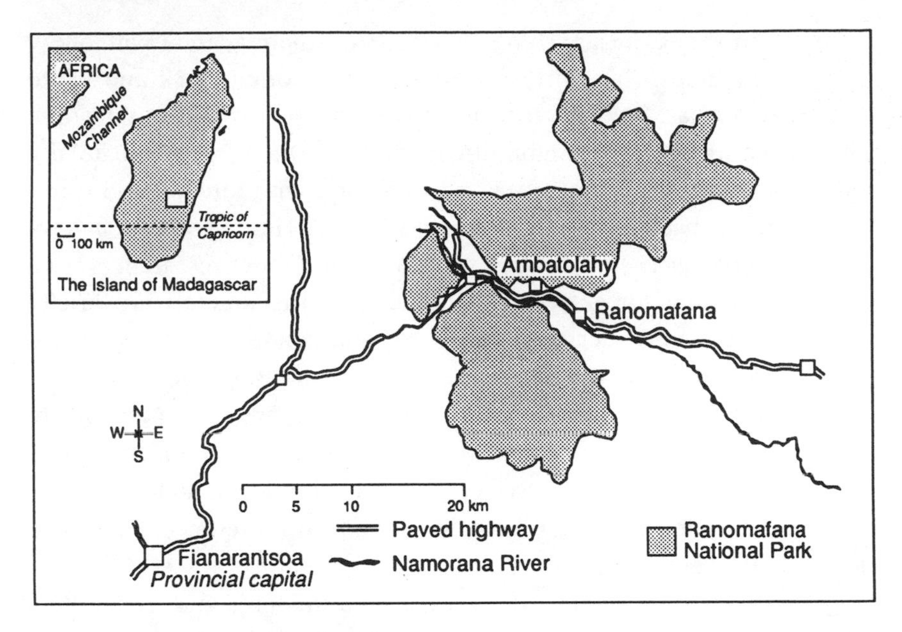

Map of Ranomafana National Park
(Adapted from a map by Lon Kightlinger)

says Pat. "AID wants us to hand responsibility over to the local people, yet many of them are reluctant to take charge. That's the reality for now, and we must work with it." A partial solution is to enlist Malagasy counterparts who may or may not come from the local region to work one on one with foreign personnel. This way the burden of accountability is shared.

LEMURS AND THE FOREST

Evening comes swiftly in the forest. First the cicadas kick in, *tchh tchh*, monotonously high-pitched, then the tree frogs—just like back home, I think, tossing in my sleeping bag and wondering if a scorpion has snuck past the tent's zippered fly to join me. When rain comes it is heralded by growling thunder but very little lightning. Water swirls around the tent platform within seconds, channeled into ditches dug by a previous occupant. Overhead the canopy takes tremendous punishment: Tall traveler palms, Madagascar's national tree, bow in submission to the cannonade.

In the morning the sun shines. Today Pat, Amanda, and I will follow a group of lemurs, big thirteen- and fourteen-pound black and white diademed sifakas. We will write down everything they do from the time they wake up until they settle down at night. One of the Ambatolahy guides knows where they are. We set off early with lunches and water bottles in our backpacks and notebooks handy. This is part of a behavioral and ecological study of this species Pat and other researchers have been conducting for six years. Once a year the animals are briefly tranquilized, sexed, measured, weighed, and collared so that they are easy to identify. We will refer to individuals as Blue-Green, Yellow-Green, and Red-Red, their names reflecting the colors of their newly attached collars and tags. When we find them upslope of one of the few marked trails their heads swivel on their shoulders, following our movements, but they do not seem disturbed by our presence. They have lovely amber eyes.

We note they are feeding on fig leaves and small red guava fruit. "It's important to know what they eat so that we can know what trees are important in the reserve," says Pat. Guava, however, is an introduced and now ubiquitous tree that we find throughout the disturbed part of the forest. Its fruit is only available in April. Does its availability change the sifakas' behavior at that time of year? This is one of today's unanswered questions, but only an analysis of lots of data collected over many days will yield an answer, and perhaps not even then.

While we wait for the sifakas to make a move we sample the tart, delicious fruit. One by one the lemurs swing off through the canopy, leaping from tree to tree in great arcs that set the vacated tree swaying for a moment in frenzied counterpoint. We are hard-pressed to keep up: Ferns, vines, some with two-inch thorns, bamboo thickets, bogs, and fallen rotted logs on precipitous slopes obstruct our progress. Sweat-soaked and breathless, we press on for the sake of science. So much depends on the observer's training, alertness, perseverance.

Total diademed sifaka numbers are unknown, but there are not many and the species is already listed as endangered by the IUCN. What kind of space do they use? What do they eat? How do they interact with each other? With other lemurs? With other species? Pat hopes information from this study, as from all other research being conducted in the forest, will help guide park managers to make wise decisions in the future so that this species and others will survive.

"The difference between a biologist and a conservation biologist is the questions we ask," Pat says. "Our questions all relate to conservation"—of species, of habitats, of landscapes. Pat calls herself a conservation biologist, but here at Ranomafana she is also a manager. Someone must make decisions about trails and boundaries and who has access to the park.

Researchers come and go at Ranomafana, taking up residence in a cluster of tents that surround but are concealed by jungle from a large airy log cabin Pat has had built on stone pilings about a mile from the road. To reach it, one crosses the Namorona on a precarious swinging bridge and hikes up a short, well-marked trail. The cabin is festooned with rain gear and research equipment—compasses, cameras, surveyor's tape, mist nets, a centrifuge. There are boxes and baskets of food. Socks and towels hang drying under the roof of the porch. Huge spiders weave intricate webs in the sunlight. Tiny green spotted lizards crawl along the walls while their eyes roll in search of insects and their narrow anticipating tongues flicker in and out. Pat decides who comes to do research here. In addition to good science she looks for compatibility to stave off cabin fever. Pat says she has experienced it herself but will not say with whom or when. It is obvious that field conditions here—long hours in the rain, the mud, the leeches, the insects, the humidity—are stressful.

Some researchers study plants, others birds, butterflies, rodents, snails. A few have possibly discovered species. A fish, a carnivore, and countless insects are currently under review for scientific authentication. Other researchers conduct comparative studies of disturbed (previously cut) and undisturbed forest to determine regenerative processes. One student is following the germination speed and success of various endemic seeds when they are eaten and gut-passed (defecated) by lemurs as compared to being dropped directly on the ground from parent trees. On the average it appears that gut-passed seeds sprout about three months earlier and two and a half times more successfully than those that merely fall from trees, for sharp teeth and/or digestive processes crack or soften seeds' outer casings and droppings serve as fertilizer. At least one tree seed relies completely on lemurs for dispersal.

The forest needs lemurs to regenerate, and lemurs need the forest to survive. Conservation biologists argue that the park must be managed to support this important link.

We lean against the base of trees to watch the sifakas rest, entwined every which way in the branches of a high tree. "I was in the forest not far from this spot one day in July 1989," Pat says, "when someone brought me a blue paper telex which instructed me to telephone a Chicago number. Putting a call through from Ranomafana village to anywhere is a daunting experience. Trying to place a call to the States was impossible. Three days later I finally called from Fianarantsoa, the provincial capital, forty miles away. Earlier that year I had applied to the MacArthur Foundation for a grant to document the biological diversity of the park. I thought the call must have something to do with that. Instead, someone I had never talked to before told me I had received a John D. and Catherine T. MacArthur Fellowship. I didn't know what it was. He explained: $250,000 would be coming to me over the next five years *to do anything I wanted.*"

These fellowships are chosen each year by a secret selection process. Poets, chemists, artists, musicians, physicists, and biologists are among the recipients, twenty individuals each year. The jury—whoever they are—picks Americans it thinks are or will be innovators in various intellectual and cultural fields. A MacArthur Fellowship is recognition of one's worth and one's potential.

"Overnight my life changed," Pat says in understatement. Suddenly she was dogged by the press and by lecture-circuit impresarios. Duke University doubled her salary; two years later she had tenure. She paid off outstanding graduate school debts first and set a little money aside for Amanda's college fees. Then she spent most of the rest of the first year's stipend on the park, meeting obligations "before the AID money kicked in." During the weeks we are together I watch her dip into her black shoulder bag more than once to slip a few francs to a villager to help build a house, to buy a bolt of cloth for the women's village cooperative, to build a display case for Ranomafana's tiny museum. Clearly, sharing her good fortune is a joy. "I could never afford to be generous before," she says, but adds somewhat wistfully, "Since the MacArthur I have had so little time."

Overhead one of the sifakas stirs and changes place with another, a sleepy, fluid motion. Ecology is a branch of biology that deals with relationships among organisms and between them and their surroundings. While there is no precise threshold en route to extinction, an understanding of these lemurs' social systems may help show their minimum viable population size, that is, the point "below which a species might go extinct. An understanding of their demographics, genetics, and disease—among other aspects of population biology—will also help future managers."[11] Thus, what Pat and her colleagues are learning about these animals in this natural setting will influence how they are protected in the wild and in captivity in the future. If reintroduction to wild settings from captivity becomes possible or necessary in years to come, such data will help guide programs.

In the forest Pat and I are always on the lookout for Ranomafana's three species of bamboo lemurs, but they prove elusive. The most visible sign is broken, stripped bamboo stalks three inches in diameter—the 5.5-pound greater lemurs have been here recently and cracked open the bamboo with their teeth to get to the pith, which they eat. The remains are shredded "like spaghetti," says Pat, handing me a piece of the evidence. Finally I spot a few tiny gray bamboo lemurs almost wholly camouflaged in the dappled forest light. They are munching on bamboo leaves. Pat has learned that golden bamboo lemurs—which I never do see—eat yet another part of bamboo, succulent young stalks just emerging from the ground.

"Our first question was, Why are all three bamboo lemur species here?" Pat tells me, picking her way through a wild pig wallow. "We looked at what they were eating and found the new stalks contained 30 percent protein, while the leaves held only 15 percent and the pith only 5 percent. If this were so, why weren't all three species eating the new stalks? Purely by chance, we tested for cyanide and found these emerging stalks were riddled with the poison—enough to kill a man! How does the golden bamboo lemur eat this and survive?" Discovering the golden bamboo lemur's secret may someday help doctors develop an antidote for cyanide and perhaps reveal other antitoxin benefits as well.

Is the golden bamboo lemur another rosy periwinkle? What other medicinal or industrial benefits lie locked within Ranomafana's heart?

THE CREATION OF A DREAM

One day Benjamin delivers Pat's duffel of U.S.-manufactured T-shirts to the park museum, a small, freshly whitewashed building perched on a short rise just on the edge of town. They are stacked neatly by color on a display table inside the door—pink, gray, navy, white. The price for villagers is about four dollars but for foreigners like myself, ten. Everyone considers this such a good deal that all 200 are gone within an hour. Contrary to expectation, the villagers won't wear them until the day of the park's inauguration, May 31, after I have left Madagascar. When I ask why a local woman replies, "This is one way we can honor our park." Bystanders nod in agreement.

Unexpectedly, trouble brews. Those few families not quick enough to buy a T-shirt before the supply runs out are envious. Quarrels break out. The villagers come to Pat, worried about village harmony. Pat places a rush call to Antananarivo which is relayed to her office back at Duke. "Send 500 more shirts with the next traveler! We must have them in time for the inauguration!"

Pat's ability to mix micro–problem solving like this with policy negotiations and high-level decision-making impresses me. Back in Tana I had watched her juggle meetings with government officials and shopping expeditions for sewing machines. Here she begins a typical day at a dawn breakfast with youth leaders, hops into the Toyota to drive two hours to the provincial capital for flashlights, wire, light bulbs, wheelbarrows, mattresses, and paint, and locates a contractor (after some searching) who promises to deliver bricks for the new schoolhouse within the week. During our return trip she stops at a village at the park trailhead to present a toilet seat she had brought from the United States for installation in its privy. (Will other villages be envious? Will she have to order twenty-five more?) At her suggestion this village has also built a thatched-roofed snack bar. Here the villagers sell soft drinks to thirsty hikers with an appealing shyness bordering on diffidence. A noncash economy is reaping its first monetary payment from the park; a service industry is being born though no one quite realizes it.

Then Pat dons rubber boots and disappears into the forest for two or three hours of lemur tracking with Amanda. Sometimes she worries that she spends too little time with her teenaged daughter. Taking the unspoken hint, I return to the hotel for a quiet evening on my own.

Pat seems focused on the upcoming park inauguration. At the same time there is a faraway look in those almond eyes of hers. I sense a pulling away, a letting-go even as she rushes about organizing people. She plans to return to the United States soon after the celebration and has hired another American to take over the project's management duties within a few weeks. He will have a Malagasy counterpart who will be named soon. Will she be back? Of course. "At least a couple of times a year, mostly to help remotivate any flagging spirits and to continue lemur research, especially to follow up the cyanide mystery."

On my last day in the forest we hike past an ancestral resting place, tumbled moss-covered stones and one or two upright stelae overgrown with vines. The Namorona River sparkles in the distant valley while thunder rumbles behind the range of mountains to the east. The families of Ambatolahy whose ancestors these are have removed the bones, but the place is still revered. We step carefully. The presence of spirits is powerful in this shady spot.

Pat's mind ranges widely as we move up the slope. "I love being a part of something which is history. Ranomafana is history. I'm having so much fun making it happen. I've had to learn leadership talents really fast. I was frazzled at first. What you're seeing now is a very pleased Pat Wright. My dream was to mix biologic and development projects in depth, to build a rapport for truth. Everything is just beginning here—the park, family planning, improved health and education. The inauguration is a beginning, but in many ways for me it's an end. The fun part has been the creation of the dream.

"I don't know what my next project will be. Perhaps I'll take a two- to three-year break to write science and a popular book about my experiences. I've still got over half the MacArthur grant left. . . . Now others can continue the on-site Ranomafana project management while I can help direct it and raise funds in the U.S."

For Pat, it's time to move on. As for Ranomafana and conservation in general in Madagascar, the road ahead will not be smooth. Conservation and development goals are in constant "creative tension," as one foreign expert put it. Professional conservationists, mostly foreign, mostly nongovernmental, worry, as Pat says one day, that "we may be swamped by development experts and lose sight of our main focus, the protection of biological diversity.'' But she also worries whether foreign conservationists are talking the Malagasy's language.

Others worry that competition among Malagasy ministries and among foreign environmental groups will dilute the conservation endeavor. Several suggest that a nonpolitical Malagasy should be named to coordinate these competing interests. He or she would have to be a consummate diplomat whom everyone could trust. Like Pat. But she's not Malagasy, and she's leaving.

Since 1987, when a shift in government policy opened pro-Western doors, foreign investment in Madagascar has increased exponentially. Consumer goods have become available, and there is an aura of bustle throughout the country that Pat says was missing when she first visited in 1984. Over a period of three years (1990–93) about $60 million will be pumped into the Madagascar economy by the World Bank, the European Community, AID, and others. Some of the money is slated for environment/development projects in and around parks. WWF and Conservation International have negotiated ''debt-for-nature swaps'' totaling over $6.5 million; under these agreements, Madagascar can reduce its external debt by agreeing to pursue conservation activities in exchange for the nonprofit organizations' purchase and cancellation of a portion of its foreign debt. Despite signs of civilian discontent, mostly in Tana, since my return to the United States, a once-discouraged nation may be gaining a new lease on life.

Until recently the lack of a national family-planning strategy has been a serious problem. In May 1991 the American embassy in Madagascar cabled the U.S. Department of State: ''Madagascar's population growth rate of more than 3 percent per annum threatens to negate any progress made in overall economic growth and to accelerate an already alarming pace of environmental degradation. To respond to these concerns, the government of Madagascar has approved a national population policy.'' For the first time, Madagascar has said officially that population planning and environmental management must go hand in hand if balanced economic growth is to occur. The World Bank has responded quickly. In collaboration with AID, the European Community, the UN, and others, the bank will contribute $8 million to an emergency family-planning program over five (1991–96) years.[12] Madagascar itself will come close to matching that amount.

This initiative provides some hope for environmental conservation in Madagascar, as do a high-level government commitment to Madagascar's fifteen-year environmental action plan, the continued input of scientific and technical expertise, mostly foreign, and ongoing adequate economic support. Most of all, the willing involvement of local people in places like Ranomafana is key. If any of these ingredients come up short in the near term, this "naturalists' promised land" will surely disappear. Much already has.

Hope lies in the fact that the education and training of Malagasy are required ingredients of all conservation projects. Every foreign expert has a Malagasy counterpart. Every foreign researcher has Malagasy associates. At Ranomafana, an American will coordinate park activities for the duration of the AID project but a Malagasy will be named as park director. These two will work together closely. The Malagasy, or his or her replacement, will be there long after the American is gone.

On the day I leave Madagascar Benjamin Adriamihaja accompanies me to the airport. As we drive past rice paddies gleaming in the setting sun outside of Tana, past ochre-tinted farmhouses and wooden fences, he asks me what my overall impression of Madagascar has been. Unaccustomed to being on the receiving end, I respond inadequately, "Tremendous economic need, terrible odds. I fear for the future of this finite land. The poor have nowhere to go when the forests are all gone, as surely they will mostly be if hillside farming is not slowed. I worry foreign monetary assistance may dry up too soon." I am a worrier by nature. I would rather be surprised if I am proven wrong than further saddened if proven right.

When the three-year AID Ranomafana grant expires, expenses will be picked up under another AID program for two more years. But will the park and the local village economies be self-sustaining after five years? Will the leadership be adequately trained?

Benjamin jumps on me. "You've missed the motivation! You've missed the spirit of the people! I have tremendous hope for Ranomafana, because the people there are truly excited about the park and about their opportunities. The people of this region are especially *vivant* ("lively")—

that is not true everywhere in Madagascar. Pat, especially Pat, has gained their trust and projects her own enthusiasm. They are infected by it. The Americans who have come with her have entered right into the life of the town. They are not standoffish, they do not act superior. Not all foreign aid–givers are like that. You Americans have a pioneer spirit. You have fire. The American way—Pat's way—is special. The people respond to that. Pat seeks solutions with input from the people. The villagers appreciate that. Pat is truly the mother of this project. The people love her."

We are inside the airport terminal now, inching our way down the long customs line toward passport control. We are running out of time. "Give conservation in Madagascar five years," Benjamin pleads. "Then we can measure if there has been improvement or decline in the standard of living. We have our base-line data at Ranomafana, so we'll know. Do you not see the motivation here in Madagascar? The power of the dream? It's very strong."

With that, I say goodbye and slip through the departure gate. Only time, and not much of it at that, will tell Madagascar's future. Meanwhile there is the dream.

CHAPTER 2

David "Jonah" Western: People, Wildlife, and Mobility

THE *ORINGA*: MASAI SYMBOL OF LEADERSHIP

The Masai begin gathering at Namelog at dawn. They come on foot and in trucks and cars that have given them lifts. Red volcanic dust swirls at their passing, reflecting slanted, early light. To the south Tanzania's snow-capped Mount Kilimanjaro hangs hugely ethereal in the dissipating mist just south of the border with Kenya, where I now stand. Amboseli National Park, a 150-square-mile wildlife sanctuary created in 1974, is a few miles away. Excluded from the park by government fiat in 1977, many Masai, originally a nomadic people, have settled just outside its boundary.

It is August 1990. The Masai leaders have called for a *harambee*, a "pulling together" in Swahili, to raise money for a nursery school in this tiny community of no more than 150 families. Living close beside the Engumi River, one of the only permanent watercourses in an otherwise semiarid landscape, Namelog children must cross a dense swamp choked with papyrus and tall sedges to attend school at another town. Recently a child was killed by a Cape buffalo along one of the swamp's many shadowed paths.

The amount of available arable land will ultimately limit this community. Except along the river and around the swamps the ecosystem is a mosaic of savannah grassland, clumps of dense, thorny brush, and occasional acacia woodlands. The savannah becomes green when the "long" rains come in March but turns to a dry monochrome as the year progresses. Now, in August, dust devils waver and dance on the horizon.

Small homes, some thatched with traditional cow-dung patties, others roofed in tin, dot the rocky landscape. Here irrigation ditches have turned the red soil productive: onions, beans, tomatoes, *sukuma wiki* (a kind of spinach), corn, and radishes grow year around. Barefoot children guard goats nearby, herding them with short flexible switches among the brush and termite mounds. Most of the cattle, which even a Masai-turned-farmer still considers his primary wealth, graze farther afield on land owned communally by the local tribe.

Everyone has come: schoolteachers from Mombasa and Nairobi; grandmothers gaily wrapped in red-and-white-checked shawls, their ears and necks festooned with finely strung beads; schoolchildren in sharply pressed navy shorts and pinafores; aloof *morani*, young warriors with elaborately corn-rowed, ochre-tinted hair, their burnt sienna wraps worn regally; other young men in Western garb who from time to time bend down to polish city shoes with bits of cloth. Several leaders in khaki or business suits circulate among the crowd, somehow making order out of chaos so that everyone eventually has room to sit on the wide meadow in front of a speakers' podium and small officials' tent.

I have flown in from Nairobi with David "Jonah" Western, an ecologist and Kenyan citizen. Jonah is director of East African programs for Wildlife Conservation International (WCI), the research/conservation arm of the New York Zoological Society (NYZS) with which he has been associated for many years. We spent last night at the bungalow he built more than twenty years ago at Ol Tukai, not far from Amboseli's airstrip. The only private "inholding" in the park, the house stands alone on a broad expanse of short grass savannah surrounded by an electric fence and shaded by acacia trees and thorny brush. This morning zebra, wildebeest, and gazelle were grazing a few yards from the compound while a troop of yellow baboons foraged nearby. In the distance five elephants marched slowly left to right in single file. They were headed for the swamps, the heart of Amboseli's ecosystem. I was reluctant to leave this wildlife treasure, but Jonah made it clear he wanted to attend and contribute to the *harambee* of his neighbors. By seven we were on the road, a dusty, potholed, sometimes unidentifiable track.

Now we stand shoulder to shoulder waiting for the songs and dances and speeches to begin. Though practical in purpose, a *harambee* is also a celebration, a rare occasion for far-flung families to reunite, for young people to meet, for an enormous feast to be eaten of savory (though tough) goat stew, rice, unleaven bread and fruit, and copious amounts of bottled water, beer, and Coca Cola. I study Jonah covertly, squinting in the bright, hard light.

In his mid-forties, Jonah is compactly built. He carries himself like a schoolboy on report, his posture at all times impeccable: straight-backed, a little tense. When Jonah smiles his eyes crinkle slowly, almost warily. A smile bestowed by Jonah is all the warmer for its rarity. "You know, I am a very private person," he told me when we met. Did that mean I shouldn't pry? Not at all, he reassured me, but I sensed that it was not easy for him to open up to strangers.

"A loner who doesn't suffer fools gladly," Canadian economist Frank Mitchell, who worked closely with Jonah in the early 1970s, had told me many months before. "Extraordinarily shy," other colleagues had said. "Reticent, stoic, very controlled." Close friends avowed that he had loosened up since his marriage to primatologist Shirley Strum in 1982 and the arrival of their two tow-headed children, Carissa, now five, and Guy, just three.

I puzzle over these characterizations as I watch Jonah move easily among Namelog's Masai, greeting officials and small children with quiet, equal courtesy. Today as the crowd ebbs and flows kaleidoscopically around us he seems relaxed, forthright, in his element. Some say he is more at home in this kind of environment than in a Western urban setting. British by birth, Jonah grew up in Africa from the age of three, mostly in the bush, revisiting England for the first time when he was sixteen. Never completely at home there ("My accent was never quite right," he says with that enigmatic smile), he returned to Africa as soon as he had a degree from the University of Leicester.

While we wait, Jonah gives me a short course on Masai traditions. Theirs is a pastoral culture whose welfare is intimately linked to that of livestock, on which they rely for milk, blood (mixed with milk), and occasionally meat. Until recently vegetables were rarely eaten. Hides are used for clothing, water containers and blankets. Cow dung is used in housing construction and as fuel. Prestige, indeed survival, depends on the size and health of a Masai's herd. Access to water is therefore his number one priority. Traditionally, the Masai migrate with their livestock toward or away from water sources that rise and fall with the seasonal rains. Masai and their livestock have been constantly moving about southern Kenya for five centuries; other nomadic tribes preceded them.

Until the 1960s there was no permanent settlement at Namelog. Then droughts in 1961 and again in 1973–74 decimated livestock even while human numbers steadily increased.[1] As their per capita milk yield dwindled, many Masai families turned to farming,[2] learning their skills from nearby agrarian tribes, the Warush, themselves once herdsmen, and the Wachaga. What has happened at Namelog reflects the gradual settling down of the Masai people, as encouraged by the colonial government in the 1940s and 1950s, and their tendency toward private landholding, as encouraged by the post-colonial government. To support permanent settlements, several water bore-holes were dug in the savannah surrounding Amboseli, "although local elders were rarely consulted."[3] Today, except where there are national parks or wildlife preserves, Masailand has been largely carved up into individual *shamba*s (farms) and loosely held cooperative ranches managed by traditional Masai elders.

Amboseli is a place where for centuries permanent springs and swamps have provided an important synergistic haven for wildlife as well as livestock during dry seasons. Called *ampusel* or "salty dust" in Maa, the Masai language,[4] the Amboseli ecosystem was formed by volcanic activity. While the salt pan still referred to as Lake Amboseli occasionally floods in a heavy rainy season, the Masai's only permanent water source is a series of springs seeping from the Mount Kilimanjaro watershed. These meet at the heart of the ecosystem to form luxuriant swamps of tall sedge grass and papyrus, which attract a wide variety of migrating birds and herbivores. Thousands of animals congregate in and near the swamps during the two annual dry seasons (June to October, or November and January to March). During the long (March to May) and short (November to December) rains they fan out far into the adjacent bush.

Jonah first came to Amboseli in 1967 to collect data for his doctoral thesis. At the time Amboseli was still technically a reserve where the Masai could move freely. His aim was to understand the reserve's ecological significance for wildlife and for the Masai people, as well as their significance to its ecology. Tourism was just beginning to be an important source of foreign exchange in Kenya, and the reserve was the most lucrative tourist attraction in the country. (Until the 1991 Persian Gulf war the industry was bringing in more than $350 million annually; it remains high on Kenya's economic agenda.) About this time the government began to believe the Masai and their cattle were turning Amboseli into a dustbowl and endangering the future of its wildlife.

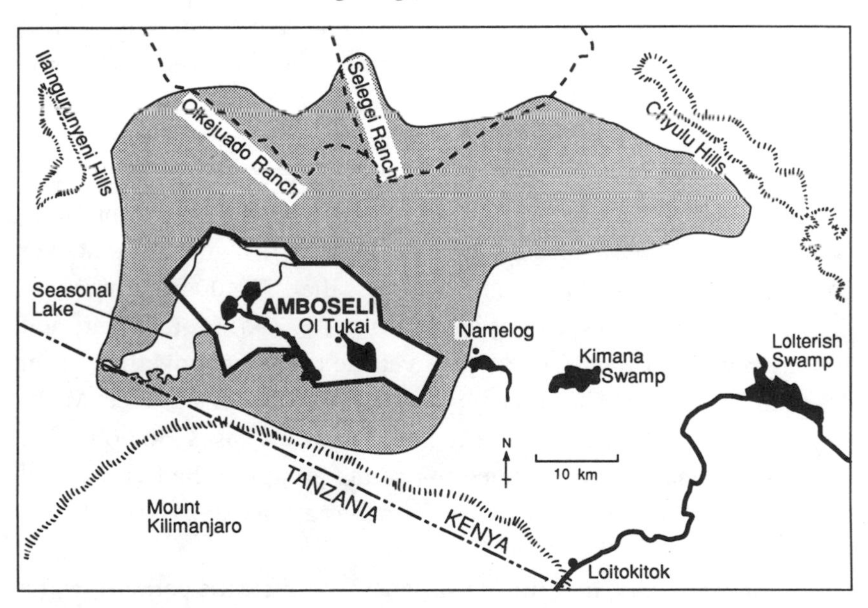

Location of Amboseli National Park and Namelog, showing the main wildlife dispersal area (shaded) *of the ecosystem*

For their part, the Masai using Amboseli were facing two realities, one societal, the other political. First, their way of life was becoming less nomadic. Second, the national takeover of Amboseli was imminent. Ten years after Jonah first came to Amboseli, it was declared off-limits to them.

Amboseli, though small compared with many Kenyan parks, still earns more from tourism than any other: Some 200,000 tourists come here every year. In 1990 gate receipts amounted to $1.4 million a year (if lodge receipts are included the total would probably exceed $15 million, but not much tourist money ends up in local Masai hands). Today, the Olkejuado County Council, sitting sixty miles away in Kajiado, gets about $200,000 a year from lodge operations. The local Masai cooperative ranch earns about $18,000 operating a public camp site and another $18,000 from other concessions just outside the park.

On our flight from Nairobi to Amboseli the day before the *harambee*, Jonah had told me a little about Masai politics. County councils are regionally elected bodies recognized by the central government as representing tribal interests. Over the years, however, inefficiency and corruption has meant that local needs are seldom met. Tribal elders are almost as wary of their county council representatives as of the central government in faraway Nairobi.

Just as almost no income from the park reaches the Masai, little of it filters back to bolster infrastructure in the park. In 1990 Amboseli's chief warden is Francis Mkungi. Jonah introduces us. Generally an optimistic and jovial man, Mkungi is obviously not happy. He complains that over the past several months he has received less than $1,400 from his superiors in Nairobi, the Kenya Wildlife Service. Roads, equipment, and buildings are in disrepair. Every park vehicle (there are only three) is in the shop for repairs. A 55-mile pipeline installed in 1979 to meet Masai water needs outside the park is broken and will now cost $150,000 to fix. He does not have enough money to operate pumps at the few artificial wells still working. Masai are returning to the park seeking water. No one has the heart to kick them out.

It is thirteen years since the Masai agreed to vacate the park. Now, the summer of my visit, they again face critical decisions. In July Kenya Wildlife Service director Richard Leakey announced that 25 percent of Amboseli's gate receipts will be turned back to them provided they can agree on how the money should be spent. Leakey promises the money will be distributed by October. For the locals, who have seen promises evaporate before, relations with the central government are as confusing and tenuous as ever.

The *harambee* finally gets under way at midday with a number of introductory speeches and children's songs performed for Masai officials who sit in semishaded tents. Then Kerenkol ole Musa, a government-recognized "subchief" of the local Masai, steps to the microphone. In his midforties, Kerenkol grew up in the Amboseli region and was a young *morani* when Jonah first met him. Kerenkol carries an *oringa*, or "authority stick," a two-foot-long, tapered piece of wood with a knob at one end. This identifies him as a spokesperson for his people. He beckons Jonah forward.

"Jonah Western is the Masai's friend," he tells the suddenly hushed crowd in Maa. "He is white, but he is a true African, as African as we are. He has helped us in so many ways. He has spoken for us before, and we need him to speak for us now." A venerable Masai elder then hands Jonah an *oringa* intricately covered with fine beading. Further gifts are bestowed: *morani* necklaces draped across his shoulders by laughing Masai women, bags of onions and tomatoes, a roan goat of truly magnificent proportions. Jonah thanks the Masai with a few understated remarks. Only the faintest glimmer of a smile shows how pleased he is.

Sometime later I will meet Kerenkol again in Nairobi and he will tell me, "We gave Jonah the *oringa* because it is a great honor. In this way he is appointed as a leader. Wherever he carries the stick he will be recognized as a wise man. He has worked for us for a long time and always takes the initiative when talking to the Ministry of Tourism to be mindful of Masai needs."

The Masai are banking on Jonah to help them sort out and deal with the central government's new intentions. Jonah the scientist, Jonah the head of a leading conservation group in Kenya, is being asked now to be a politician as well.

We fly back to Nairobi the next day. At his office later Jonah invites me to sit in on a meeting with his WCI staff. Before the group gathers he tells me about an American sociologist, Wesley Henry, who came to Amboseli in 1977. Wesley called himself a recreation scientist. He studied the psychology and behavior of visitors with a view to determining tourist

SHIRLEY STRUM

Jonah Western receiving the oringa *from Masai leaders at Namelog*

"carrying capacity," that is, how many tourists Amboseli could support without harming the animals and the ecosystem, and without ruining their own experience. Together Jonah and Henry projected that with careful planning of wildlife viewing circuits and control of tourist behavior to limit harassment of animals, the eighty thousand tourists visiting Amboseli annually (in 1977) could double without significant damage.[5]

Thirteen years later, tourism and its appropriate management are still controversial topics. John Waithaka and Chris Gakahu work with

Jonah. John is looking at tourist attitudes and behavior in the Masai Mara, a vast reserve bordering Tanzania where 200,000 visitors a year are beginning to damage the ecosystem, disturb the wildlife, and by their very numbers destroy the "wilderness experience." "In August their vehicles look like herds of grazing animals," John tells me. "They fan out across the savannah in swarms, with no regard for fragile savannah vegetation, nor for the animals." The results of John's research will provide guidance to park managers in handling the flow of tourists. Chris, a conservation biologist with a PhD, has done similar surveys. Now with the help of graduate students he is investigating Masai attitudes about tourists. He says, "We need input from local people, the tourists, the scientists and the politicians, first, to get our data, and then to make conservation work."

Helen Gichohi, a PhD candidate who works with Jonah, shows me some 1989 survey maps of the Mara in the dry and rainy seasons. According to the maps, all animals except elephants are now using the surrounding ranchlands more than the reserve. Cattle are excluded from the reserve, she points out, while tourism is at an all-time high inside it. Could it be that the wild animals are finding the ranchlands more hospitable than the reserve created for them? This, says Jonah, is justification enough for treating regions like Amboseli and the Mara as entire ecosystems. Otherwise "you may create 'segregation effects' downstream," that is, static species separation instead of mobile interaction.

Helen is studying the effect of controlled burning on wildlife grazing areas in Nairobi National Park, just outside Kenya's capital. This park is fenced to keep wildlife from penetrating the city's sprawling suburbs and slums. At the same time, migration corridors to the south and west are becoming more and more constricted as suburbs there continue to expand and farmers fence their lands. The normal come and go of seasonal migrations is being greatly altered.

A tall handsome woman, Helen radiates enthusiasm for her work and for her boss. After the meeting in Jonah's office, I spend the day with her bumping over fire-blackened ground in the WCI van, measuring startling new growth in burned-out areas of Nairobi National Park. Helen is learning that fire judiciously set in the right season can be used to maintain open, nutritious savannah that attracts wildlife. "Fire keeps the unpalatable grasses and brush in check,'' she says, as we watch wildebeest, gazelle, and zebra graze the burns. ''Fire creates 'grazing arenas' which the wild animals then maintain and enlarge by grazing on them.'' For centuries the Masai have used fire to improve forage for their livestock, she tells me. Cattle also help open up these arenas, but cattle are not allowed in the park. Using data from her experiments, Helen now advises park managers where and when to set fires. They must be doing something right: In a morning's visit one can see a higher density and a greater variety of animals, including rhinos, in Nairobi National Park than in many other Kenyan parks. This is biology serving management, I realize—ecosystem manipulation to maintain vegetation to attract wildlife. It helps maintain the quality of wildlife viewing, and here in Kenya the bottom line is the tourist dollar.

About Jonah, Helen says, ''Bright people are usually impatient, but Jonah is very patient. He's a great teacher. I've learned more from him in a short time than I could have from anyone else in ten years.'' It bothers her that Jonah's intelligence and ability to articulate his views sometimes irritate colleagues. ''The conservation community is intimidated by Jonah,'' she says, bristling a little. ''They're afraid he knows too much.''

THE AMBIVALENT BUSH CHILD

Helen and I finish our fire-plot survey. We drive on through Nairobi National Park to Jonah's house outside Nairobi, a large rambling structure partially carved into the rock face of the Magadi River gorge, where I will spend the night. Every room in this imaginative house has a view, usually of wild animals. Through one window I see two giraffes browse slowly across the upper slope, their ears flicking to and fro at the faintest sound. With Jonah's guidance I spot the dark shadow of a Cape buffalo resting in the midday heat. Jonah says rhinos, leopards, and lions also often come here to drink, mostly at night. Jonah's wife, Shirley, has lunch with us and retires to the spacious office she and Jonah share in the other wing. Helen heads back to Nairobi. Jonah and I settle back in comfortable bentwood chairs on the terrace, soft drinks in hand.

Jonah's father, Arthur Western, was a Kiplingesque character with a pinch of Hemingway thrown in. ''He was and still is the key person in my life," says Jonah. Born in 1906, Arthur left England as a teenager for India, then still a British colony, to join the Third Hussars, a mounted-horse regiment stationed at Lucknow. After eight years he went back to England to court and win Beatrice Slack, a pretty nineteen-year-old. World War II altered their plans to leave the country together. Instead, he was sent to train the King's African Rifles in the Rift Valley north of Nairobi. On leave he would go hunting with bow and arrow, camping along remote, wild rivers, learning the lay of the land and the ways of its people. After the war he convinced his wife to move to Tanganyika (now Tanzania), to a small village near the coastal capital, Dar es Salaam. There were three children, a girl and two boys. A second girl would be born later. Jonah, called David by his family, was three.

In the 1940s the outskirts of Dar teemed with wildlife. Arthur hunted regularly to stock the family larder, bringing back eland, warthog, and bushbuck. As soon as Jonah and his brother were old enough he took them with him. The boys carried shotguns almost as tall as they were, but they were not allowed to shoot until they had learned tracking and bush craft to their father's satisfaction.

"All I can remember of those earliest days was the tall grass. I was that small," Jonah tells me.

His children, Carissa and Guy, are playing nearby under the watchful eye of a young Kenyan woman. Yesterday Guy tumbled into a small decorative lily pond, so she is taking extra care today. It was a near thing, Jonah says. He is thinking about surrounding the pond with some sort of wire cover so that the family can continue to enjoy its beauty and small amphibian life with less anxiety.

Carissa comes up and climbs into her father's lap. Jonah recalls a certain childhood ambivalence, a word he will use more than once this afternoon. Helping his father's tracker skin dead animals, he could never quite reconcile the excitement of the chase with the silence of death. Sometimes the muscles of a dead animal tremble right after the shooting. "It's calling for its mate," the tracker would tell Jonah. One day the boy watched as a huge sable antelope bull stepped out of the forest to within six paces of where he was hiding with his father. "It was mesmerizing," Jonah says. "For the first time I identified with an animal as an individual." He was not sure how his father felt.

"Don't shoot!" he begged.

"I have no intention of shooting," his father said quietly, setting aside his gun. From that time forward, the younger Western began to prefer stalking and observing wildlife over hunting.

He was absorbing other important lessons: Wildlife was sometimes useful, indeed essential, to human nutrition and well-being. Extremely poor, the local people hunted for meat to feed their families although it was illegal. White colonials could get licenses to kill; local blacks could not afford to do so. He also discovered wildlife can be an enemy. His father was often asked to eliminate maurading lions, hippos, and elephants that stole livestock, trampled *shambas*, and destroyed crops. Sometimes Jonah and his brother went along, sleeping and eating in the *shambas*. On one of these excursions, Jonah met his first Masai, the Wakwapi Masai, who dress mostly in black rather than the more familiar burnt sienna. He admired their quiet self-possession and bush craft.

When Jonah was eight the boys went off by train to boarding school at Kongwa, 300 miles inland. About four hundred boys and girls attended this progressive school, formerly a ground-nut plantation set in the middle of wild, bush-covered hills. Many of the children were like the Western boys, bushwise and almost impossible to control in the classic British scholastic tradition. Jonah soon formed a gang with six other boys, called the Silver Fleet after a comic strip about space flight. Each took the name of one of the characters. Up to this point still known as David, Jonah now acquired the name of the Fleet's flight engineer. It has stuck, sometimes causing confusion. (Before we met, I thought there might be two men with the last name Western in Nairobi, a David and a Jonah. And as I got to know him better there did indeed seem to be two men within: the reserved, single-minded, urbane conservationist on the one hand, and the straightforward, self-sufficient, lighthearted outdoorsman on the other.)

"Kongwa was my freedom," Jonah says, as the shadows lengthen along the Magadi River and we sit silently sipping Coke.

The Silver Fleet roamed the countryside on weekends, sleeping in the forks of trees for safety and exploring as far afield as they could walk out and back in two days. They grew their own carrots, tomatoes, and onions, carved slingshots, and made *kibori* guns out of the metal legs of school chairs. The powder charge for these weapons was usually a firecracker, the scatter shot scrounged ball bearings. It would take two boys to shoot this unpredictable gun, one to aim, the other to light the fuse. The boys ate almost everything they shot—dove, spur fowl, and other small game—cooking the meat over open fires. None of this conflicted with Jonah's emerging ambivalence about hunting. Hunting for mere sport bothered him; hunting for the pot was acceptable.

Arthur Western continued to kill troublesome animals as well as a few extra elephants and rhinos every year. The sale of then–legally obtained ivory and rhino horn helped pay the boys' school bills. Jonah's first elephant hunt when he was ten was a disquieting experience. He recalls the rush of adrenalin during the chase, the overwhelming fear as he closed in on the towering animal, and the sorrow that struck him once it had fallen. "It's just a big prefab animal cutout," he says, "not very real against the sky—until you see its amber eyes and long, beautiful eyelashes." He has killed few elephants since, only when they endanger people or are in great pain.

One weekend the boys and their father came upon an abandoned village of the Mogambo tribe. Huts and fences were crushed, vegetable plots trampled, and one of the Mogambo villagers had been killed. Jonah recalls the people complaining bitterly to his father that white men were making money from ivory tusks but doing nothing to help them protect their *shambas* from marauding elephants. "This really hit my father where it hurt," Jonah says. "By the mid-1950s there was an upsurge in poaching. Initially the poachers went after game for meat. Now they were also going after elephants and selling the tusks to middlemen who shipped the ivory overseas." Their primitive muzzle-loading muskets wounded the big animals more often than they killed. His father spent more and more time shooting rogue elephants and helping local (white) authorities arrest poachers.

As the 1950s waned East African political independence was imminent. Fearing Africa's wildlife would disappear under lax and untrained African management, British administrators began creating parks. Jonah's father, named an honorary warden, spent most of his time at the Mikumi Controlled Area 150 miles west of Dar. "Mikumi was awash in wildlife!" Jonah recalls. Local people, a mix of hunting and agrarian tribes, were summarily removed.

"I couldn't see Mikumi without people," Jonah says. "All I saw was a war: elephants messing up *shambas* outside the park, the people kept from going after them inside. They called Mikumi *Shamba la Bibi* ('The Woman's Farm'). They resented being turned out of the park and being told the animals there belonged only to the Woman, their name for Queen Elizabeth. I could understand why the animals needed protection but not how the park would work, because I saw the tremendous antagonism it generated." It hurt that the local people would no longer talk to his father or track for him. They said he had betrayed them by siding with the government. Why was the distant monarch more interested in protecting animals than people? they would ask.

"I guess I was always more interested in people than in biology," Jonah says, "and more in conservation than in pure science. At the age of eight, I knew I wanted to be a warden like my father. But I had a real ambivalence toward parks."

In 1957 the boys and their father went by Land Rover to look at the area around Lake Manyara and the Ngorongoro crater with a view to reporting on the prospects for tourism there. The boys were given their first cameras. Elephants were everywhere in Manyara, and tame compared with those at Mikumi where people and animals were at war. On foot the boys could get close to snap pictures. Unlike today there were almost no permanent settlements, and only a few Masai moved seasonally through the area. Confrontations between elephants and humans were infrequent, battle lines not yet drawn.

On the second day they drove up to the rim of the crater. "There below us stretching from horizon to horizon was wave upon wave of animals—zebra, wildebeest, impala, gazelle, rhino, elephant. They seemed oblivious to the Masai tribesmen and livestock moving about among them."

The difference between Ngorongoro and Mikumi? Most of Mikumi's people had lived in permanent settlements and their ouster from Mikumi created real hardship. On the other hand, small groups of Masai and their animals had shared water and land with Ngorongoro's wild animals for centuries, each giving way to the other in a delicate, hardscrabble dance of survival. Thrown out of kilter by human population growth and the creation of legislated, artificial boundaries constricting movement, this fragile, mobile balance has now been lost, not only in Ngorongoro but nearly everywhere in East Africa.

That day at Ngorongoro occasional four-wheel-drive vehicles could be seen, here circling a pride of lions and there following a solitary cheetah as it hunted across the plain. These were the first of what in the decades ahead would become hundreds and then thousands of vans and buses to crisscross East Africa in search of "photo ops" for tourists from Europe, America, and Asia. (In 1991 Tanzania banned overnight camping in the Ngorongoro crater. Too many vehicles were destroying the vegetation and driving out the wildlife.)

Jonah went on to become a champion of East African tourism, turning cash earned from it to save vanishing wildlife. But he would also see in this activity the beginnings of its own demise. He was one of the first to recognize that the notion of carrying capacity should refer not only to how many wild animals or species a park can support before ecological damage is done, but also to the number of human visitors.

One holiday Jonah's father failed to meet him and his brother when they returned from school. He had been killed by a wounded elephant that had already trampled two farmers. Jonah's father had come upon the herd when the big bull was off to one side; he probably never saw it charge. "Mother never wanted us to go into the bush again," says Jonah. Almost a year to the day after his father's death one of Jonah's closest friends was drowned while they were spearfishing together off the coast. For Jonah's mother this was the end of the African sojourn. She packed up and returned to England while Jonah finished out the school year. Jonah was sixteen when he followed her. "I owed it to her to go back, but I already knew Africa's wildlife was my life. Someday I would return."

After passing stiff entrance exams, Jonah chose Leicester University over Oxford or Cambridge because of its curricular emphasis on ecology, molecular biology, and physiology. "I became a biologist almost inadvertently, but I had already guessed biology could be an important tool for conservation." He became president of Leicester's biology society at the end of his first year and met many top British scientists who encouraged him to continue in academia. Against their advice, he returned to East Africa in 1967. "However prestigious a doctorate from a major British university might have been, I knew that if I wanted to be a modern African in Africa, I had to go to Nairobi to finish up." The fledgling

University of Nairobi already offered a master of science program in conservation biology, probably the first such comprehensive course offered anywhere. It was tailor-made for Jonah, who would receive one of the program's first doctorates.

We have long since finished our Cokes. At some point in the afternoon the buffalo has slipped away like quicksilver in spite of its bulk. A Sykes monkey calls its short staccato high-pitched cry somewhere between a whoof and a bark. On the lawn two hyrax chase each other, the pursuer displaying a raised white patch of hair on its back like a wound. A frog in the lily pond lets go a huge, deep-chested bellow. Rain-flecked clouds gather over Nairobi. We are only forty minutes from downtown yet we could be in another world. Like the Amboseli bungalow, this house is a statement of the man: private and remote, yet somehow in perfect harmony with its surroundings.

EARLY DAYS IN AMBOSELI

In search of a site for his doctoral research, Jonah drove his battered Land Rover first to the Serengeti Plains in Tanzania where he met a number of fellow researchers. Just twenty-three and open to suggestions, he was surprised to find they thought any prior human activity in an area eroded the quality of ecological research undertaken there. "Find some place untouched by man," they urged.

In the 1960s this approach to ecology, that reliable information about the natural world was best gleaned from pristine areas, was not uncommon. But what was pristine? Jonah wondered. Where had human beings *not* been? To these people, keeping an area protected and uncontaminated meant maintaining stability—that is, preserving conditions and staving off change. They talked about balance but were in fact referring to a kind of stasis.

Jonah had two concerns. His childhood observations made him distinctly uncomfortable at the thought of alienating local people from parks. Second, he did not think it appropriate to treat humans as aliens if they were already an integral part of the savannah ecology. There were not many places left on earth, if any, that could claim to be "prehuman." And he wasn't sure balance in nature was so much a static condition as an ongoing process of thesis and antithesis. Back in Nairobi he told his doctoral advisors he wanted to look at human-wildlife interaction as part of a natural process.

Jonah arrived in Amboseli late one afternoon in 1967 having taken a back road across the plains from Kajiado. His destination was Ol Tukai, a small settlement inside the reserve then administered by the Masai Olkejuado County Council. Two tourist lodges had been built at Ol Tukai. The council was receiving rent from the owners, all park entrance fees, and fees from hunting concessions just outside the reserve. Ongoing difficulties in trying to retain control of remaining water and grazing resources had hardened local Masai distrust. A new tarmac strip had just been completed behind the lodges. Jonah was so euphoric about arriving in Amboseli that he failed to notice the change in the roadbed. He bumped along, unaware that his tires were leaving deeply patterned tracks in soft, uncured tar. Standing at the side of the new road was Daniel Sindiyo, the newly arrived first warden of Amboseli. Arms akimbo, he was the embodiment of Masai outrage.

The day after I spend the night at Jonah's house in Magadi I call to arrange an appointment with Sindiyo, now the operator of a family owned safari business. He suggests we meet in the hospitality lounge of the Nairobi Hilton, a little corner of a pseudo-London tea room on the second floor. An impeccably polite majordomo guides us to a table laden with small sandwiches.

Sindiyo is a distinguished, soft-spoken man. From about 1980 to 1988 he was director of Kenya's Wildlife Conservation and Management Department. A former high-school teacher, he worked in the Game Department in the early 1960s, then spent a year at Colorado State University studying wildlife management. When he returned home, "Amboseli's problems were at a boiling point," he recalls. The Masai knew there was mounting pressure to give a core area of Amboseli full park status to the exclusion of their livestock. Tourists were paying to see wildlife, the authorities argued, not cattle and goats. Sindiyo asked to be assigned to Amboseli, hoping to intercede with the central government on behalf of his people.

Jonah was upbraided by Sindiyo for ruining the new stretch of road. Sindiyo grins when I tell him this. "I could see he was a very determined young man." Despite Jonah's inauspicious arrival, Sindiyo marks the event as the start of their friendship. He ended up inviting the doctoral candidate to his modest home a few hundred yards away.

"Amboseli exemplified the kind of human-wildlife interaction I was looking for," Jonah says later. "The ecosystem seemed a small enough unit for one person to take on, and no one else was doing similar research there. Above all, I wanted to help resolve the antagonism that had grown between the local people and reserve officials since independence. I found a kindred soul in Sindiyo, on the management as opposed to the scientific side."

Before Jonah arrived, Sindiyo had convened a committee of local Masai elders, the first time the people who used the Amboseli ecosystem were consulted by any official representing the central government. Jonah began to sit in on their meetings and learn the ways of Masai decision-making. The Masai reach agreement by consensus after selected spokesmen from different communities and age groups have expressed their views.

"I could have died happy right then," Jonah tells me. He was doing exactly what he had always wanted to do—living and researching in a wild place, among wild animals, answerable only to himself. After living in a tent for a year and a half, with Sindiyo's permission he built a small mud-brick and stucco house in a grove of acacia trees half a mile from Ol Tukai. He began his study of the Amboseli ecosystem by building several exclosures—six-foot-high fenced plots fifteen feet across—at random sites throughout the park in order to compare changes in vegetation within the fences to those outside.

In the late 1960s the dust bowl Amboseli had become was blamed largely on Masai livestock. It was clear to everyone the Masai would soon be ordered out. Jonah and Sindiyo hoped to defuse Masai belligerence—many rhinos, elephants, and lions were being speared in protest—and find a solution that would meet local needs as well as national objectives. By monitoring the diversity and tempo of vegetation growth inside the exclosures and then comparing that information with the diversity and growth rate of grasses outside them, Jonah wanted to learn exactly which animals used which grasses and when. He also began driving back and forth across the reserve in a grid pattern called transects, sampling vegetation and counting wildlife species as he went. He hoped to use biology as a tool to arrive at wise management decisions.

A few days after my meeting with Sindiyo Jonah and I fly back to Amboseli. Because he juggles responsibilities in Nairobi and Amboseli, Jonah is likely to make this trip every few days. This time he has a date with Andrew Muchiru, a graduate student who is mapping former Masai settlements in order to study changes in vegetation at these sites over time and to see what wildlife now frequent them. He turns me over to his assistant, David Maitumo, with whom I go off looking for Parashino ole Purdul, one of the first Masai Jonah met when he came to Amboseli. I've been forewarned this somewhat unpredictable man may not talk to me, but he has known Jonah since 1969 and so I hope he will.

To postpone what may be disappointment we stop first for tea with David's wife, Joyce. She serves it the Masai way, adding tea to boiled milk and bringing the mixture to a second boil before lacing it liberally with sugar. One by one the Maitumo children come up to bow slightly and whisper, "*Sopa*," a respectful greeting. Copying what the other adults do, I touch their foreheads gently in return. They are dressed in spotless shorts and pinafores, though barefooted. One says, "Good morning," giggling. David's home is on the edge of Namelog, a neat tin-roofed house, the first with solar-powered electricity. Although today David and Joyce both wear Western-style clothes there are pictures on the wall of their wedding and both are in ceremonial Masai robes and jewelry. David's mother joins us. She is bent and twiglike, her earlobes stretched by Masai beaded rings, her feet bare, her hands gnarled and arthritic. For all that her smile is no less welcoming than her son's, and he introduces her proudly. Not long ago this woman roamed the Amboseli basin on foot with family and livestock. Now she lives next door to her educated, English-speaking son.

We find Parashino overseeing a garden supply store in the village. Someone has run off with money from the shop; Parashino is guarding what is left. At his somewhat brusque invitation we retire to a back room where I buy everyone soft drinks. Parashino's face is finely chiseled with sunken cheeks, a prominent jaw, deep, penetrating eyes. "I will speak with you only because you are a friend of Western, and Western is my best friend," he says.

"I was a *moran* about the same age as Jonah when we met," he begins. One day Jonah drove up to one of his exclosures to find the wire gone. Parashino and two other *morani* dressed in traditional wraps and carrying long spears and rhino-skin shields hovered nearby. "Jonah was very angry," Parashino recounts with relish. His weathered features, at first reserved, become more animated. His hands never stopped moving, suspended just above the rough-hewn tabletop between us. Like so many Masai he is a vivid storyteller.

" 'Who swiped my wire?' Jonah said. The two other *morani* ran away but I stood my ground.

" 'What are you doing here?' I answered. 'Are you taking this land for a park? I don't like war, but I don't want our land to be taken either. *We* took your cages.'

"Jonah then told me he was trying to find out if cows and wildlife are kept from eating the grass, how fast it will grow, and what different grasses there will be. I told him, 'I know the answers!' " Parashino told Jonah how the wild animals and the Masai moved toward Amboseli's swamps during the dry season, dispersing when the rains came, giving the vegetation time to recover from the previous months' concentrated grazing. He showed Jonah what the different species ate and explained that his people occasionally speared animals, especially lions and elephants, when they endangered the herds or *enkangiti* (family compounds). This created a constant tension between the people and the wildlife that kept them naturally wary of each other, although in migration they often moved along the same trails. The key was the mobility of both groups: Neither stayed in one place so long that they overgrazed the land.

"I told Jonah, 'You must understand our cattle and our ways. Only then can I respect your views.' " Still suspicious but showing typical Masai hospitality, he invited Jonah back to his *manyatta* (warrior compound) for milk.

Through Parashino, Jonah met other young Masai. Jonah told me he was grateful for having learned how to throw a javelin as a schoolboy because the *morani* promptly challenged him to a spear-throwing contest. Impressed by his skill with a spear, his running speed, and bush craft, the *morani* gradually accepted Jonah into their "age group" (the

Masai divide themselves into such groups; young people learn skills and responsibility and eventually move into the leadership positions of an older group).

When we part Parashino grips my hand urgently. "Tell Jonah I need him to help me write my book," he says. He gives me a sampling: "A long time ago in the time of my forefathers, there was water everywhere. As late as the 1960s Amboseli was still very dense with thickets and there were many animals. Now it is all open plains. There is more salt in the soil than before. The Masai don't destroy trees and don't usually kill animals. The salt has killed the trees and the animals have moved. The rhinos are gone, the lion are gone, they don't like open spaces. There are few hyena left. The animals always move. The people used to move with them, away from the park when it rains, but then the government told them they couldn't return. Now only the elephants stay. There is more dust. The soil is changing. It used to be very soft."

Jonah says this cycle has happened before. In 1883 explorer Joseph Thomson described Amboseli as an area almost devoid of trees. But Parashino says that around 1914 Lake Amboseli had water year round and was host to thousands of flamingos and other water birds, and that there were many young trees. His statements are confirmed by turn-of-the-century photos. When the watertable is low groundwater is liable to be less salty, allowing a larger variety of plants to thrive. When the watertable is close to the surface salt becomes concentrated there, inhibiting the growth of many nutritious plants and trees and hastening the death of others.

Until the early 1950s Amboseli boasted extensive yellow-barked acacia woodlands. (A haven for breeding mosquitoes, these are also called fever trees because early explorers camping in their shade often contracted malaria and other mosquito-borne diseases.) According to Jonah, about 90 percent of Amboseli's trees were lost between 1950 and 1970. At first he blamed the problem on increased salinity alone. Later based on detailed observation he decided that the increase in salinity was the result of trees dying rather than the reverse, and that elephants were killing the trees. Trees wick moisture into the air, lowering the watertable and reducing surface salinity. If too many trees are killed, salinity increases.

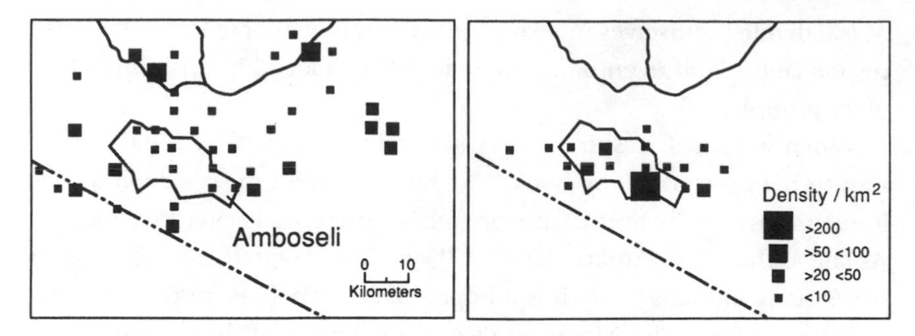

Seasonal distribution of a typical Amboseli migrant, the wildebeest, showing (left) *dispersal during the rains and* (right) *concentration in and around the park and its swamps during the dry season*

Elephants frequently browse among fever trees, debarking some and knocking over others. Where there are plenty of trees and not many elephants this is not a problem, but today too many elephants inhabit Amboseli. Today the silver, sandblasted carcasses of thousands of trees can be seen scattered across the Amboseli plain.

What Jonah learned from Masai oral history was reinforced by his own observations. During rainy seasons wildlife ranged throughout some 2,000 square miles of the Amboseli ecosystem savannah and competition with cattle was negligible. However, in dry seasons 95 percent of the animals dependent on water moved into a 190-square-mile area surrounding the swamps. Because of the scarcity of water competition among wildlife and the Masai was most fierce at these times. In either case, vegetation outside Jonah's exclosures was relatively diverse, acceptable to a wide variety of grazing animals. Inside, thorny brush predominated and shaded out diversity.

Most wildlife continues to graze at night while cattle and goats are returned to Masai settlements for protection from predators. Sometimes as many as two thousand domestic animals are confined in one place nightly. Their inability to graze unrestricted at night limits their nutrient intake, accounting for their poor health at the end of the dry season or during droughts. Research shows that ancient Masai settlements, well fertilized by such nighttime confinement, are "nutrient sinks." Once abandoned, their compact but fertile soil eventually generates new and diverse vegetation to which wild animals are attracted. From the air these sites are obvious: distinct round blushes of green several hundred yards across and stands of grasses and (later in succession) trees surrounded by miles of semiarid brushland. They are dotted with gazelle, zebra, and giraffe. The surrounding terrain is relatively empty. This seems to say that, over time, shifting human settlements have played an important role in the changing ecological mosaic of the landscape.

In times of drought, livestock losses are much greater than wildlife losses, Jonah tells me. However, livestock recover faster when the rains return. As milk production drops off during a dry period Masai first supplement their diet by eating the meat of dying domestic animals. Then, but only then, do they begin to kill their "second cattle," the wild animals around them. Thus has wildlife been their insurance against starvation in the past. With hunting now banned in Kenya the Masai no longer have this option.

Jonah's initial vegetation research and animal counts showed that vegetative diversity was usually higher where several different species, including cattle and elephants, grazed, as long as there was seasonal movement. (Since then, the role played by elephants in Amboseli has greatly changed.) Nairobi's scientific and conservation elite did not agree with Jonah, blaming the evident decline in forage variety on the Masai and their cattle. They hoped to defend the "natural" stability of Amboseli from deteriorating further by removing human influence entirely. Jonah responded by recommending a small livestock-free area "in the interest of securing an undeveloped core for wildlife," but only if local Masai were involved in the decision and received income from the tourism that resulted. He lobbied for a plan whereby they would receive, in exchange for giving up grazing rights, benefits equivalent to their loss. The Masai would lose their primary natural water source when this happened, and although they would be denied access to the proposed wildlife sanctuary, nothing would prevent the wild animals from migrating back and forth across Masai lands outside it. Wildlife would have the right to roam at will. Humans would not. As a small boy, he had seen this happen at Mikumi and had watched resentment build. Similar forces were at work in Amboseli.

Historically, a ratio of about ten cows to one Masai had provided adequate subsistence to these pastoral people. By 1969, as human populations surged, the ratio became closer to four to one. Some Masai were selling their cattle and buying grain, depressing the ratio even further.

Others were leaving increasingly underproductive rangelands to try their luck in Nairobi. Many who remained would soon turn to killing second cattle illegally. Jonah, Sindiyo, and Parashino well knew the central government wanted to protect the tourist industry and would no longer countenance Masai spearing of wildlife, even for subsistence.

"The interactions between the Masai and wildlife are as complex as the ecosystem itself, and any study of wildlife ecosystems within Masailand cannot justifiably ignore the human factor," Jonah argued.[6] Prominent conservationists of the day, among them Leslie Brown, Louis S. B. Leakey (father of the present head of the Kenya Wildlife Service), and Kai Curry-Lindhal, accused him of being overly emotional about his Masai friends. They said he had contracted "Masai-itis." As a young PhD candidate Jonah didn't have much clout. "The conservationists wanted to discard the Masai but keep the wildlife," he says. Today he feels somewhat vindicated, for human ecology, that science which considers the role of people as a part of nature, has become an important component of nearly all modern conservation thinking. It has taken over twenty years for attitudes to change.

Jonah explains how he envisioned the Masai's role as their traditional economy faltered: "Daniel [Sindiyo] and I did some crude calculations and figured that tourist revenue per acre earned twenty times what their livestock could earn using the same space. We knew protecting a core area for wildlife viewing was politically necessary. But we figured that if the future park could be called a *Masai* park and the *local* people could earn income from the tourists who came there, this income (used to buy cash crop foods) could become the equivalent of their second cattle. The Masai would then have a reason for protecting 'their' wildlife. Unfortunately, those in power heard the word *park* but ignored the word *Masai.*"

In 1969 Jonah gave a talk at the Natural History Society in Nairobi outlining the problems Amboseli faced and possible solutions as he saw them. There he met Frank Mitchell, then attached to the Institute of Development Studies at the University of Nairobi, about the same age as Jonah and teaching at the university while pursuing his own PhD in economics. Mitchell was intrigued that there was an ecologist thinking in economic and sociological terms because "the attitude at the time about wildlife was 'get rid of the people and their cattle and nature will take care of itself.' " The two men had long talks together. "As scientists," Mitchell said, "we needed a model to manipulate. I hoped Jonah could provide an ecological model which could directly relate to economics, but the models were too simplified in those days. . . . The entire landscape of Amboseli needed modeling. We never did achieve explicit modeling, but that was the direction we would have liked to go."

In science, the process of modeling attempts to reduce the complexity of the real world to a computerized, mathematical formula, often to analyze the consequences of certain actions or to predict the future. Ecological models are usually based on data about the controlling mechanisms operating in a defined time and space. Models are a way of checking up on scientific assumptions, but as the product of human choice they are imperfect.

The result of his meeting with Mitchell was a 1969 paper by Jonah, "Proposals for an Amboseli Game Park," which became a turning point in the planning for the reserve's future.[7] A 30-square-mile area where no cattle were allowed had already been set aside for wildlife and tourism. Annual revenue from tourism was almost $110,000. The county council was receiving all of that amount, which was 60 percent of its total annual income. Jonah argued that by 1980 the annual income from tourism in Amboseli could be as much as $910,000, whereas if the area was used exclusively for livestock the income potential would be no more than $70,000. Hoping a significant portion of this amount would be returned to the Masai, he suggested that the Amboseli wildlife reserve be increased from 30 to up to 250 square miles to encompass at least 95 percent of the dry season ecosystem. However, if this were done the Masai must be given alternate, preferably better grazing areas and new, preferably better water sources. Jonah argued that they should also receive economic and social benefits: income from the park, new schools, cattle dips, and their own cattle market. At the same time plans for the park itself—better roads, lodge distribution, and tourist regulations—must be developed. Perhaps too optimistic, he saw this as a way to satisfy everyone. Once again the Nairobi conservation establishment was critical. "You've lost sight of conservation in the fog of economic analysis," said one senior colleague.

Daniel Sindiyo and Jonah still hoped for a *Masai* park, but the Olkejuado County Council, which had been receiving revenues from gate receipts and concessions in the park since 1961, began to give Sindiyo less money as it foresaw a hostile takeover. Although Jonah tried to dissuade him, Sindiyo was so discouraged that he asked for a transfer and soon left Amboseli for another post.

Mitchell returned to the United States in 1972 and took a position with the World Bank in Washington. Using Jonah's data and his own as well as that of other analysts, he began to promote Amboseli as a model for how national governments and local people could earn money from wildlife on a sustainable basis. Donor agencies were just beginning to accept and base their actions on what now seems obvious: Third World countries could justify protecting their wildlife only if there was adequate monetary return, only if, that is, they could prove wildlife's usefulness to their constituencies. Meanwhile Jonah, working with an American economist, continued to fine-tune an Amboseli plan. Their data "showed that the total revenues earned from all sources could be more than doubled by planning wildlife use at the ecosystem level, rather than exclusively for the park. More importantly, through the financial incentives made possible by the greater visitor capacity, the net revenues to the landowners within the dispersal area of the park could increase by 85 percent over their maximum projected agricultural earnings."[8] Local people would benefit from the presence of wildlife, while the wildlife (and the tourism it drew) also thrived.

In 1973 the World Bank loaned Kenya $37 million for a major livestock improvement program. Included in the plan was funding for Amboseli, Masai Mara, and Samburu parks. Thanks to Mitchell, Amboseli was used as the economic model for the grant proposal. A key component demonstrated that by improving roads and infrastructure one could improve wildlife viewing, lessen adverse impact on the ecology, and increase profits.

In 1977 the Masai finally agreed to vacate the park if the following conditions were met:

- A guarantee of adequate water outside the park by means of strategically placed bore-holes and a 55-mile pipeline laid from the swamp to beyond park boundaries.

• Compensation for "tolerating" wildlife on their group ranches. Jonah comments, "This 'wildlife utilization fee' was to equal the theoretical market value of cattle which could have been raised instead of the equivalent biomass of wild herbivores which migrate across the group ranches." The amount was initially set at $40,000 per year and would increase if wildlife populations grew as expected.

• Direct economic benefits to the Masai, including the development of wildlife viewing circuits, camp sites, and hunting concessions, and possibly harvesting of wild meat for sale in Nairobi and elsewhere. These incomes would eventually replace utilization fees.

• A school, dispensary, and community center at the new park headquarters.[9]

It had taken almost a decade of negotiation. Many Masai doubted the plan's promises would be kept. "Although the Masai were upset that their land had been taken away from them, they became somewhat mollified by the few benefits that immediately came their way," Jonah recalls. About $120,000 was paid out over three years as compensation for allowing wildlife to use their ranchlands, and the new school and dispensary were completed. However, the group ranches saw no more wildlife grazing fees after 1980. With hunting banned shortly after the agreement there was no more income from lucrative hunting safaris. Then, too, 1976 was a bad year: Amboseli's Masai lost half their cattle to drought, there was only enough milk for the children, and Masai adults had to accept government famine relief. Excluded from the park and no longer legally allowed to hunt, they had no access to their second cattle to see them through bad times.

Parashino's story was typical. He sold some of his cattle and bought a small piece of land on the lower slope of Kilimanjaro where he planted corn and beans. Proudly he showed Jonah around his new *shamba*. Jonah asked him, "How can you foresake your traditional ways for this?" Parashino just glared.

"His look made me realize the agony was mine, not his," Jonah tells me. His family starving, Parashino had done the only sensible thing. The drought, the hunting ban, and expulsion from the park had transformed his way of life forever. Now cash crops were his second cattle.

Water was the key to salvaging what was left of the Amboseli plan and money was needed to supply it. One day Jonah showed an American financier, Royal Little, around Amboseli. Little was a well-known wildlife conservationist and ardent supporter of the NYZS. Returning to the United States, he quickly convinced NYZS director William Conway to support construction of a pipeline. Buried entirely by hand over fourteen months, the 55-mile pipe began pumping water in 1979. However, within a few years it fell into disrepair. While some wells at the edge of the park continue to work (when there is money to buy fuel for the pumps), the artificial water supply is still dependent on central government approval. (Since my visit and thanks to Jonah, NYZS, through WCI, has again stepped in with dollars and technical assistance to salvage the pipeline. WCI is now also paying a full-time manager to run not only the pipeline but the nearby bore-holes as well.)

The 1979 world recession hit Amboseli hard. There was no money to support tourism, to maintain the pipeline, to control poaching. "The only constant during this period were the Masai," Jonah says. Only the camp site managed by the Masai just outside the park brought in revenue, as it does today. When the world climbed out of recession similar revenue-producing programs were introduced in the Masai Mara. For a long time these parks were the only two areas in East Africa where elephants—heavily poached elsewhere—increased their numbers. The message seems to be that where wildlife benefits local people, even minimally, poaching becomes less severe.

Only in his thirties, Jonah found himself swept into increasing responsibilities. He was already on the NYZS payroll as a resource ecologist. For a time he headed Kenya's wildlife planning unit. He became a consultant to the United Nations development program, traveling to the United States, Canada, Central and South America, the Middle East, and Southeast Asia to help develop wildlife research and management plans. Everywhere he went he would point out the value of science to planning and planning to management. For two terms in the 1980s he headed the African elephant and rhino specialist group of the International Union for the Conservation of Nature (IUCN), and for three years he was director of WCI, a position he relinquished in 1990 to become, as mentioned earlier, its East Africa program director. Now he wants to devote more time to writing and to a new interest, "ecotourism," the encouragement of tourist behavior that treads lightly on fragile ecosystems and brings maximum benefit to local people. He is chairman of the Wildlife Clubs of Kenya, probably the most successful national conservation-education program in any developing nation today, and has recently helped found a new nonprofit group modeled after The Nature Conservancy in the United States. The goal of the Kitengela Conservation Project is to conserve wildlife on private lands and to protect important wildlife migration corridors by preventing further fencing and development along the southwestern border of Nairobi National Park.

Daniel Sindiyo tells me, "The local Masai still carry Amboseli on their backs and receive peanuts in return. If one of them drives a cow to market and sells it for 7.000 KS ($320), he pays a small tax and the rest is his. What is he getting from the park?"

"Sometimes all you can do is minimize the impact of change," Jonah says a little ruefully. Today continuing and profound societal change among a new generation of Masai is altering the ways conservationists are responding to their needs.

At Namelog David Maitumo showed me one such response that seems to be working. Aware that conflicts between humans and wildlife escalate around human settlements, Jonah suggested that the Masai build a solar-powered electric fence to protect their *shamba*s. The voltage is strong enough to knock a *moran* off his feet. I watched four of David's friends challenge each other to grasp the wire. To the delight of spectators the fence delivered its expected jolt, but its more serious purpose is served: It keeps large animals from trampling crops and threatening the village while allowing them to pass alongside the settlement in seasonal migration. Built in 1990, this $7,000, 7-mile fence has already paid for itself in terms of property protected. Other villages like what they see and may follow suit. In this landscape where agriculture and wildlife meet, "a hard-edged response may be the only way to go," says Jonah. Briefly I think of the lily pond in Jonah's garden outside Nairobi where a wire shield may soon separate frogs and children for a different reason.

WATER, WATER EVERYWHERE

On the day we go up in the Cessna to count elephants—a monthly task for Jonah—the sky is steely and the wind calm. We taxi the runway once to drive away animals. Even so, a few Thompson's gazelles skitter aside as we take off and a solitary wildebeest bucks and kicks at our shadow. Below, the plain gives way to shimmering ponds and connecting waterways etched with papyrus, sedge, and grass. Small family groups of elephants move single-file toward the swamp—one or two babies no more than six months old, middle-sized teenagers, older, slightly larger "aunts." The largest of all, the family matriarch, leads. Farther away a solitary bull uses his trunk to toss dirt over his shoulders. Herons, egrets, sacred ibis, and smaller water birds wheel below us or stand like statues in the shallows, hunting. Ahead, elephants step ponderously down a steep embankment into the marsh to luxuriate shoulder deep in the cooling waters and feed on weeds. From time to time one sprays her own back or that of a neighbor, using her trunk with dexterity and, it seems, a little humor. Gleaming backs with prominent backbones are broad, well muscled, prime. Ears flap in contentment. These elephants are well off, I think. But my optimism is ill-founded.

Owing to compression of the elephant population within its borders, there are now so few trees in Amboseli that Jonah fears seed dispersal has been hampered. His experimental exclosures and the newer electric fences around his bungalow and around Ol Tukai's lodges prove this point: Trees are regenerating within the exclosures but have little chance where elephants browse freely in great numbers, as is currently the case. For the last few years the rains have been unusually heavy; now in 1990 the watertable is exceptionally high. Water has spread into long-forgotten riverbeds and flowed across access roads and into tourist lodges. "So?" I say, remembering Jonah and Parashino's description of the swamps' ever-changing nature. Jonah explains: The level of water and of salt has increased especially where trees have died out. Elephants are killing trees. In the 1970s there were about seven hundred elephants using the park, but on a seasonal basis. Forty percent of these were later poached; by 1977 there were only 480 left. After the Masai quit the preserve, however, poaching slowed. Elephant numbers climbed to 680 by 1988 and to 730 by 1990. What makes the present situation so critical is this: Of all the animals that use the Amboseli ecosystem only the elephants have stopped migrating. Elephants took refuge in this park when poaching elsewhere was at its worst. Known for their intelligence, they apparently noticed when the Masai were no longer using the park and may have deduced that they had less to fear from humans if they stayed put. Thus during the 1970s their range contracted by 90 percent.

"I got 'into' elephants in the early 1970s because of their dwindling numbers and the heavy poaching then going on in Amboseli," Jonah says. "By the mid-1980s I also began to see how important they were to opening up grasslands." Where, when, what, and how much they eat are all factors contributing to landscape change. Biologists call elephants a keystone species because they play a crucial role in maintaining habitat in certain ways. If a keystone species disappears, its loss may precipitate a domino effect and many other species may be jeopardized. Because of their eating habits (an adult elephant eats up to 350 pounds of plant material a day), elephants indirectly support numerous other species, especially herbivores, by retarding the regeneration of forests and by opening up areas for grazing. They also help seed dispersal through their droppings.[10] However, Amboseli's elephants are now consuming more vegetation than can recover. As the supply and variety of edible plants diminishes, Jonah has noticed, other herbivores are being seen in greater numbers outside the park than in, often grazing not far from Masai cattle. The implications for the ecosystem and for continued high-grade wildlife viewing are profoundly disturbing.

Some scientists, including Jonah, believe the importance of a species in some ecosystems is related to its individual biomass. Biomass is a dry-weight measure of living and somctimes dead biological tissue that is used to measure different things. One biomass calculation equates weight with size, emphasizing the individual of a species over the aggregate weight of all individuals within that species. This stresses scale, showing that big animals rearrange landscapes more dramatically than small ones. For example, in a study area there may be twenty elephants, each weighing an average of 2.5 tons for a total of 50 tons of biomass. But in the same area there are millions of termites and trillions of bacteria, with a total species biomass far exceeding that of the elephants. Over time such tiny creatures play vital roles in landscape design, but it is what the big animals do that we notice first.

"Look! The elephants have created what I call a grazing lawn," says Jonah as we bank, pointing out wide swaths of tall sedge cropped to one or two feet. "Now the swamp has no reserve if a drought occurs, and there's very little cover."

Later when we land on the dry bed of Lake Amboseli to stretch our legs we meet some young *morani*. They come running when we land and walk with us across the pan, throwing small curved spears with deadly accuracy at outcrops of brush ahead of us. They point to the north, far beyond park boundaries. "The lions have followed the game up there. In the hills. We have seen them."

Jonah's bungalow at Ol Tukai was originally surrounded by shoulder-high brush and large shade trees, primarily acacias. So dense were the thickets in the early 1970s that a visiting primatologist, killed by lions only a few yards from the house as she walked back from Ol Tukai Lodge, was not found for several months. Now no one has seen a lion in the park for a long time. According to one theory most of the lions were poisoned by Masai.

"I'm not so concerned about whether the lions have disappeared due to the Masai or to habitat change," Jonah says. "The key issue is that a fivefold increase in elephants has impoverished the habitat. This has caused the disappearance of many species. Overall, biodiversity is way down, and biodiversity, not elephants, is what the park was intended to protect.

"Until recently there was a creative balance among the users of Amboseli," Jonah tells me. "The elephants would open up the bush for the Masai cattle and other wildlife. The Masai would then drive out the elephants to allow their livestock to graze. When the brush and taller grasses upon which the smaller animals did not feed began to regenerate, the cattle would move elsewhere. There was constant spatial and vegetative change, a shifting mosaic that benefited all players.

"Not discounting climate, I now believe the critical element in these savannah ecosystems is movement. If the Masai are to settle, as they are doing, adequate space becomes important because we must create satellite areas to allow for continued circulation of their herds. Space is also important for the wildlife, especially elephants. So at the same time we must build in to any future wildlife plan wide migration corridors through which they can move seasonally. Species diversity is better where the land is heavily grazed, *provided* there is movement."

Today many scientists believe this kind of instability is the norm in most ecosystems and that trying to hold one or more species within fixed boundaries may court disaster. Whether or not one agrees, and however desirable it would be for natural landscapes to evolve unimpeded, human population growth means that some hands-on management of parks and species is inevitable. Where, when, and how much intervention is permissible, necessary, or possible? These are some of conservation biologists' most urgent questions.

"Today we have a segregated ecosystem in Amboseli," Jonah says. "We have grassland inside the park and bush outside, to the detriment of both the pastoralists who cannot use the park and the wildlife within and without it. There is no longer much movement of two key actors—the elephants and the Masai."

Poaching has eliminated another important animal, the rhino. In the 1960s there were two hundred in the park. Now there are ten. Because elephants have destroyed so much of the woody vegetation that is prime rhino habitat, the future of even these few is tenuous. In fact, in all of Africa there are no more than 3,400 black rhinos left, whereas the population once numbered in the hundreds of thousands. Kenya has fewer than five hundred, nearly all closely protected and guarded around the clock. Jonah has suggested that a sanctuary be built near Ol Tukai to which rhinos from less secure parts of the country could be moved. A high-level electrified fence would deny elephants forage, allow woody vegetation to recover, and provide food and cover for rhinos.

Jonah has another more radical idea. He has argued that if Amboseli's elephants could be kept out of the swamps at least temporarily by fencing, one might encourage them to migrate elsewhere and thus reestablish a seasonal pattern of movement. Cynthia Moss, who has studied elephants in Amboseli since 1972, disagrees. "The problem now in Amboseli is that there is an elephant population concentrating in the park which is keeping the trees from regenerating. I don't think creating an artificial drought by fencing will help. The elephants are there because they are terrified of the Masai." Amboseli's warden, Francis Mkungi, feels differently: "If the fence doesn't work, the only alternative is culling," that is, killing off excess elephants until the habitat is no longer stressed by those that remain.

"I don't rule out culling as a conservation tool," Jonah admits. "But it won't solve Amboseli's problems. . . . Getting the elephants back on their migration can help the park and the Masai more."

A natural cull, that is, as a result of starvation, disease, or some such phenomenon, is a possibility. Literally eating themselves out of house and home, the elephants may begin to move of their own accord. But where to, in safety? Unless the Masai are receiving benefits from the park, they may spear migrating elephants. Political helplessness could cause the Masai to lash out in frustration once again.

As we count elephants from the Cessna, Jonah makes note of the expanding water below us. There is now so much water in the swamps that several strong currents are visible from the air, some carving new channels along formerly well-graded roads, some gliding into imperceptible depressions. He shows me where Cynthia Moss's research camp stood until a year ago. Now the area is flooded. He studies the headwaters to the southeast, banking the plane twice around, and looks at the lay of the land as it falls away particularly to one side. "Let's go get Mkungi," he shouts over the engine. We collect Mkungi from park headquarters and are airborne within the hour.

Based on what Jonah shows the warden, park personnel go to work the next day digging a short, deep channel, directing the rising waters away from roads and lodges. They had dug an earlier channel but in the wrong place and to no avail. While the waters may continue to rise at least until the onset of a drier period, for the time being they are no longer threatening the comfort and convenience of tourists. A manipulation of nature undertaken for economic reasons: If the swamp waters had continued to destroy roads and spread into the lodges (where septic systems were backing up), tourist revenue would surely have fallen off.

ELEPHANT POLITICS

Over dinner at Ol Tukai Lodge following our afternoon in the air, and surrounded by boisterous German and Japanese tourists, Jonah outlines for me the complex history of how science has influenced national policy with regard to elephants. In 1979 biologist Iain Douglas-Hamilton completed a three-year African elephant survey for WWF, the first such continentwide survey ever attempted. He reported that about 1.3 million elephants were left. In twenty-eight of the thirty-five countries covered in the survey elephant populations were declining, in some cases crashing. He estimated that 100,000 to 400,000 animals were being killed annually, mainly from poaching but also because of habitat constriction, local warfare, and skyrocketing ivory prices.[11]

A parallel study of the ivory trade by Ian Parker, a wildlife-management expert based in Nairobi, was released at the same time. Parker disagreed with Douglas-Hamilton. He showed that only 630 tons of ivory reached world markets each year, the equivalent of 45,000 elephants killed, not 100,000 or 400,000—an amount low enough not to harm the overall population. He believed a vast number of uncounted elephants were hidden in central and West Africa's forests, and that the total continental number was more like 3 to 4 million. He said habitat loss was the chief cause of the elephants' decline, not poaching. Raw ivory prices rose rapidly during the 1980s, peaking at about seventy-five dollars a pound just before a worldwide ban on ivory trade was imposed by trading countries in 1989.

Thus began a tale of ongoing international controversy involving nonprofit groups, international organizations, even presidents of countries.

In 1989 Richard Leakey, an anthropologist and native white Kenyan, was appointed director of the Kenya Wildlife Service by President Daniel arap Moi primarily to stop poachers at a time when elephant poaching had reached critical proportions. Fewer than 20,000 elephants remained in Kenya, down from some 140,000 only sixteen years earlier. Poaching was particularly rampant in parks like Kenya's largest, Tsavo, due east of Amboseli. Here only a handful of rangers were assigned to guard more than 3,000 square miles of open savannah, volcanic hills, and riverine forests. They were ill-trained and underequipped to battle ruthless *shiftas*, as the Somali bandits blamed for most poaching are known.

To halt the carnage, Moi had previously announced a policy to shoot poachers on sight. Leakey promptly set about training paramilitary units capable of high-speed deployment. At the same time, a worldwide ban on ivory trade had shriveled international markets.

By the summer of my visit to Kenya elephant poaching has become negligible. Many Kenyans tell me that, given historic tribal rivalries and rampant corruption in government, Leakey's appointment came at a crucial time. To dramatize Kenya's commitment, Leakey encouraged Moi to order the burning of twelve tons of tusks the government had confiscated from poachers during the previous five years. The pile of burning ivory, televised worldwide, galvanized anti-ivory trade forces.

Jonah has been just as active as Leakey, but behind the scenes. In 1982 Jonah became head of the African elephant and rhino specialist group (AERSG) of the IUCN (now the World Conservation Union). He was to head this group twice, from 1982 to 1985 and from 1988 to 1990. The AERSG is a body of scientists, wardens, and conservationists dedicated to determining the status of elephants and rhinos throughout their ranges and to recommending conservation measures to protect them. "Good science is the key," says Jonah, but when it comes to elephants there is often disagreement.

Jonah began his job by asking Douglas-Hamilton to update his 1979 survey. Douglas-Hamilton replied that most elephant counts had occurred within national parks and therefore any estimate of losses was probably too conservative. He feared his own figures might be too optimistic. Meanwhile Parker continued to analyze ivory exports. He concluded that a continued continentwide harvest of between 800 and 1,000 metric tons was sustainable and recommended that annual national quotas be established at that rate. Because trading in wildlife products is an important source of revenue for some societies, "maximum sustainable yield" has become the accepted formula among utilitarian-minded conservationists. Maximum sustainable yield is determined by what it takes to replace members of a species in adequate numbers to maintain their population at healthy levels.

Parker's data were initially influential. The Convention on International Trade in Endangered Species of Wild Fauna and Flora (CITES), an international agreement to monitor and manage wildlife trade, has been signed by over one hundred countries. Largely based on Parker's findings, CITES countries that have elephants on their land established national tonnage quotas for the continued harvesting of ivory.

Then Jonah asked Tom Pilgrim, a postdoctoral student from the University of California, to help him design a computer model looking at the impact of hunting on elephants. They used information from Uganda to help calibrate the model. The Uganda data had analyzed the age structure of three thousand elephants killed and compared the ivory they carried with actual trade figures. (Tusks continue to grow throughout an elephant's life, so for maximum yield one should let elephants die naturally of old age before harvesting their ivory.) What Pilgrim and Jonah found was that younger and younger elephants were being harvested. In the past individual tusks had sometimes topped a hundred pounds; by the 1980s ten- and twelve-pound tusks were common in the marketplace, some from elephants not yet in their teens. Thus many more young elephants were being killed than Parker's tonnage figures implied.

"If Parker was right," Jonah says, "Africa's $50 million-a-year ivory trade was no threat to elephants and was in fact a boon to strapped-for-cash governments. If we were right, overhunting would eventually doom the elephant and, inevitably, slash ivory revenues too. The unknown factor was the forest elephant." Estimates for the more easily observed savannah elephant were considered quite accurate at 0.5 million. Estimates for the slightly smaller forest elephant ranged from 400,000 to 3 million. This meant anywhere between 900,000 and 3.5 million elephants remained in Africa, figures much too rough for wise conservation decisions.

Because of the uncertainty, and with NYZS backing, in 1986 Jonah commissioned British biologist Richard Barnes to get a more accurate count of forest elephants. Beginning in 1985 in Gabon and the Central African Republic, Barnes had devised a way to count dung on the ground, dividing the number of fecal boluses by the average amount produced per elephant. From this information he plotted the distribution of animals.

To help set up the project, Jonah flew to West Africa with author Peter Matthiessen in 1986. Bad weather, poor charts, and unfriendly tribes almost derailed this fact-finding odyssey, and Jonah returned with a new appreciation of the difficulty of Barnes's task. He describes Barnes's research technique as "comparable to estimating the population of New York by counting cigarette butts in trash cans sampled from a few apartment houses randomly chosen on a street map." Putting their heads together, however, the two men agreed that high numbers of forest elephants were not there and may never have been, not even before poaching. "Before our forest survey, I was open-minded about whether the ivory trade threatened Africa's elephants," Jonah wrote in *Discover* magazine upon his return. "Now I am convinced that only firm trade regulations can invalidate the projections [Tom] Pilgrim and I have made—that half of Africa's elephants will be lost in the next ten years."[12]

Some populations of elephants were suffering from poaching more than others. Tanzania had lost 53 percent of its elephants in a decade; Uganda had lost 89 percent; Kenya had lost 85 percent since 1973. But others were holding steady or increasing, especially in South Africa and Zimbabwe. Both countries allow hunting, in fact often selectively cull entire elephant families to keep habitat from being overgrazed.

Behavioral and age-structure studies have found that when the matriarch of an elephant family dies the entire family is prone to become disorganized and more vulnerable to poachers. Stressed elephants congregate more heavily than normal, perhaps in a misguided effort to defend themselves. Heavy poaching in places like Tsavo National Park, Kenya, has eliminated most older, larger males with big tusks as well as big matriarchs. Today it is not unusual to see families in Tsavo headed by young teenage females.

In November 1988 Jonah attended an unprecedented meeting of representatives of ivory-trading nations in Nairobi. Called the CITES African elephant working group (AEWG), it was chaired by Perez Olindo, then head of the Kenya Wildlife Service. Thirteen exporting countries and nine importing nations were present. Nearly all hoped well-regulated trade in ivory would continue. After several days of debate Jonah announced he was establishing an ivory trade review group within AERSG and suggested that AEWG ask it to rcport on the trade and on methods to conserve the elephant. At the meeting an African elephant action plan was adopted calling for the selection of high-priority populations to be protected. Selection would be based on the viability of their habitats, the importance of their ecosystems, their vulnerability, and the political will and ability of their host nation to carry out conservation projects. The plan called for the development of national strategies, the regulation of legal trade, the control of illegal trade, and an unprecedented public awareness campaign.

''The value of an elephant can be calculated far beyond its tusks,'' Jonah said to the AEWG. ''It is intrinsically valuable, an agent of landscape change, a keystone species in ecology. It is also a 'flagship' species, capable of attracting international attention—a ship that can save the entire fleet.'' He called for $18 to $25 million over five years to help save the African elephant. The key ingredient for success would be the political commitment of each country's leaders.

The CITES secretariat and most trading nations were still thinking of allowing trading quotas. Others, including Jonah, began worrying that CITES would be unable to control the flourishing illegal trade. In the spring of 1989, bowing to irrefutable evidence that poaching was out of control, eight African range states (those with elephants) led by Tanzania and including Kenya called for a CITES-backed halt to the ivory trade to take effect the following January. As most of these countries relied on tourism for foreign exchange, the loss of elephants would be a telling blow to their economies. Their action coincided with the publication of new data collected by the Ivory Trade Review Group, twenty respected scientists, economists, and trade specialists who had recently met in London. The review group went one step further: It recommended an immediate worldwide emergency ban as the only step that would prevent a killing spree before January 1990 when the ban would go into effect (provided it was approved at the next CITES meeting in October 1989). Jonah announced this recommendation at a press conference in Washington, D.C., in May 1989. A few days later President Bush announced that the United States would impose just such an emergency ban to remain in effect at least until CITES met. Canada, the twelve-nation European Community, Switzerland, and the United Arab Emirates quickly followed suit.

In October CITES members voted seventy-nine to eleven with four abstentions to place the African elephant on CITES Appendix I, that is, to ban all commercial trade in African elephant ivory or other products. (The Asian elephant, more endangered, has been listed on Appendix I for several years.) Botswana, Zimbabwe, and South Africa immediately said they would take reservations, a legally acceptable way of not honoring a CITES vote.

A special technical group was set up within CITES to evaluate whether the South African, Zimbabwean, and Botswanan elephant populations were safe and to determine if those countries could resume trade without endangering other countries' elephants. At the next CITES meeting in Kyoto, Japan, in 1992, these countries sought a "split listing," that is, they sought to remove themselves from the Appendix I trading prohibition. However, they withdrew the request when faced with overwhelming opposition. The sticking point was and is the inability of governments to find a fail-safe way to identify "legal" as opposed to "illegal" ivory should the trade be reopened. Scientists are now scrambling to see if new techniques of DNA fingerprinting can discriminate between tusks from legally and illegally exploited populations.[13] Another investigation is trying to determine if the source of ivory can be identified by measuring the ratios of isotopes of carbon, nitrogen, and strontium in samples of ivory and bone.[14]

In 1990 the "battle for an Appendix I listing was won on technical grounds," Jonah says, referring to irrefutable evidence about the extent of elephant losses that CITES members had been unable to ignore. "But the technical arguments of the southern Africans have validity, too." Today, however, he is still opposed to reopening trade in any country until better controls and identification procedures are in place.

Whatever one's views—whether one appreciates an elephant's intrinsic value, what Jonah calls its "essence," or is an "instrumentalist" who believes in the pragmatic use of wild elephants—the bottom has fallen out of the international ivory market. Today the price for ivory is less than $1.50 a pound, and no one is buying. Poaching has dried up almost everywhere, and there are even signs some populations are beginning to recover. For now, the battle against poachers may have been won, but the war to protect Africa's dwindling wildlife goes on. The continent's human population is destined to double in the next twenty to twenty-five years. The human need for food, fuel, and shelter is already the dominant force molding political decisions.

It's my last evening in Amboseli. Jonah and I are sitting on the verandah of his bungalow. The sun is setting behind us as we face east, casting a reddish glow over the wandering wildebeest and zebra just outside the fence. In the distance an elephant family of four straggles away from the swamp, their shadows growing longer as we watch. Hundreds of squabbling starlings settle in the acacia trees behind the house. "The world as we know it is changing at an accelerating rate," Jonah muses, hands cupped around a mug of boiled tea. "Sometimes conservationists seem to be the only ones trying to keep it the same.

"As to the land surrounding Amboseli, its future will be agricultural, but only 5 percent of the area has agricultural potential. I believe in a hard edge between the development activity—agriculture—and the wildlife conservation area. I'm for judicious fencing in conflict areas, but not for fencing parks entirely, which would be untenable biologically. I hope we can work out a process whereby the larger ecosystem can be kept open for wildlife as well as for mobile livestock. That other 95 percent can be utilized flexibly if we play our cards right.

"The Ministry of Tourism wants to increase the numbers of tourists and is building more and more lodges to accommodate them, but high numbers are not necessarily proportionate to income and can erode the experience. As congestion builds, higher-paying guests will go elsewhere. The whole essence of visitation is its uniqueness and naturalness. As crowds build, this will be taken away.

"You cannot be driven solely by emotion. The result of being a conservationist in science or a scientist in conservation is a split personality. Choices must constantly be made between the head and the heart. It's not easy."

The starlings have quieted at last. On the dark plain outside the fence moving twin sparkles of light reflect from a rising moon the eyes of a hundred grazing animals, zebra, wildebeest, impala. We get up slowly to go inside, to close shutters before the mosquitoes come out in full force.

BEARING THE *ORINGA*

"Jonah's the only one of us looking at the big picture," Mark Stanley-Price, head of the African Wildlife Foundation in Nairobi, tells me over a Chinese lunch at a restaurant near his downtown Nairobi office. Not that he and other Nairobi-based conservationists don't see their own local and regionally based work proceeding within a global context. But Jonah is the one, thrust into the public eye during CITES negotiations, who jets from London to Sweden and California and Washington to participate on panels and boards dealing with ecosystem management, climate change, and biological diversity—global issues requiring innovative global solutions. One reason he has been invited to so many international gatherings is the 1989 publication of *Conservation for the Twenty-first Century*, a provocative volume of essays by leading conservation thinkers coedited by Jonah and the WCI's director of research and conservation, Mary Pearl.

Fundamental research on how nature operates is still important, Jonah avers, but the changing human condition and how it is affected at the local, political, and global levels increasingly occupy his thoughts. As his time becomes more precious Jonah is more likely to suggest and direct research paths for younger up-and-coming scientists like Helen, Andrew, John, and Chris, than to conduct his own inquiries. Amboseli is often still his testing ground. Jonah remains fiercely loyal to the Masai and hopes his status as an *oringa* holder has been helpful. He says, "Progress is slow. Revenue-sharing schemes have still not been perfectly worked out. That's quite a setback to everything we had planned in Amboseli." Two years later, as I put the finishing touches on this book, Jonah is less discouraged. He writes that for a long time communication about the amount and mode of payment was fruitless, until the Masai threatened to fence off the park unless payments were forthcoming. Finally the Masai received $154,000 from the Kenya Wildlife Society in late 1990. Richard Leakey has since promised an additional $705,000, but when this payment will occur is anybody's guess. Sideline observers say Jonah has worked hard, mostly behind the scenes, to keep dialogue among the players going, and helped immeasurably by designing an acceptable revenue-sharing scheme based on ecological data.

What about the future? Privatization of land has far-reaching implications for wildlife, Jonah believes. How can wildlife and landowners coexist? "An entirely new set of principles must be worked out for many wildlife conservation areas worldwide." One of the places Jonah and fellow Kenyans hope to make a difference is in the Kitengela region just south of Nairobi National Park, where many Masai reside. Here spreading human settlement threatens the seasonal mobility of the thousands of plains animals that regularly thrill tourists and schoolchildren on game-viewing treks through the park. Fenced on the north, the park remains open to the Kitengela plateau to the southwest where wildlife and Masai cattle have mingled peacefully for centuries. "Without this dispersal area Nairobi Park would lose most of its migratory ungulates which comprise perhaps 70 percent of its wildlife population," says the Kitengela Conservation Project outline drafted in 1991.[15] "The social fabric of the Masai community in the Kitengela is threatened by an influx of land-seeking outsiders." The area is being rapidly carved into "an unplanned suburban slum which will soon destroy the Masai way of life and choke off the Nairobi National Park."

The project's goals? "To provide the Masai with information, contacts, technical assistance and financial advice to enable them to pursue their development aspirations while at the same time preserving the pastoral sanctuary that their way of life has (until now) preserved." Working through individuals and private organizations, the Kitengela conservation project is bringing landowners and tour operators together to set up income-producing concessions south of the park. Efforts to repurchase land or to create easements for migratory corridors based on methods perfected by The Nature Conservancy in the United States are under way. While Amboseli's future seems to be on hold for now, Jonah's pragmatism has found this other outlet. Pastoral, wildlife, tourist, commercial, and social interests are all at stake.

As I pack my bags to leave on the midnight Nairobi-Frankfurt flight, I mull over how to sum up David "Jonah" Western, this man of conflicting ties who walks the halls of conservation power almost as comfortably as the wildlife trails of Masailand. Perhaps the words of others are best. Here is Jonah's contribution in the eyes of Frank Mitchell, World Bank economist: "The trouble with conservationists is that there are strong emotions at play. They don't have all the answers, but they think they do. There has to be a balance—you have to listen, keep the channels open and act, even though your solutions may be imperfect. Pure ideology, pure knowledge is not enough. We have to find political mechanisms to achieve results. This is what Jonah saw." And in the eyes of Perez Olindo, former head of the Kenya Wildlife Service: "I don't believe Jonah aspires to the front line, but he does want his views to succeed. Jonah's principal contribution is in making sure local people benefit from wildlife and that they have a say in what happens. In the early days he was a lone voice. . . . Time and small people will be behind the survival of wildlife. There is no other option. It is the way of our ancestors."

CHAPTER 3

George Archibald: Dancing with Cranes

LABOR INTENSIVE, HANDS-ON CONSERVATION

Ramsar fixes me with a daunting round eye and stalks slowly from the far side of her large outdoor enclosure toward a board-and-baton shelter that, inside, is divided by a strong wire fence. I am sitting on one side of this barrier with George Archibald, twenty-year veteran in the battle to save the world's wild cranes. Ramsar prowls along the other. Six feet tall, snow white with black wing tips and a face strikingly marked with red, she is a Siberian crane.

George speaks softly: "Hi, Rammy. We have a visitor. It's okay, Rammy, even if she is wearing white pants." Then, to me, "She thinks you're another crane. I think she's jealous. Visitors almost never come here. Isn't she beautiful?" Ramsar was born ten years ago in Baraboo, Wisconsin, site of the International Crane Foundation (ICF), which George heads. The setting is a 160-acre former farm, once badly overgrazed and eroded, now being carefully restored to its preagricultural condition.

It has been two decades since George and his friend Ron Sauey, at the time both graduate students at Cornell, decided to create a foundation to preserve the world's cranes through research, public education, habitat conservation, captive breeding, and reintroduction to the wild where feasible. The foundation was first housed at Ron's family's Arabian horse farm nearby; contributions allowed the purchase of the present site in 1979. Today more than a hundred birds representing all fifteen species of cranes are housed at "Crane City," the site's 12-acre fenced breeding complex. Located on a knoll at the end of the property, as far from buildings and traffic as possible, Crane City has four internal roads separating sixty-five crane "dominions" or cages. Its exterior fence is electrified and partially buried to discourage raccoons and dogs. Elsewhere on the property are an exhibition "pod" where a few cranes are on public display; an interpretive building, auditorium, and shop; a place for the incubation and raising of chicks; an exercise yard for young cranes; offices; and a large library to be dedicated in a few days in memory of Ron, who died suddenly of a cerebral hemorrhage in 1987. Later a guest house for foreign visitors and interns will be added.

Of the fifteen species of cranes, seven are considered endangered by experts and others are becoming rare. The product of 16 million years of evolution, these various species are increasingly menaced by revolution and war, by hunting, by the building of dams and drainage of habitat for agriculture, and by the mishandling of toxic wastes. Flooding, draining, and poisoning degrade and destroy essential wetland habitat where cranes nest and raise their young. Their long-distance migratory habits are also their undoing: Tall mountains, bad weather, and all-but-invisible power lines take their toll. Furthermore, cranes do not adapt easily to change—as, for example, deer sometimes do to suburban development—and their reproductive rate is low. In the wild they usually lay only two eggs a year. Generally only one of these survives.

Found on all continents except the Antarctic and South America, these enormous, graceful birds do not recognize national boundaries. Wintering in the south, nearly all cranes migrate vast distances north, from the southern tip of Africa to northern Europe, from India and China

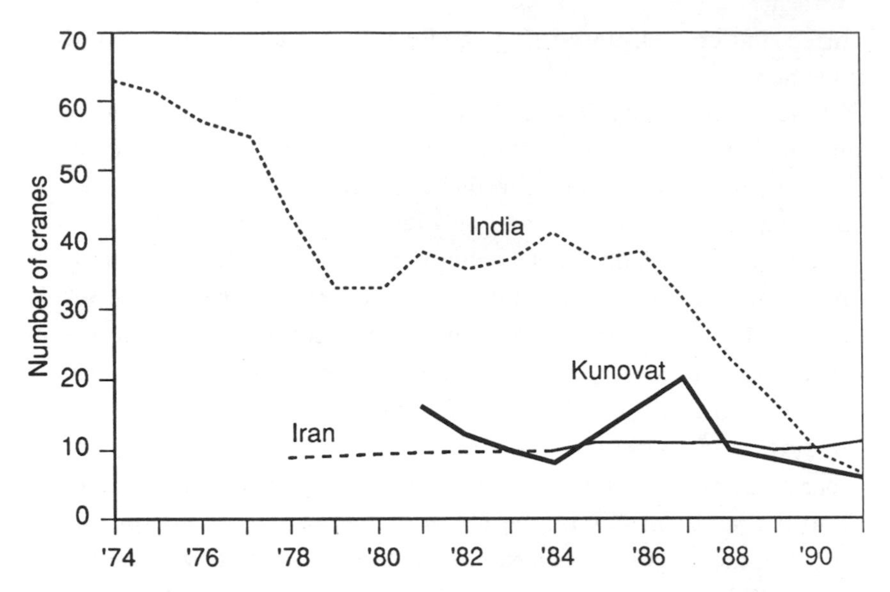

The parallel decline in the number of Siberian cranes wintering near Bharatpur, India, and the number of cranes on the nesting grounds of the Kunovat Basin, Russia, suggests these are the same birds. The flock that winters in Iran is holding steady at around ten cranes, but their breeding grounds have not yet been discovered. (International Crane Foundation)

to Siberia, from the lower forty-eight to Canada and Alaska, to nest and raise their young during summer.

In terms of numbers, Siberian cranes, or Sibes, as George calls them, are the third most endangered cranes in the world after whooping and red-crowned cranes, but in terms of immediate threat, Sibes are probably most endangered. A western flock of no more than ten birds of this species winters in Iran; their breeding grounds in the former Soviet Union have not been discovered. A central flock winters in India, passing through Pakistan and Afghanistan and the Ural Mountains to reach Siberia's subarctic wetlands. This flock has dwindled from over a hundred birds in the mid-1960s to six in the winter of 1991–92. Only two pairs have returned to Russia's Kunovat River wilderness to nest. If something happens to these four birds and if the other two remain unaccounted for, the flock could well be finished. Another flock of Siberian cranes winters in China. While there are more than two thousand in this group, a planned hydroelectric project in the upper Yangtze River valley threatens to destroy their winter habitat.

Reared by humans, Ramsar is uninterested in males of her own species. Imprinting is the process whereby certain young animals learn to recognize and be attracted to members of their own or of a substitute species. Cranes are monogamous, and if they imprint on humans they may never mate with their own kind. Wild-crane chicks remain with their parents for about eight months and experience sexual imprinting during that time. George says, "They later choose to mate with an animal that looks like their parents. If it has been raised by humans, it imprints on humans and will perform its ritual mating dance and pair with humans, not other cranes."

Imprinting is just one of many problems captive breeders face, not the least of which is concern that their breeding efforts may mask the real battle, which is to save habitat. (Preventing disease and inbreeding are other problems.) However, most captive breeders including George see their efforts as a means to that end. Reintroduction of captive-bred birds to the wild where they can resume normal breeding is his ultimate goal, *provided* appropriate wild places and migratory corridors still exist and can be protected and/or restored to adequate condition. Much of his field work is dedicated to securing such places and learning how wild birds use them successfully.

Since the early 1980s there have been some notable reintroduction successes for captive-bred species, among them reintroduction of the peregrine falcon to the United States and of the oryx, a relative of domesticated cattle, to Oman. But there are difficulties. Captive-bred animals are sometimes clumsy in the wild and may not know how to feed themselves. They may carry human diseases or diseases from other captive animals to animals in the wild. They may be killed by wild predators or by wild members of their own species. As I will learn, captive breeding is labor-intensive and costly. Every failure is mourned, every small success a cause for celebration. Above all, patience is a virtue.

Conservation biologists are beginning to realize that "small populations of animals are at far greater risk of extinction than anyone had guessed."[1] Captive breeding is therefore more in vogue today than it was a decade ago when it was more likely considered a mere function of zoo exhibits. Opponents argue that wild animals should not be collected for captive-breeding programs under any circumstances because unpredictable changes in vacated habitat might destroy them upon reintroduction to the wild. However, by the time its numbers are so low that it is in danger of becoming extinct, removal from the wild may indeed be a species' only hope. Other critics are opposed to the very idea of caging wild creatures. George and his mentor, William Conway, director of the NYZS, would reply that saving species that would otherwise disappear from the face of the earth is reason enough for breeding them in captivity, even if, and sad as it may seem, some may be held forever after in a zoo. To these men, captive breeding and (where feasible) reintroduction *are* conservation.

Conway is to tell me later, after I am introduced to Ramsar, about his first meeting with George over twenty years ago. "This guy just appeared one day at the zoo. He had a determination and spark which he retains to this day. He has never wavered from his original interest, which is cranes. He is single-minded, but he has made cranes the model for addressing all conservation problems."

"Academia by itself is a waste," Conway advised George shortly after that meeting. "Do conservation," he said. "If capable people like you don't, it's all down the tube. Be careful, because science is very mesmerizing." George hopes he is successful at linking the two.

In an effort to get a viable egg, George first "danced" with a crane in 1976. Tex was a whooping crane, the sole survivor of injured parents captured in the early days of the U.S. Fish and Wildlife Service's efforts to save this endangered North American species. Scientists theorized that Tex probably had wild genes no other "whooper" then in captivity possessed, but she was already imprinted on humans when she came to Baraboo. After five years of failure, George's six-week stint with Tex in 1982, dancing and nest building, resulted in the production of one egg, artificially fertilized. The hatched chick was named Gee Whiz, the only surviving member of this family tree until 1992 when he fathered four chicks. Television crews loved this story. I had been one of the intrigued viewers at the time and dreamed of someday meeting this man crazy enough to dance with cranes. Now I have my chance.

George has spent fourteen hours a day for the past six weeks with

Ramsar. His cramped half of the shelter contains a table and two chairs, a word processor, a few books, fading wildflowers in a small vase, a sleeping bag. Every hour or so he has entered Ramsar's enclosure and pretended to be a male crane. Female Sibes are receptive to mating for about six weeks in springtime. George is glad the season is almost over. "I'm tired," he says. "Really tired." He misses his wife, Kyoko, a Japanese-American who first came to ICF as an interpreter, then as a volunteer, and his lawn needs mowing.

Ramsar was three years old when these experiments began, her human-oriented preference already well established. Now she is in love with George. He has responded by prancing about like a courting male Sibe, making frequent friendly "contact" calls (*chrr, chrr,* way back in the throat), stroking her back, and helping her build a nest. This looks something like the child's game of pickup sticks. George plucks grass and small twigs from the ground and drops them in front of Ramsar. She weaves them into a circular mat perched on an artificial mound of dirt built to simulate an arctic tussock. George looks silly as he bobs and weaves and flaps his arms like a bantam-weight boxer, but he doesn't *feel* silly—his behavior seems appropriate for this time and place. Moreover, his play acting has paid off. Female cranes do not lay eggs unless they have a mate, and Ramsar believes she has found her mate in George. She has laid three eggs this month, all artificially inseminated and fertile. Artificial insemination is accomplished by injection through the vagina while the egg is forming inside the bird's body. Just before I arrived, two of these eggs were flown to the Soviet Union. If all goes well the chicks will be introduced to wild cranes and will migrate with them back to Iran or India. They will be fitted with tiny radio transmitters in hopes their 5,000-mile migration route can be pinpointed. Experimental transmitters have already tracked another kind of crane from Siberia to Asia, but imperfectly. Ramsar's other egg is "cooking" here, says George, that is, being incubated by two red-crowned cranes who have proved to be good parents in the past. As with captive breeding of many birds, eggs are removed from the natural parent to encourage more frequent laying.

Ramsar draws closer, and gives me a baleful stare. "If looks could kill," George whispers, eyes twinkling behind thick owlish glasses. I am sitting in the spare chair close to the wire. Suddenly Ramsar's four-inch

DAVID THOMPSON/ICF

George Archibald dancing with the Siberian crane, Ramsar

beak plunges through the mesh like a striking cobra. Furious, she may injure herself if we don't leave. We oblige her.

During our first half hour together George has talked mostly about crane husbandry. Now as we walk away he turns philosophic. This is Aldo Leopold country, summer home to many of America's sandhill cranes. George reminds me of that great environmental writer's words. Describing the marsh not far from here and close to the summer cottage he and his family had fashioned from an abandoned chicken house, Leopold wrote, "A sense of time lies thick and heavy on such a place. Yearly since the ice age it has awakened each spring to the clangor of cranes . . . When we hear his call we hear no mere bird. We hear the trumpet in the orchestra of evolution. He is the symbol of our untamable past, of that incredible sweep of millennia which underlies and conditions the daily affairs of birds and men. . . . The sadness discernible in some marshes arises, perhaps, from their once having harbored cranes."[2]

Crane City is not exactly what George wants for cranes, for he too knows their haunting cries and has seen them soar in freedom. "This is a prison," he says grimly as the high metal gate clangs shut behind us. "But it's a prison with a function. My real love is the wild birds, but to save the wild ones we must have this breeding facility. To build species banks. To develop programs for returning birds to the wild."

Seeing ICF's caged birds for the first time I try to share his vision. It is greatly diminished by chain link.

Then, out of the blue, "I believe harming the environment is a type of sin, an injustice to our planet," George says. "But I deal spiritually with this kind of thing, which gives me hope." This is how I first pick up that George is deeply religious, a born-again Christian who identified his faith in 1979. His speech is peppered with religious maxims: "The Lord works in wondrous ways"; "It was a gift from God to love birds"; "You do your best, He'll do the rest." What happened was this: In 1979, exhausted and ill, George was on a flight from Korea to Japan when "a sudden peace overwhelmed me. Things began to happen. I got well. I got invited to China—I'd been trying to get that invitation for years." A short time later he had a dream about the disciple Peter walking on water. "In the dream Peter sank if he looked down, but if he looked up toward Jesus, he would survive. If there was a Power that could raise Peter, why can't it help me and ICF? I asked myself. I began to study Jesus." Now he believes this power can heal the whole world. "What a wonderful opportunity!"

I wonder how all this connects with the scientist in George. On Sunday we go to church. Almost everyone holds a well-thumbed, annotated Bible and follows along as the minister refers to scripture. He says, "Don't ever forget, we are not animals. Creation is God-driven. Evolution is human-driven." What does George think about this statement? Anticipating my question, he later says privately, "I don't entirely agree with him. I have difficulty with this part of my religion. I believe evolution is a part of creation. It is our spirit and our ability to see past, present, and future that sets us apart."

So this is George Archibald. Crane dancer. ICF administrator. Thinking Christian. Scientist.

"George lives and breathes ICF like no one else," says Jim Harris, deputy director of ICF. We are sharing our sandwiches at the oil-cloth-covered table in the staff lunchroom. "George always has a thousand irons in the fire," he continues, "but he's a true leader, with the capacity not to show stress. A creative optimist. From being an idealistic student he's had to evolve into a manager and diplomat. The cranes and the science are still important, but he's had to develop other skills. He's had to learn to accept institutional structure."

Belinda Wright is on the board of ICF and here in Baraboo to help plan the dedication of the Ron Sauey Library. She is staying at Ron's old place, a small white house not far from his parents' farm. Spirea and lilac bloom outside. Out back an unpruned apple orchard overtaken by honeysuckle slopes away. A photographer and social scientist from India, Belinda met Ron in 1974 when he went there to study Sibes at Bharatpur, an artificial wetland in central India. She met George in 1976. "He's a never-say-die person," she begins in her clipped British accent. "He has an unbelievable flair for stirring people up, a person with big ideas. Ron was the one who would make sure there were no loose ends. Both were extremely charismatic. It was a good combination." Belinda gets up to refill our tea cups. She adds, "George likes to be free. He likes to be in the limelight, but he also likes to disappear. He's very complicated. Ron was always the rock of Gibraltar in the background."

Bird curator Claire Mirande has been at ICF since 1984. When we meet she leads me to the shade formed by an overhang between the ICF offices and the nursery where eggs are incubated and some chicks raised. We perch on the waist-high wall and watch dust devils spiral up from the parking lot and across the newly seeded lawn in front of the library. Later in the week I will help plant annuals along this wall. Nearby a volunteer is exercising a tiny red-crowned crane only days old.

Researchers have found that if a captive crane chick is in visual contact with other cranes and human contact is minimized, the birds will normally pair with each other. To avoid human imprinting George and others at ICF go to elaborate lengths to conceal their identity, first when the chicks are small, using hand puppets sculpted to look like parent cranes, later disguising themselves in human-size costumes resembling cranes. This is called isolation rearing, a technique pioneered at ICF in 1985. For some unknown reason this gangly baby red-crowned crane has been imprinted on humans. Its destiny is thus set: It will spend the rest of its life in captivity, perhaps as a breeder of another generation that will see liberty. Crane chicks grow an inch a day—they must be ready to migrate long distances when they are only three or four months old—and in a few days this chick will have doubled in size.

Claire says, "The behavioral aspect of bird breeding is an art. You can teach the science but not the art of getting inside the bird's head. George has a green thumb with birds." She tells me ICF is breaking new ground by using behavior as a management tool in captive breeding. Does a bird like its proposed mate? Is he or she comfortable in his or her surroundings? What environmental factors might enhance egg-laying? These are questions a manager sensitive to bird behavior must address. George, for example, has discovered that artificial light simulating long arctic summers stimulates the breeding and egg production of Sibes, and that periodic deluges from sprinklers simulating monsoons are necessary to the survival of captive brogla cranes native to Australia.

"George is the brainstormer. Fortunately, as he has evolved, so has ICF. He now has a team to do the nitty gritty and to filter out some ideas and implement others. We have to find a balance between the dreams and the reality. There is so much more we could do here than we can accomplish. . . . We all work so hard!"

The next morning I get a taste of what she means. At eight o'clock I go with aviculturist Ann Burke in a van back to Crane City. The daily task is to clean cages and feed the birds. A chill wind whips across the hillside, flattening prairie grass outside the fence. We wear rain gear and knee-high rubber boots, the first because rain threatens, the second because we'll be stepping into a Clorox solution whenever we enter or leave a cage. ("We take a number of disease-prevention steps," George told me, recalling a terrible week in 1978 when twenty-two ICF cranes that shared a common meadow died of herpes.) My job is to dump yesterday's disinfectant, wash the foot baths and refill them. My second task is to scrub buckets and fill them with fresh drinking water from faucets located outside of each shelter. Step. Dump. Scrub. Refill. The work is nothing if not monotonous, though I relish the interplay with the cranes. Before entering shelters we close the doors to outdoor compounds so the cranes cannot attack us; we keep a broom handy to fend off unexpected assaults. Most of the birds ignore us, but Ramsar's aggressiveness has taught me respect. I don't turn my back on any bird.

Ann and I work in tandem along "Whooper Way" and back up "Sibe Street." She wears heavy rubber gloves and crawls into each shelter on her hands and knees to sift waste into an empty grain bag. When we finish three hours later we'll carry this back with us in the van for disposal elsewhere. Prompt removal of waste is part of the cleanliness regime.

On our way back we run into Claire and assistant curator Scott Swengel, who are worrying about Ramsar's egg now being cared for by the red-crowned cranes. The surrogate parents' cage is too close to the entrance gate and they are nervous from the comings and goings of people like us. A decision is made to remove the egg to isolation rearing, but they will check with George first.

CRANE GLASNOST

George is not always easy to pin down, busy as he is with Ramsar, with planning the library dedication, with meetings, phone calls, and the sudden appearance of the occasional "big" donor. Throughout all this flurry of activity he seems unflappable, serene. Each day we manage to share at least one cup of coffee during which time he always seems focused on my questions, as if I am the only person in the world who matters.

I learn a lot in a short time about Siberian cranes. In the early 1970s there were only a few elderly Sibes in captivity, and none had bred under those conditions. ICF managed to get four of these cranes sent to Baraboo. With lights placed over her enclosure to simulate conditions of the land of the midnight sun, one female that had been in captivity for thirty-one years and never laid an egg laid ten her first spring at ICF. Fertility continued to be a problem, however, until 1981 when a healthy chick, Dushenka, hatched. Subsequently Wolf, the oldest Siberian crane, fathered a chick at the age of seventy-nine. To secure additional genetic stock from the wild and thus avoid the deleterious effects of inbreeding, in 1976 George met with Dr. Vladimir Flint, the leading Soviet Siberian crane expert, to discuss the possibility of receiving eggs from the USSR. In 1976, in response to a letter from Ron, then studying Sibes at Bharatpur, Flint invited George to Moscow.

Vladimir, a great bear of a man with a huge grin, a salt-and-pepper beard, and thick glasses, has come to Baraboo with his wife for the library dedication. "We were brothers at first meeting," he says of George. Flint has studied Sibes at their arctic breeding grounds for most of his professional life. He theorized that removing one egg from nests that had two would not harm the wild population. Crane *glasnost* became a reality in 1977 with the shipment of the first four eggs collected by Vladimir in Siberia. They were flown to Baraboo, nestled in plywood and styrofoam packaging and warmed by a hot-water bottle.

George recalls, "On July 14 I telexed Vladimir, 'Two eggs addled. Two eggs hatched. Congratulations.' Vladimir was ecstatic." There were five more successful hatchings from artificially incubated eggs in 1978. "Crane eggs incubated by cranes usually produce stronger chicks than machine [incubated] ones," George continues, but it wasn't until 1981 that the first chick to be incubated naturally, under sandhill cranes, survived. Life inside an egg is tenuous at best. Sometimes a sudden change of temperature is all it takes to kill the embryo. Sometimes parents or surrogate parents break the egg. Sometimes the embryo just dies and all the theorizing around the staff lunch table cannot explain why.

Today there are twelve Sibes at ICF. Flint brought colleagues to Baraboo in 1978, returning home with plans to build a similar facility at Oka, 200 miles south of Moscow. By 1991 there were twenty-five more at Oka and several more at Vogelspark Walsrode in Germany.

The international captive flock may be growing, but the wild one continues to decline. There are several problems. Successful mapping of the migration route of the western Sibe flock, of which fewer than ten individuals remain, is still an elusive goal. If it can be mapped, efforts will be made to protect stopover locations and to educate people along the corridor to protect, not hunt the birds. The amount of time and effort that has already gone into trying to track so few birds is extraordinary. In the late 1970s George went to Iran to mark common (Eurasian) cranes with colored ribbons so that they could be identified later on their taiga (coniferous forest) nesting ground in Siberia. Although Siberian cranes had not been seen in Iran for over fifty years, the idea was to place Sibe eggs under nesting common cranes the following summer in hopes the resulting chicks would migrate with their foster parents back to Iran, thus reestablishing this Sibe winter destination. George managed to drug, tag, and release ninety-two common cranes under arduous field conditions. Exhausted and sick with hepatitis, he returned to Moscow to do a television show with Vladimir urging people to report the tagged birds. Then the revolution in Iran and the resulting shutdown of normal communications put an end to the experiment. With no way to find out if any young Sibes returned to Iran with the common cranes the next summer, George and Vladimir decided not to waste their precious supply of Sibe eggs; the probable travel route and winter destination—*if* the eggs hatched and *if* the young birds migrated—simply could not be monitored. A disappointing example of how the vagaries of global politics can interfere with conservation biology. More recently the first attempt to attach tiny radio transmitters to a few common cranes to track their return to Asia was only partially successful. The experiment will be tried again.

The number of Sibes returning to Bharatpur in winter also continues to decline. (To differentiate these birds from those believed to winter in Iran, George now identifies the Sibes in India as the "central" flock. When Ron Sauey was studying them in the 1970s and early 1980s, they were not yet considered a separate group.) While natural forces and hunters' bullets are undoubtedly causing some of this decline, well-meaning overprotection of the Bharatpur marsh is a new worry. In 1982 Belinda set up a meeting between George and the late prime minister Indira Ghandi. "I told her how Bharatpur was overrun by cattle and people in search of water, food, and firewood," he says. As a result, "Mrs. Ghandi ordered the wall around Bharatpur repaired and guarded. All the water buffalo which had been a natural part of the ecosystem for a long time were removed. Now much of the wetland is clogged with invasive plants, and the ecosystem is changing." Will the few Sibes that may return here next year be able to cope?

Genetically, hope for this species may hinge on China's larger population. In 1979 Chinese orinthologist Cheng Tso-hsin invited George to visit him. George pressed Cheng for word about where Siberian cranes might be wintering, and two years later Cheng reported hundreds of Sibes had been seen at Poyang Lake, a seasonally inundated wetland bordering the Yangtze River. In 1985 George and two ICF board members, Abigail Avery and Fred Ott, traveled to Poyang, China's largest lake. In late winter it shrinks to one-tenth its springtime size, becoming a series of mud flats, shallow lakes, and ponds swarming with swans, geese, ducks, and cranes. From Poyang George wrote a friend, "Mounting an outcrop and on hands and knees we peered below to behold the army. What a sight! Standing beneath us and emitting choruses of flutelike calls were 1,317 Siberian cranes, near them 1,162 white-naped cranes and 107 hooded cranes."

George chuckles. "This trip of ours hit the news media in China in a big way, especially the story of the elderly lady—Abigail was seventy-five at the time—who came from Boston, walked miles in the mud, and burst into tears upon seeing the cranes. Elderly people and cranes are revered in China. Abby's tears did more good for wetlands in China than a lot of our research."

The Chinese asked for guidance in building a research and breeding center as well as an observatory at this site. George promptly invited them to visit ICF and the wintering site of North American whooping cranes in Texas. They also needed advice on how to protect the area, given the subsistence needs of local people. George says, "It's an awesome responsibility to be asked what should be done to resolve the conflicts in land use between fishermen, farmers, and conservationists. Somehow a balance must be achieved." This is the same problem Pat Wright and Jonah Western face: Should protecting a natural area, be it a wetland or a rain forest, take precedence over farms or rice paddies or pasture when the only way local people can get enough to eat is to drain, or burn, or clear it? Are there compromises that can benefit both the ecosystem and the people, or at least minimize damage to each?

Poyang was declared a nature reserve in 1983, but George is still worried about China's Sibes: "Ninety-nine percent of this species is concentrated in wintertime in this one area." A species confined to a restricted habitat, whether naturally as in this case or artificially as in zoos or captive-breeding complexes, is more vulnerable to epidemics than if its range is more widespread or variable. Similarly, a major storm, flood, or earthquake could kill thousands of cranes or alter the environment so suddenly and significantly that a given species might not be able to adapt quickly enough to the change. Such are the nightmares of conservation biologists like George.

Of all the threats to these birds and thousands of other waterfowl that use the Yangtze seasonally, the greatest is man-made: the Three Gorges Dam, a $10 billion hydroelectric complex planned for the upper Yangtze. Although it has been controversial and delayed a number of years, in April 1992 the Chinese legislature finally voted to go ahead with the dam. As presently planned it will undoubtedly affect the seasonal flooding so vital to the plants the Sibes eat in winter. The makeup of the Poyang wetland will be permanently altered.

NORTH AMERICA'S LARGEST BIRD

George spends a final night at Crane City. I meet him the next morning in his office, a sunny room with tall windows looking out across the prairie and toward a shady oak forest carpeted in wildflowers. There is a birdhouse in one window, a feeder in the other. A leather sofa is piled high with notebooks, files, and slide trays. Framed prints as yet unhung and rolled posters and maps crowd the corners. Overhead a mobile of paper cranes turns lazily in the breeze. The four-year-old child of George's assistant sits quietly coloring at a table. "Zachary is my surrogate son," George says, tousling the boy's hair in passing. "Kyoko and I don't have children yet. Zach helps fill that gap." Zach tells me he is drawing whooping cranes.

George sinks tiredly into his swivel chair and tilts back. He has saved this hour for talk. "Last night we were watching a pair of whoopers," he begins. "They are copulating on their own, but they broke their first egg, so now we've mounted a round-the-clock watch. We've tried giving them an egg full of hot mustard, and then a wooden one to teach them the futility of breaking another, but we're not sure it will work, so we want to grab the next egg before they break it."

He is talking about Wanda and Fred, members of the most endangered crane species in the world. With an eight-foot wing spread and standing roughly five feet tall, these are North America's largest birds. Once whooping cranes migrated in large numbers from Texas and northern Mexico to north-central United States and Canada, but by 1890 they had all but disappeared as pioneers plowed their way westward and drained wetlands in their way. Hunting and egg collecting also took their toll. By 1941 there were only twenty-two of these birds left and not until 1955 was their breeding ground discovered, at Wood Buffalo National Park in the Northwest Territories of Canada. In 1967 the U.S. Fish and Wildlife Service (FWS) in cooperation with Canadian wildlife biologists took "one egg from each of six two-egg clutches" and moved them to FWS's Patuxent Wildlife Research Center in Maryland, where they were hatched. In ensuing years forty-four other eggs were taken from the wild and raised successfully. This new generation of birds began producing eggs of their own in 1975, when most of the females were between seven and eleven years old.[3] Sandhill cranes were used as surrogate parents. Sandhills are America's other native crane, more numerous and adaptable than whoopers.

In the 1980s a number of birds at Patuxent suddenly sickened and died, and the FWS realized how dangerous it was to keep all eggs literally in one basket. To forestall another disaster that might wipe them out, twenty-two whoopers—almost half of Patuxent's flock—were shipped to Baraboo in 1989. George is proud of this event, as it confirmed FWS's recognition of ICF as a partner in the national effort to save the whooping crane. Wanda and Fred are from the Patuxent flock.

In the last fifteen years, various efforts have been made to create new wild whooper flocks. One involved taking eggs from Wood Buffalo nests and transferring them to Grays Lake National Wildlife Refuge in Idaho, where they were placed in the nests of wild sandhills. The idea was that the sandhills would hatch and rear the whoopers, which would then follow their foster parents to safe winter haven in New Mexico. However, drought, power lines, and predators caused heavy losses. Worse, for unknown reasons the whoopers raised by sandhills did not pair easily with each other. (Fortunately for the species, they did not pair with sandhills either. Breeding between crane species is unlikely.) This experiment was discontinued in 1989.[4]

George tells me there are now more than 210 whooping cranes, about

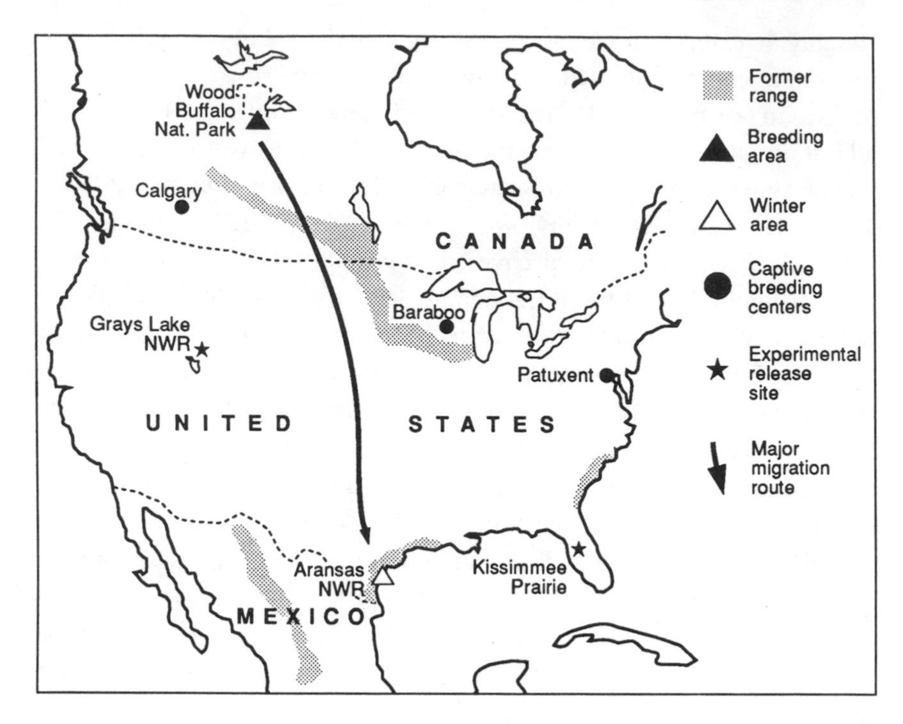

Whooping crane range
(Adapted from a map by the International Crane Foundation)

70 in captivity (29 at Baraboo) and about 140 total at Wood Buffalo, Grays Lake, and the Aransas National Wildlife Refuge in Texas. This is by no means a large number, and whoopers remain high on the U.S. endangered species list. The FWS is planning to release nine captive-reared whoopers on the Kissimmee prairie in central Florida with a view to establishing a nonmigratory flock. The assumption is that the birds, having not been taught to migrate by their elders, will not do so. Experimental evidence suggests that for cranes migration is learned, not innate, behavior. There is some concern, however, that these birds might catch equine encephalitis, a disease endemic to nearby parts of Florida and to which some birds are susceptible.

George goes off to answer a call and I head for the ICF lunchroom. Jim Harris is there with Richard Urbanek, who has just driven 300 miles from Michigan and wants to go back today with twenty red-crowned eggs in an incubator box on the seat beside him. Richard is working on new ways to reintroduce whoopers into migratory situations. His effort is different from that at Grays Lake in that chicks will be reared in the field with puppets instead of being turned over to sandhill parents. Because there are so few whoopers and a relative surplus of captive red-crowned cranes at ICF who share close genetic ties, red-crowned eggs will be used in this experiment. Raising more red-crowns at ICF is still a desirable goal, but not using this particular blood line, because it is important to maintain genetic diversity in a captive population. One might say that, at least for now, these individual chicks are expendable.

Red-crowned cranes are native to China and Japan, not the United States. What happens if they hybridize with sandhills? To be safe all males will be sterilized, Richard explains. No one seems too worried about the females hybridizing, because it is unlikely that wild sandhill males, already imprinted on their own species through early association with their real parents, would choose to mate this foreign species. The experiment is not about breeding, however. It is about an established wild species teaching migration habits to a captive-bred, isolation-reared species so that the latter learns behavior consistent with its wild ancestry. The ultimate goal is to increase the number of genetically viable whooping cranes in the wild.

Richard holds a PhD in zoology from Ohio State University. He seems the prototypical field scientist—five o'clock shadow, yawning with fatigue, but a certain fire in his eye. He says, "I wouldn't be here if it wasn't for George." They met five or six years ago at a conference in Florida. George was immediately impressed by Richard's "commitment to crane research and conservation, his deep understanding of cranes, and his contagious enthusiasm." It is this last quality, coupled with seemingly unshakable determination, that leads George to call him "the Indiana Jones of crane field research."

Richard wants to see George before he leaves, but time is running out. The eggs must be on their way back to Michigan soon if they are to survive.

Richard is not at all sure the red-crowned introduction will work. He tells me these birds are relatively heavy and do not soar like other cranes. In China their average migration is only 500 miles, the maximum 900 to

1,000 miles. The distance from their starting point, the Seney Wildlife Refuge in upper Michigan, to south of Orlando, Florida, where the Seney sandhills go in wintertime, is more than twice as far. Richard's red-crowns will have tiny radio transmitters attached to their backs "so we'll know if they stop somewhere halfway. If they do stop, the Fish and Wildlife Service wants me to *drive* them to Florida! We would have to net and drug them, but dressed in crane costumes so that they do not imprint on humans." The idea is that if migration does not work well in the north-south direction perhaps it will work the next time when the birds head north again.

Later, George reappears. He sees Richard off, calls me back to his office, and begins to reminisce. Now forty-six, George grew up in Nova Scotia in a small house his father, a schoolteacher, built. "We always had food on the table, the basics," says George, the second of six children, "But we were never wealthy. My first memory is of crawling after a duck and her brood. One of the next was getting angry at my father because he shot a duck and hung it on the back porch. As I grew older I kept peacocks and ducks in the backyard. My parents were very supportive. They paid for the birds' food. I know it was a sacrifice." His cousins and schoolmates thought he was weird, George recalls wryly, raising ducks and bird-watching.

Like Pat Wright, George is a MacArthur Fellow. "Did you know nearly all MacArthur Fellows have supportive parents?" He has invested much of his grant. The income helps pay for his own research and travel and he gives regularly to his church.

"I never thought I'd be an ornithologist because I'd never met one," he grins. Then in the autumn of his senior year at university he hitchhiked across the U.S.-Canadian border to Ithaca, New York, site of Cornell University and its ornithological lab. Exploring the lab, he came upon "a guy in lederhosen smoking a big pipe, surrounded by birdcages." This was ornithologist William Dilger. The college student and professor talked for over an hour. "I told him about my summer job working with cranes at the Alberta Game Farm. I told him cranes now captivated me more than any other bird. I'd never been able to really talk to my friends about this interest. Here was a man who listened and asked all the right questions. The final one was, 'Why don't you come to Cornell?' "

In the fall of 1968 George moved to Ithaca to attend Cornell as a graduate student. The university lent him space at an abandoned mink farm where he could begin to breed and study the behavior of cranes in captivity. He rebuilt the mink cages and fixed up a small house for himself. Then he went in search of cranes.

His quest led him to William Conway at the NYZS in the Bronx. George says, "That meeting was really important to me. I needed cranes. Wet around the ears, I barged into Conway's office. His stockinged feet were propped up on the desk. I said, 'Mr. Conway, please lend me some cranes.' Bill's face fell to the floor. 'Who are you? You have no experience,' he said. I blithered. He gave me a hard time, then put on his shoes and showed me the whole zoo. By the end of the walk I had twenty-two cranes and a grant to pay for my pens. Bill provided the impetus for me to move into conservation," George says. "I'd always wanted to do conservation, but the idea never crystallized until I talked to Bill."

Altogether, George borrowed fifty-six cranes from zoos around the country and began to study the comparative behavior of thirteen of the fifteen crane species. Inevitably, the old mink farm became known as the Cornell Cranium. "I was in my element. When one white-naped crane pair began producing chicks I got the idea for a captive-breeding center for endangered cranes."

It wasn't until he met Ron Sauey, who came to Cornell as a graduate student three years later, that the idea took shape. "This was another wonderful moment in my life. We went on a field trip together to help do the annual waterfowl count on Cayuga Lake. The weather was so foul you couldn't see the birds in the wave troughs, so we went to a pub for coffee." The two began dreaming out loud. Ron mentioned his parents were moving to Florida from their farm in Baraboo, Wisconsin, and that perhaps the farm would be available.

In 1971 George completed his doctorate studies in ecology and systematics. Now he wanted to check his observations of captive cranes with cranes in the wild. NYZS paid for his first trip overseas, to Japan and Australia. (The final version of his dissertation was to be submitted in 1976, the PhD conferred in 1977.) Having worked during most of 1972 on wild cranes in those countries, George returned to Wisconsin in December of that year to establish roots and start ICF. He missed his flight from Chicago to Madison, the nearest large airport to Baraboo, by fifteen minutes. The flight he was supposed to have been on crashed. "The Saueys were waiting for me but I couldn't reach them," says George, who credits the Lord for his good fortune. The final decision to start ICF was made when the Saueys and George were reunited hours later. Ron's parents agreed to rent the farm buildings to the two young men for one dollar a year. Armed with hammers and saws and joined by a number of friends, they set about turning horse stalls and paddocks into indoor/outdoor pens suitable for cranes.

The sun is low on the horizon as George and I walk toward the ICF parking lot, he to his battered Volkswagen, I to my rental car. Although he is no longer spending nights at Crane City other ICF staff have continued the round-the-clock vigil at Wanda and Fred's cage. Someone stops to tell us that Wanda has laid an egg. Someone else has grabbed it before the cranes can do damage, but the egg is deformed—soft at one end and flat on the other, double-shelled. Is it stress that has caused this pair's bizarre behavior and such deformities? Are these problems the result of the caged, unnatural setting, George's "prison"? Are there ways ICFers can improve the way they handle the birds or change environmental conditions so that Wanda and Fred will breed and raise chicks successfully? This is and will continue to be the stuff of daily lunchroom talk.

THREATENED WETLANDS OF HOKKAIDO

The next day George and I walk ICF grounds on a mowed path that cuts through the mid-May blush of prairie grass and wildflowers, lupines, shooting stars, and buttercups. In the shade of oaks, sugar maples, and birch, fiddlehead ferns are up, still coiled tightly. A pair of rails are nesting in the marsh below. We hear their calls but do not see them. Orioles, grosbeaks, wrens, and goldfinches are staccato notes of action and color overhead. A school group is moving away from the exhibition pod and through the wildflowers toward us, laughing. Although the dew is barely off the grass, three charter buses are already lined up in the parking lot. A senior citizen's group is just starting out, led more slowly than the children by one of ICF's forty volunteers.

George resumes his story. NYZS provided the impetus—and $4,000—for George's first trip abroad. Japan was an eye-opener. Traveling to Hokkaido, the most northern island of the Japanese archipelago, he was to find cranes surviving "in the world's ultimate civilization, where brutality and sensitivity to the environment are so mixed." The birds he went to see in Hokkaido were red-crowned cranes, like all cranes revered for thousands of years in Asian art and poetry as symbols of long life, fidelity, happiness, and marriage. Today the Hokkaido population numbers about five hundred, and there are perhaps a thousand others that winter in China and Korea. Twenty years ago the Japanese knew that a few pairs of cranes nested on the wetlands of Hokkaido, but they thought most of them migrated to the mainland to breed.

"Just as Bill Conway affected my graduate-school experience and introduced me to the idea of conservation, it was Dr. Soichiro Satsuki, a Japanese obstetrician from a small town in northeastern Hokkaido, who affected my life profoundly in the real world. Neither Cornell nor the Bronx Zoo were the real world. Hokkaido was." For George, Dr. Satsuki was "an example of the power of kindness and selfless generosity." While the people of the Kushiro area were proud of their long history in crane conservation—a feeding program had begun in 1952 and by 1972 there were almost two hundred birds—to George's dismay, "many of the people involved were jealous of each other, a pattern I subsequently observed worldwide. The Satsuki family was above such pettiness and through their unconditional help to all parties, great progress in research and conservation was made on many complex interpersonal frontiers. The Satsukis were ethics in action. To follow the example of Dr. Satsuki was perhaps the most important lesson I learned in international conservation."

Shortly after George arrived on Hokkaido, Dr. Hiroyuki Masatomi, a scientist from Sapporo, told him there were cranes near Kushiro, at the far end of the island. George climbed onto the train one blustery day in January 1972. "My anxiety level was very high," he recalls. "I was alone and unable to communicate a word in Japanese." Six hours later he stepped off into blowing snow and darkness. He knew no one and had no hotel reservation. Out of a great swirl of snow stepped Dr. Satsuki, who had been forewarned of his arrival by Masatomi. Satsuki swept

George out of the station and into a taxi where his wife and daughter and a Japanese graduate student were waiting. George slept for the first time that night on a *tatami,* the tightly woven traditional floor mat used still by most Japanese.

The next day he headed for the marsh. "It was golden brown with last year's grasses and phragmites," George says. Phragmites are tall papyruslike reeds found in wetlands throughout the world that form dense concentrations of undulating fronds, crowding out nearly all other vegetation. Smoking volcanoes formed dark purple silhouettes on the horizon. The sky was bright blue and it was freezing. George set up camp in an abandoned shack. His PhD dissertation was about relationships among cranes as revealed through their behavior, especially their calls, but until now he had studied only captive birds. He was looking forward to the next three months.

"There used to be cranes all over northern Japan," he tells me. For centuries red-crowned cranes had been revered and protected by an aristocracy that lost power in the late 1860s. The Ainu, an aboriginal tribe of Hokkaido now almost totally assimilated into Japanese culture, also worshiped the cranes as gods of the marshes, but they could not stop ordinary citizens' retaliatory slaughter of cranes following the hated rulers' downfall. The sacred birds were believed to have been wiped out, but in 1924 a small colony was discovered in the remote southeastern corner of Hokkaido. They had been spared, as it turned out, because they were nonmigratory and remained throughout the winter, unnoticed, around hot springs where they fed. Because of a limited food supply their number is believed to have hovered around thirty for many years. Then in 1952 the springs froze for the first time in memory. Sympathetic children started feeding the cranes, a task soon taken over by the government, and the crane population has increased ever since.

Everyone assumed the cranes would leave again in springtime to summer somewhere in the Soviet Union, and indeed, they seemed to do so: Family groups began disappearing in mid-March. A few days later George noticed most of the juveniles had returned, and he could still hear adult pairs calling to each other from some inaccessible place deeper in the marsh. He suspected the birds had not really migrated at all. "I was frantic. I knew some of these marshes were destined to be drained for development soon, yet now I was sure endangered cranes were nesting here. How could I, a *gaijin*, or foreigner, convince the Japanese?"

George rushed back to Kushiro. Together with Dr. Masatomi he hired a small airplane to fly over the marsh. They counted fifty-three nesting pairs of red-crowned cranes, bright flashes of white perched on small raised nest islands scattered throughout the sparkle of shallow lakes and channels. Here was proof that this population did not migrate as previously thought. This being so, the case for protecting the Kushiro wetlands was greatly strengthened, for the wild cranes could not long survive if the marsh was drained. Well known as an ornithologist, Dr. Masatomi was the credible Japanese witness George needed. Back at the airport their enthusiastic and forewarned volunteer partner, Dr. Satsuki, waited with the press.

The news hit Japanese newspapers and television in May. "From then to the end of August I was a robot. I had beautiful slides of the marsh and of the birds, and maps of the planned development." On his own time and strictly as a layman interested in crane conservation, Dr. Satsuki organized a tour for George to television stations and universities. "In the end, I had an audience with the crown prince, who is now emperor. Dr. Satsuki also gave parties for researchers from all over Hokkaido so we could build a conservation program together." Much of the Kushiro wetland region is now a national park.

"That was the year ICF started," George reminds me as we head back across the fields. "We could point to Hokkaido as our baptism in conservation: ICF was not only raising captive birds, it was helping to save wetlands too."

We are hurrying now, late for the weekly staff meeting. I slip into a chair at the back of the room. While I listen to the various department heads give their reports, I watch George reluctantly put on his managerial hat. His style is low key and polite. He reacts with phrases like "May I suggest . . ." and "What if . . . ?" All very Japanese.

WETLANDS RESTORATION

After a week at ICF I meet the resident ecologist, Jeb Barzen. In his early thirties, Jeb has a masters degree from the University of North Dakota in biology. He first met George at an international conference in Ottawa, Ontario, in 1986. "George was chair of a panel debating different approaches to the management of endangered species. There was a big discussion going on about the importance of zoos. I was just a brash young kid, but I stood up and said, 'It seems to me zoos are here to stay, so why not use them?' George came up to me afterwards and we talked." A year later Jeb started work at ICF.

We head off along the path toward the fields where George and I had walked earlier. Today there is little bird activity over the marsh. Even the insect hum is muted. The sun beats down. I pull at stalks of prairie grass to suck minimal moisture from the stems and flick a too-friendly tick from my knee.

"Saving cranes means saving wetlands," Jeb begins as we hike down toward the marsh. Without wetlands, he says, there is no point in trying to reintroduce captive-bred cranes to the wild, for they will have nowhere to go. Nearly all cranes need wetlands for stopovers during migration, to winter and to nest.

Although wetlands are found everywhere, their importance to the biological balance of many life forms is only just beginning to be understood. Defined by some as the "biological crossroads where water and land overlap,"[5] wetlands serve as nursery to many species and resting place or home to many others. Growing and decomposing vegetation are prime food for billions of organisms from high to low throughout aquatic food chains. Cranes rearing young eat mostly small aquatic animals. These supply protein for the fast-growing youngsters. Some also feed on the roots and tubers of aquatic sedges. When they are not breeding, the so-called successful species such as sandhills often feed on upland farmland gleanings, corn kernels left on the ground after harvest, for example. The endangered cranes all seem to be locked into wetlands even when they are not breeding and raising young, making the loss of this habitat for them especially critical.

But wetlands are far more than mere havens and providers of protein. Wetlands trap nitrogen and phosphorus, which can otherwise cause algae growth in deeper water and ultimately deplete oxygen. Their complex vegetation also filters toxic wastes and pesticides and controls flooding. Sometimes wetlands store water that eventually helps replenish underground aquifers.[6] These functions are in many ways as important to humans as they are to the thousands of wild species that use wetlands.

Some 200,000 to 400,000 acres of wetlands, from vast coastal salt marshes to pond- and streamside bogs to seasonally wet prairie "potholes" like the one where Jeb and I have paused, vanish each year from the United States. In the lower forty-eight states, 53 percent of our original wetlands have been lost since colonial times,[7] drained or filled to create new farmland and, more recently, for interstate highways and suburban sprawl. Worldwide, particularly in developing nations, wetlands are being converted even faster to meet the urgent need for rice and other foods. Yet such drainage projects threaten major fisheries and the breeding grounds of fish, shrimp, and waterfowl—important protein sources for humans. The long-term costs to mankind of losing wetlands are beginning to appear far greater than the benefits of draining or flooding them for other purposes.

One of Jeb's jobs is to restore ICF's 160 acres to its preagricultural state, a task begun in 1980 by another ecologist shortly after ICF bought the land. Before it was farmed the land had been a mosaic of prairie and oak savannah (grassland with scattered trees) and boasted at least two wetland depressions. By 1980 the wetlands had been silted in by soil eroded from nearby plowed fields and invaded by woody vegetation. The prairie had disappeared under the plow and many original trees had been cut. ICF's restoration effort is based on historic scientific data about how this area of Wisconsin appeared before humans altered it so profoundly, including what wild species may have moved through and within it.

"When I came some of the professionals here had a narrow view of what a 'good marsh' is," Jeb says. "They thought—as does the public—that open water surrounded by reeds makes a good marsh, but there are all kinds of marshes. People have great difficulty understanding the dynamic qualities of wetlands and how they change by year or by season. Many go completely dry at some times of year, as this one does occasionally. Nineteen eighty-eight was the driest year here since the Depression. When this marsh dried up some people said, 'What's wrong?' They had a fixed image of what a wetland ought to be.

"We call cranes ambassadors for conservation, but that can be a two-edged sword. You have to decide if you are going to do community management or single-species management. If I was managing solely for sandhill cranes in Wisconsin, I'd have a marsh, corn, and pasture. Instead, I go for biological diversity. My main goal is to manage communities that *in part* serve as crane habitat, not to create crane exhibits. In restoration ecology it's the process that counts." By process, Jeb means the natural dynamism of an ecosystem as it responds to changes in light, temperature, rainfall, fire, water levels, and flow. It is this process he hopes to restore at least partially, but because the site is so small considerable management is and will continue to be required, such as periodic controlled burns and the removal of exotic trees.

"Areas managed for single species frequently fail precisely because they are artificial," Jeb says. "Let's stick with what worked before the acreage was a farm."

There are no sandhills on ICF land this year, but a pair is nesting just across the road. Briefly we hear them calling and pause to listen. The notes drift toward us, a haunting French horn–like alto. We move on, taking one of the carefully mowed paths that wind across the property. These along with strategically placed interpretive signs serve ICF's educational function. A few hundred yards away an elderly couple with binoculars and bird books are seated on a rustic bench studying their surroundings intently.

Now we are climbing a long hill. "Ecological 'succession' means you ought to be able to predict what's going to happen next as an ecosystem changes," he continues. "But the presence of native and nonnative plants here makes you realize lots that is happening is based on random factors. Whatever got here first or is most adaptable or most invasive may dictate a unique community of species." There is no guarantee that an isolated habitat—a biogeographic island such as ICF, surrounded as it is by dairy farms—will ever recover its previous full complement of diversity; that it will be more impoverished than it once was is more likely. The best people like Jeb can hope for is an approximation of what has gone before, avoiding if they can the loss of dynamism that worries Jonah Western in Amboseli. Playing God, perhaps, but what are the alternatives?

I think to myself: If natural dispersion is random, while the science of ecology tries not to be, then restoration ecologists are making choices and decisions about managing sites that may be arbitrary, but are seldom random.

Jeb points toward the northern edge of the property where another small marsh is barely discernible to my inexpert eye. "We talked about building a permanent pond over there to be attractive for cranes, but that would have meant we'd have to dig past the clay pan to reach groundwater. That sort of construction, eliminating an existing marsh to create a pond where none existed before, is *not* restoration. In the end, we didn't dig.

"Fire is one of the most important ecological factors on the prairie," Jeb says. "In a marsh, where fire may also play a role, it's the presence of water over time, its depth and its chemistry which dictates what species will flourish."

We are passing through one of last year's "controlled-burn" areas, about three acres of blackened soil through which the tiny shoots of native grasses and wildflowers are already apparent. Long ago, natural fires set by lightning and fires set by Native Americans to drive wildlife, helped shape these prairies. Fire stimulates native prairie and savannah species, Jeb explains, and prevents forest encroachment. "We don't have grazing buffalo any more to keep out invasive plants, so fire may have to do it all." A hundred years ago buffalo might have also helped disperse, fertilize, and plant native seeds through their dung. It would be impractical to reintroduce buffalo to this small site today. Will the prairie species planted on these old corn fields be able to maintain and reproduce themselves well enough without the buffalo? Since most prairie natives are perennials, only time will tell. "A very long time," says Jeb.

I think about Jonah Western's discussion of the role of biomass in shaping landscapes, and for a moment I mourn this landscape's loss far more profoundly than for scientific cause alone. What was and might have been will now never be again.

Overall, the ICF site exhibits a variety of ecosystem processes in microcosm—the marsh, the prairie, the oak savannah—a fine demonstration of the possibilities inherent in restoration efforts. "Wisconsin is our lab," George tells me later. "Every April and September we invite and pay for . . . people from overseas to come here and then we throw neighbors together—Tibetans with Bhutanese, Outer Mongolians with

Inner Mongolians, South Africans with East Africans. We want them to become friends. Then we tailor their trips around the United States so they can visit habitats similar to their own. Mongolians go to Idaho to see short-grass prairies like their own, Vietnamese go to the Okefenokee Swamp in Georgia."

ICF has helped convene four international workshops in the last fifteen years, bringing together specialists from around the world who would otherwise have never met. Meetings have been held in Wisconsin, Japan, India, and China. There will be one in Russia in 1993 and another in Botswana in 1994. Bonds have been forged to conserve border wetlands between the former USSR and China, two countries almost always at odds. Similarly, Pakistanis and Indians, North and South Koreans, South Africans and East Africans have found common ground in the common goal to save cranes.

In 1982 George and Charles Luthin, a former volunteer at ICF and founder of its habitat-restoration program, met Vietnam's foremost ornithologist, Professor Vo Quy, at an international conference in Moscow. "Charlie and I encouraged Vo Quy to search for the long-legged avian dwellers in Vietnam. A short time later, as head of the World Working Group on Storks, Ibises, and Spoonbills at Vogelpark Walsrode in West Germany, Charlie visited Vo Quy and quickly saw that field research was impossible because of lack of funds. Vietnamese ornithologists could scarcely feed their families." Support came soon thereafter from Vogelpark's Brehm Fund for Bird Conservation. In 1986 Vietnamese ornithologists found eastern sarus cranes on the Mekong Delta and invited George to visit. Until this discovery, Westerners had believed this formerly abundant subspecies had vanished from Asia. (A relatively healthy flock of the subspecies still breeds in Australia.)

With George Schaller of the NYZS, the indomitable Abigail Avery, and three Vietnamese scientists, George visited in January 1988 the former Plain of Reeds just north of the Mekong and stretching from Phnom Penh in Cambodia almost to Ho Chi Minh City. "This enormous shallow basin had once been a wetland wilderness with wooded islands and a plethora of wildlife," George tells me. "It was also a sanctuary for the Viet Cong. During the Vietnam war the entire basin was dredged, drained, and burned. Now, in the 1980s, the Vietnamese wanted to restore a part of the wetland and to once again grow the rot-resistant malaleuca trees (a kind of mangrove) that supplied sturdy stakes on which to keep homes above flood levels of the Mekong."

George invited several Vietnamese scientists to visit ICF, but, Jeb tells me, "it wasn't until we showed them Horicon Marsh, a huge wetland near ICF which had been ditched years ago for farming, and showed them what had happened to it that they began to get the picture." Horicon's drained soil proved inhospitable to agriculture. The state and federal governments stepped in to restore the area as a wetland, at vast expense, then after reflooding found that the marshland's hydrology had changed and the soil had been altered. Monostands of cattails appeared. Could the visitors learn from American mistakes?

Jeb has been to Vietnam four times and is helping restore 37,000 acres of wetland on the delta, quite similar to Horicon. George returns each year with teams of volunteers to help with photography, field research, and public education. Jeb explains what the Vietnamese learned from ICF: "In 1991 when I was in Vietnam some leaders still wanted to dig a big ditch in the Plain of Reeds and manage what was left of the wetland in marked-off diked squares for cranes, fishing, rice, and other purposes. The Vietnamese who had visited ICF argued with their colleagues that restoring a natural ecosystem should come first. This was a very foreign idea at first. Words like *biological diversity* are sometimes hard to communicate, but cultures *can* communicate about cranes."

The Vietnamese believe that after death one's soul goes to heaven on the wings of a crane. Vietnamese and Americans both cherish this bird, the one reverently, the other primarily because it is endangered. Cranes transcend cultures. Cranes need wetlands. Wetlands need protection. But managing wetlands for a single species may not benefit biodiversity or humankind generally, and in the long term may fail. For example, managing water level for cranes might help cranes, but one may be making the habitat less suitable for other species, including some capable of being harvested by humans on a sustainable basis. Also, if restoration or management activity involves a high level of intervention, unexpected consequences to other species and processes may result. George is single-minded about cranes, but as Bill Conway says, he never loses sight of the larger picture.

The natural habitat of Mekong birds has been radically altered, particularly in recent times. As George and Jeb and their Vietnamese colleagues work to restore this landscape to some semblance of its former functioning self, they must answer the overriding question, Do we manage only for cranes, or do we manage for restoration of this wetland's ecological benefits and services generally, of which the cranes are just a part? And when we use words like *benefits* and *services*, are we addressing ecosystem needs, human needs, or both, or neither, and to what degree?

"Let's try nature's way first," the Vietnamese who had seen Horicon Marsh eventually convinced their colleagues. "If it doesn't work, then dig your ditch, but if you dig first it will not be easy to go back." Now a management plan has been drafted by the Vietnamese with ICF's help that will protect and begin to restore the natural wetland while taking into account the needs of local people, unquestionably a part of this devastated landscape. Responding to their needs is the primary political responsibility of the Vietnamese, understood by the Americans. The plan therefore includes management activities addressing the needs of fishermen and timber and rice producers. These, it is hoped, will only minimally disrupt the natural water flow and vegetation growth required for the wetland to deliver its long-term benefits and services to all constituents. Including cranes.

RADIO TRACKING

The day after my walk with Jeb, George is worrying about China's cranes again, not just Siberians. "China has eight crane species," he tells me, "more than any other country. Six of the eight are endangered. Four of these (Sibes, red-crowned, white-naped, and hooded), depend on the Yangtze ecosystem, as do millions of other waterfowl. All of China's red-crowned cranes, about 750 of them, winter on the Yangtze delta. This is a dynamic coastline, always building with silt from the Yangtze. The Three Gorges Dam will not only drain two-thirds of Poyang Lake, it will stop this natural siltation process. Look at the map. Nanjing was once on the coast! Now it is 200 miles inland. If you prevent silt, erosion will wear away the land. The first thing to go will be the salt marshes. Red-crowned winter habitat." This kind of thing is happening elsewhere. For example, man-made flood controls on the Mississippi have led to a massive loss of salt marshland. Largely because of channelization, sediment that would have nourished the marshes now flows into the Gulf of Mexico.

"At the end of the Cultural Revolution there were only twenty nature reserves in China. Now there are more than three hundred, about 2 percent of the land. But China's reserves must support both wildlife and people. Public education is critical. We have a long way to go." George says that in order for these reserves to be successful, local people must understand their value as dynamic natural systems benefiting their own lives. Otherwise sheer human numbers will dictate other land-use priorities. How much of this is being communicated today in China is difficult to judge.

"Are you discouraged?" I ask George. There is a pause. "In this business you have to give 100 percent and not expect to get anything back," he answers. "But if you're not an optimist you're just shooting yourself in the foot.

"Who knows where we'll be by 2050? There will be destroyed pockets on earth and restored pockets on earth. There will be some good, some bad. All the work we've done until now with captive breeding and research in China, Russia, and elsewhere means we have defined the problems. The task ahead is, Can we implement solutions? We have all the ingredients. We're on the edge."

As I listen to George it occurs to me that perhaps cranes are not only symbols of fidelity and long life, as in China, but of peace as well. Perhaps the lessons learned by people meeting in the interest of cranes can someday, somehow be adapted by the players of that much more complex game, global politics.

On my last Sunday in Baraboo George, his wife Kyoko, and I drive into the Wisconsin countryside. We pass tall oaks, wide, shimmering marshes, undulating streams, wild-blue spiderwort at roadside. Pausing with windows rolled down, we hear the songs of sedge wren, flycatcher, oriole, and bobolink. Nearby the V of a beaver's whiskered nose angles across open water, its tail slaps like a pistol shot. We're looking for a pair of sandhills, one of which is carrying a small radio transmitter on its leg.

A decade ago Kyoko was photographing the behavior of a pair of sandhills. They were incubating two eggs when one evening they flew away. After dark Kyoko took the eggs under her down vest to keep them warm. "I returned in the morning but the parents did not return," she tells me as she lifts a radio-receiving antenna from the car trunk. "So I collected them and raised them at a nearby farmhouse and then in an enclosure in the prairie bordering the Leopold Preserve wetland, using isolation-rearing techniques. Later in the summer I penned them in the marsh to get them used to the wild. When autumn came they left with a wild flock. Both had colored markers attached to their legs. Last year one—I call him Leo, after Aldo Leopold—was seen eating someone's raspberries not far from here." ICF staff quickly captured him and fitted a tiny radio transmitter to his leg. "This year he's back again with a mate. They have a chick." (Later in the summer George will write to let me know that the chick has mysteriously disappeared, but he is no less proud of Kyoko's pioneering niche in the history of crane conservation. "Leo is the first isolation-reared crane to migrate, pair, and breed successfully in the wild. Now the technique is being applied to Siberians and in the near future it may be applied to whoopers.")

We tramp across newly plowed fields toward a small grove where Kyoko has built a brush blind. Nine years seems a long time to wait for the return of a single crane and confirmation of a theory, but patience is the underlying theme of captive breeding and reintroduction efforts and of conservation biology generally: Rearing chicks by puppetry, hand-carrying Sibe eggs to Siberia and red-crowns to Michigan, dancing with cranes. Each bird hatched and raised or saved from danger and ultimately returned to the wild is a hard-earned jewel in the ICF crown.

Kyoko turns the hand-held antenna slowly, right and left, but receives no signal. "I know he's out there somewhere," she says. We scan the distance with binoculars. Half an hour later we hike back to the car, defeated. "No luck today," Kyoko shrugs. She'll try again tomorrow.

As we drive back to Baraboo past fields of barely sprouted corn, we spot a sandhill crane in the distance, its shoulders "painted" with reddish soil, a camouflage trick used by these birds for unknown reasons. It's not Leo, we confirm by looking through binoculars for the telltale leg transmitter, but it might have been.

In September 1991 I learn from George that three captive-bred Sibe chicks, the two flown from Baraboo in May and one other from

Vogelpark Walsrode, were raised successfully by costumed "parents" in Siberia during the short arctic summer just past. In August when they fledged (acquired the feathers for flight) they were released near one of the last pairs of wild cranes and their chick. Although they bonded with the hand-reared chicks, the wild cranes suddenly migrated one cold morning in late August and left the three juveniles behind. The chicks were recaptured by costumed scientists and taken to the Russian crane-breeding center at Oka Nature Reserve. There are plans afoot to release them with wild cranes in India during the 1991–92 winter. If that doesn't work, writes George, they will be released with wild cranes in Siberia next spring. Patience is indeed a virtue in this game.

And when they are finally released, will their radio transmitters work? Will their migratory route be well mapped at last? If so, can someone get into places like Afghanistan afterwards to "do" conservation education, to persuade the people to protect their wetlands and not to hunt the birds? Will at least one, like Kyoko's Leo in Wisconsin, return to Siberia next year, or the year after, or the year after that?

The waiting doesn't discourage George. "The reality for me is, this is a lifetime thing." And while there's any hope at all, he'll go on dancing with cranes.

CHAPTER 4

Luis Diego Gómez: Behind-the-Scenes Botanist

EN ROUTE TO COTO BRUS

Luis Diego Gómez picks me up at the Hotel Presidente in San José at seven-thirty in the morning. The usual traffic snarl of Costa Rica's capital has not yet begun and he has had no trouble parking his four-wheel-drive Toyota on the narrow street outside. He wears freshly pressed khaki trousers, a white shirt open at the throat, and worn but clean running shoes. A clipped black mustache does little to conceal his wide smile. Under strikingly straight brows, dark eyes crinkle in welcome. He is forty-nine but could be younger.

"I'd know you anywhere," he says. But then, he had my photo in advance. I don't have his.

I lift my backpack into the Toyota and we drive to Luis's townhouse, where his American wife, Gail, and his mother, a tiny gentlewoman in her eighties, are waiting. Breakfast is laid in an airy room open to a long narrow garden fragrant with summer blossoms. Interior walls are lined with paintings, most by Costa Rican artists, Gail tells me as she serves up scrambled eggs and coffee. Against the walls stand glass-fronted cabinets filled with Central American antiquities, some as old as 3,000 years. Wildlife figurines predominate: jaguars, toucans, snakes in clay and stone. Luis says he found many of these at the edge of newly bulldozed roads or in freshly ploughed fields. (Luis drafted the 1975 law protecting Costa Rica's archaeological patrimony; his collection is registered with the National Museum.) A study on the first floor is lined ceiling to floor with books on botany, art, music, philosophy, and poetry. There is a piano piled high with scores but the keyboard is closed. Fabrics on the comfortable-looking chairs and sofas are of a rough weave in warm earth tones.

We leave soon after breakfast because there are rumors of a union strike, which may close down some roads. Right now, however, the streets are clear and we are soon climbing to rolling highlands, leaving San José's urban sprawl behind. We are on the Inter-American Highway heading south into a mountainous area called the Cerro. To our left lies the Talamanca Range, a volcanic spine of smoky-blue peaks and ridges stretching roughly north to south from San José to the Panamanian border. Behind them massive thunderheads boil to form and reform endlessly. This is July, the rainy season. Where we are going the annual rainfall averages 150 inches a year. Tonight we will sleep at a small country hotel at 9,000 feet, halfway to our destination, the 350-acre Robert and Catherine Wilson Botanical Garden some 130 miles south of San José. It will be so damp and cold I will wear long underwear, socks, and a ski cap when I bed down under two blankets, although we are only 600 miles north of the equator.

At 19,730 square miles, Costa Rica is smaller than West Virginia. It is unique among developing nations for protection of its natural areas and for innovative attempts to forestall forest loss. Twenty-seven percent of its land is protected: National parks occupy some 12 percent of the land, as high a percentage as anywhere; an additional 15 percent is protected in other ways such as forest reserves. The nation is divided into seven conservation-management zones in which a range of land-use options is monitored. In spite of these measures, about 100,000 acres of woodland

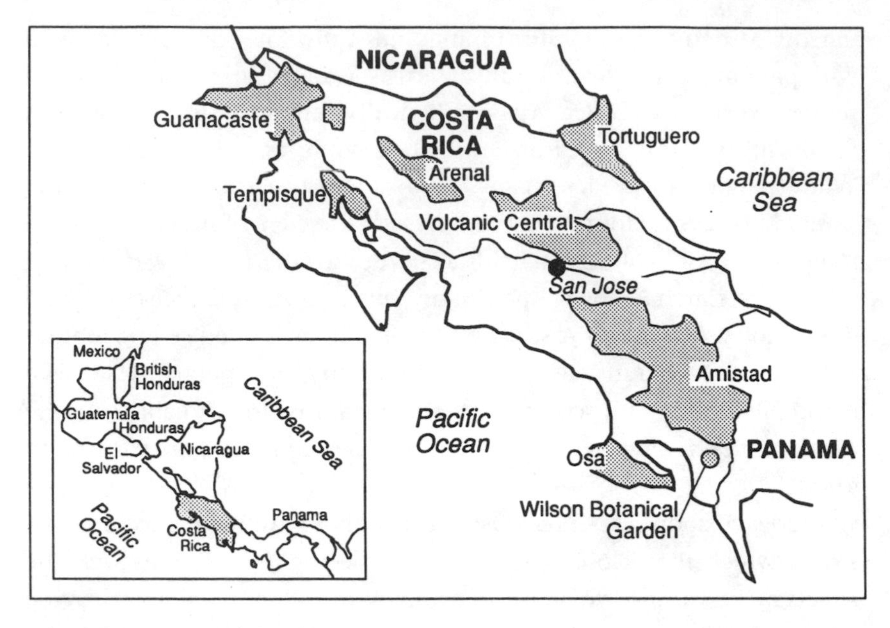

Costa Rica's seven mainland conservation areas comprise over one-quarter of its land mass
(Adapted from a map by the National Biodiversity Institute of Costa Rica)

are cut each year to create farms and for commercial purposes. Reforestation efforts are not keeping up.

Some conservationists like to call Costa Rica the little country that could, after the title of a children's book about a railroad engine that overcame great odds to pull a heavily loaded train up a long, steep hill. I have come to Costa Rica to learn if this is true. Some of this reputation stems from the country's history and political base. Costa Ricans call themselves *ticos*. *Tico* is a suffix denoting smallness, but it carries with it an underlying sense of national pride and cohesiveness. *Tico*-ism cuts across class lines and involves a deep love of the land, a strong belief in peaceful solutions to conflict. Unlike most of its neighbors Costa Rica has been an agrarian democracy for over a hundred years. There is no army, and since 1880 a free primary and high-school education has been guaranteed for everyone who wants it.[1] Major industries are coffee, bananas, and tourism. There is poverty (though according to the *World*

Almanac the average per capita annual income in 1989 was $1,352 a year, higher than many countries in Latin America). Inflation is running at about 20 percent, and coffee prices are depressed. Some observers including Luis question what the future holds, especially for the many natural areas presently protected. The problem is familiar: Rapid human population growth requires more and more cleared farmland, which may soon outstrip availability. Costa Rica has already lost two-thirds of its original forest cover, and with a growth rate estimated at 3 percent a year, its population of 3 million will double before the end of the century.[2]

"In ten or fifteen years," Luis tells me, "Costa Rica will have such a large voting population needing land that no politician will be able to keep them from invading the parks. What will happen then to our protected areas? Will our nation—the world's example of exemplary conservation—go down the drain when these persons avalanche onto our parks and reserves? Who is to stop them?" On both sides of the highway small coffee farms and eroded pastures chip away at steep, once-forested slopes. Luis points out a mudslide on the side of the road, the result of inappropriate land clearance. I cannot help but think of Madagascar.

Legislation passed in 1986 strictly controlling and penalizing deforestation has done little to slow it. In 1988 nearly 60 percent of Costa Rica's forests was already gone and the country began importing lumber.[3] "What we are talking about is the fastest possible rate of deforestation a continent has ever seen and mass biological extinctions unlike that of any other geologic period."[4]

"Twenty years ago this was a tunnel of forest," he says, one hand sweeping the view. "Now much of it is beyond the point of recovery. We must apply the concept of carrying capacity to decide how many protected areas a country can afford. If you look at the carrying capacity of an ecosystem or national land space for humans, you are going to have to compromise between conservation and development. Setting aside over one quarter of our territory may be far too much." The implication: Costa Rica's human population may soon overwhelm the carrying capacity of land currently available to it. Can needy people be denied access to natural areas set aside for other purposes?

"We humans are an overgrown herd," Luis goes on. "We need to be managed just like any other species. Nature has already begun to strike back. Look! There's cholera moving up from South America. There is AIDS . . ."

Does this mean that as humans destroy finite resources, as we pollute our environment and as nature becomes increasingly simplified biologically, malevolent organisms have a better chance of spreading? Something like that, Luis nods. He believes humans are becoming less and less a part of nature and thus are less resistant as organisms.

We ride on a while in silence. The Toyota labors upward through an oak forest reserve, where, however, I see signs of cut trees and charcoal-making everywhere. Oaks take 200 to 500 years to mature, Luis tells me, yet only three weeks to be reduced to charcoal. Still I enjoy the passing scene, a varitextured, colorful roadside replete with giant ferns, passion flowers, and "poor man's umbrellas," huge rounded leaves sometimes used for protection during downpours. Bordering the reserve, small, gaily painted houses dot the landscape, their front yards surrounded by flowering hedges. Inside open doors freshly polished hardwood floors gleam invitingly. Red, yellow, and blue laundry festoons hedges or is strung on lines.

Naturalists love Costa Rica. A biological crossroads between North and South America, species unique to each hemisphere as well as to Costa Rica mingle here. So rich is the diversity that some say "this small country . . . is home to 5 percent of all the plant and animal species known to exist." The variety of habitats is impressive: from coral reefs and mangrove swamps to dry deciduous forests, rain and cloud forests, and cold landscapes called *paramo*s that lie above the timberline. New plant, animal, and invertebrate species are discovered frequently. Current estimates list 850 bird, 35,000 insect, more than 9,000 vascular plant (Luis expects the total is close to 12,000), 208 mammal, 220 reptile, 160 amphibian, and 130 freshwater fish species.[5] Now a private effort partly financed from abroad and blessed by the government is under way to catalog all species by the year 2000. The data will be used to better manage protected areas and to discover species that might be useful (and lucrative) to Costa Rica. It is assumed that if Costa Rica can show her *tico*s protected areas and wild species are of monetary value to the country and thus indirectly to themselves, they will be less inclined to invade the parks. The income could help pay for the nation's conservation programs, freeing previously earmarked funds for other much-needed social services.

"Today we are screwing everything up faster than ever before," Luis says. "Man is a natural part of the disturbance regime, but the density of the human species has never been so high as now. We as scientists and human beings have not experienced this before." A disturbance regime is any introduced factor or event that contributes to major changes in a given ecosystem. It can be caused by nature or by humans: a landslide, a hurricane, a fire, a clearcut. Only recently have ecologists begun to recognize that humans can create a disturbance regime indirectly as well as directly. Airborne pollutants can kill a forest, for example, even though there are no people within miles. Humans have been around for thousands of years in Costa Rica, Luis says; now the sheer weight of their emerging numbers is the dominant factor contributing to ecological change.

Luis believes the forest remnants we are passing may be showing the effects of global warming, too. "This is just observation over twenty-five years, but the weather patterns here have definitely changed, and the oak timberlines are moving upslope to follow the cold." He cites work by geographer Sally Horn of the University of Tennessee, whose deep drilling of cores in highland bogs has shown that Costa Rica's oaks grew 3,280 feet lower 10,000 years ago. These thoughts are followed by a careful caveat, "Of course, this could be part of a normal cycle, just exacerbated by recent human activity."

Luis negotiates a curve. We have been inhaling diesel fumes from a transport truck ahead of us. On a brief straightaway it pulls over. Luis waves our thanks as we pass.

Luis's Spanish grandfather emigrated from Cuba to Costa Rica in the late nineteenth century and bought two square miles of land on the Atlantic side of the dormant Turrialba ("white tower") volcano. Here he raised sugarcane and dairy cattle and held a lucrative concession for all the general stores along the then-new Limón–San José Railroad. "I grew up in the forest," Luis says. "From the age of nine and a half I hiked these mountains alone, camping two or three weeks at a time. This was all pristine forest when I was a kid." Because of polio scares in the capital ("This was in the 1950s, before the Salk vaccine") Luis spent most of his time on the family plantation. The farm was four hours by horseback from the railroad. An only child, his education was "eclectic and customized." He had private tutors until he was twelve. He collected orchids, wild animals, and birds. "My father and I would study the live ones and then release them. Sugarcane is the preferred habitat for the fer-de-lance snake. My father paid five *colones* (about two cents) for every fer-de-lance head. But I had live ones in my room, and tarantulas. My mother hated it but was tolerant."

Scientists often visited the plantation and left books and reports behind. "On rainy days I would go into our library and read and read. I was consumed with the need to know." Later, attending high school in San José, he would return for holidays. Mornings he worked on the plantation. In the afternoons he went swimming, fishing, and watching otters with his father. Back in San José he occasionally attended debutante parties as befitted the children of his social circle, but he preferred the solitude of the forest.

Two hours into our trip we stop by the side of the road near an alpine bog where North American, or boreal, plants grow side by side with South American, or austral, plants. The highway has bisected the natural flow of this bog and it is slowly dying, Luis says, but it is still a place of enchantment for scientists. In knee-high rubber boots I slog down the graded road slope after him. Luis's specialty, I learn, is *cryptogams*, primitive forms of plant life that reproduce by spores rather than seeds. The bog is full of them: mosses, lichen, peat, ferns, mushrooms, algae. Luis whips out garden clippers and begins collecting plants. He hands me a plastic bag into which I slip each specimen: *puya* (a South American cactuslike plant of the pineapple family with a tall flowering stalk), geraniums, gentians, blueberries from North America, digitalis, sedges, and grasses of every description. One alga he hands me is common in high Andean bogs thousands of miles to the south. Here in isolation it has "speciated," that is, become endemic to the region.

"Don't drop it," he cautions. "That alga is very rare!"

Luis steps confidently from tussock to tussock, never wetting his shoes, while I follow less surely. Like a kid in a candy store he sucks in his

GAIL HEWSON GÓMEZ

Luis Diego Gómez chasing minnows in San Vito marsh near the Wilson Botanical Garden

breath and utters barely audible cries of delight at each find. "Don't just look, *observe!*" he cautions me, a command I will hear him repeat many times over the next several days. As I follow his instruction, the intricacies of each unfamiliar plant begin to unfold.

In fifteen minutes we collect fifty different specimens, a potpourri of color and texture in the bag I have flung over my shoulder. In his lifetime Luis has probably collected seventy-five thousand plants. On a single three-month expedition in 1982 he collected eighteen thousand, of which ten thousand are still being identified. This does not necessarily mean they are new to science, he assures me. It simply indicates how labor intensive and time consuming the identification process is.

Above us on the highway a car honks. A large white van with "O. T. S." painted on its side has stopped. OTS stands for Organization for Tropical Studies. The driver, population biologist Nancy Greig, is looking for twenty graduate students who have fanned out somewhere in a nearby forest, participants in an eight-week course on tropical biology offered twice a year by OTS to students throughout the western hemisphere. For the next several days Luis will join Nancy, Brian Boch, whose specialty is lizards, Jim Ackerman (orchids), and Don Wilson (bats) as one of their mentor-teachers. He's looking forward to this role, having honed his own botanical knowledge working side by side with an earlier generation of experts. Now it is time to return the favor.

OTS was founded in 1965 by seven U.S. institutions and the University of Costa Rica to encourage biological research and education in the tropics. Today there is scarcely a tropical biologist from the western hemisphere who has not been touched in some way by OTS. The student group we are about to meet is predominantly North American, because this course is given in English, but it includes students from Brazil, Colombia, and Costa Rica too. (An identical course will be given in Spanish later in the summer.) In two months they will visit many corners of Costa Rica, spending most of their time at OTS research sites: La Selva Biological Station, 3,800 acres of rain forest in northeastern Costa Rica, the Palo Verde Field Station to the northwest, and the Wilson Botanical Garden. Each day they will divide into groups of five or six to team-study different aspects of the tropical environment—bats, honeybees, snakes, orchids, fungi—and how these and other species interact. The teams give informal reports to each other in the evenings.

A 1988 brochure defines the OTS mission as promoting "the wise use of natural resources in the tropics" and "working to avert global catastrophe." But it was not always thus. Luis says in the early days OTS focused more on "pure" science, less on conservation. Then came the discovery in the early 1980s that La Selva was, in Luis's words, "becoming an island in a sea of developed farmland." Species loss and ecosystem simplification were feared as its isolation from other natural areas grew more pronounced.

Ecologists are familiar with this process. "Island biogeography," also sometimes called insular ecology, is the study of how true islands as well as isolated natural areas function biologically. Conservation biologists generally accept that "virtually all natural habitats or reserves are destined to resemble islands, in that they will eventually become small isolated fragments of formerly much larger continuous natural habitat."[6]

Scientists are only just beginning to describe the effects of ecological isolation of habitat fragments on species composition and diversity. As a general rule, the larger the area, the greater the habitat diversity and the more numerous the species. The reverse is also close to axiomatic: The smaller the island and the more isolated it is, the more impoverished its biota. The length of time an area is isolated will also influence species diversity, and even in a relatively undisturbed isolate, some species that need larger habitats will decline. What species will die cannot be predicted; chance plays its role, and the smaller the island the greater that role is likely to be. Consequences will be different for different species, depending on their ability to move from one location to another (by flying, for example, as opposed to walking, crawling, or being blown by the vagaries of wind), by their biological characteristics and evolutionary history, and by the closeness of other isolates or larger habitats.

Two important factors influence the survival of species in island ecosystems: size, which dictates the number of individuals an area can support, and population (the smaller its number, the higher the probability a species will become extinct within that area, owing to possible inbreeding or natural cataclysms such as hurricanes). Some immigration of other species from elsewhere can be expected to fill ecological niches left vacant by extinctions, as has been recorded especially for some birds. This view holds "that species are constantly being lost and gained, one species being exchanged for another."[7] However, this may or may not be true for species such as land-based vertebrates that normally take longer than birds to move from one place to another.

A selected park or nature reserve gives an incomplete picture of species composition because some of its species may use and need a larger area. Profound changes to species composition will occur as habitat surrounding the park is altered, for example, by clearing, ploughing or paving, and many species will disappear unless there is intensive management. This is particularly true for nonflying mammals.

Management may include providing land corridors between isolates and resources now missing from the fragment, such as certain foods.

Much more research and a greater understanding of island biogeography are needed to help humans design and maintain protected areas to benefit biological diversity. This is equally true for Costa Rica as for Kenya and Madagascar. For now, land-use managers in these different places perforce must act on the best data available to them.

In the 1980s the OTS leadership saw that one of their most valued natural areas was changing and suspected nearby human land use. Species were disappearing at La Selva before they had been inventoried. At the very least for the sake of scientific knowledge, conservation and wise management of La Selva and nearby areas had become a priority for OTS. The solution to La Selva's growing isolation was first to purchase and protect a corridor connecting the area to the nearby, much larger Braulio Carrillo National Park, ensuring freer movement of some species. The second, more long-term response was to begin offering courses on agroecology and the interdependence of economic development and ecological conservation, courses designed to reach the current and next generation of conservation leaders. Some courses are designed for local people, some for scientists. Some are given for national and international decision-makers, including foreign-aid officials whose prior focus was on economic development that depleted or otherwise destroyed nonrenewable resources.

Luis had a hand in promoting this change in focus at OTS, but he does not tell me this. Instead I learn of his role from Rodrigo Gámez, a molecular biologist who heads INBio (National Biodiversity Institute of Costa Rica), the nongovernmental organization presently inventorying Costa Rica's biological resources.

"Conservation is a young but powerful force in Costa Rica," Rodrigo tells me when we meet in San José two weeks after my arrival. "In the early 1980s what I call Costa Rica's conservation mafia had begun to emerge, people like Alvaro Ugalde, now head of the National Park Service, Mario Boza, now vice-minister of national resources, Pedro León, president of the National Parks Foundation—and Luis Diego. Mario and Alvaro were the doers, Pedro and Luis Diego were the advisors. I had known Luis when we were both teachers at the University of

Costa Rica. In 1983 I got to know him even better when I joined the National Parks Foundation board of directors. Now he's on INBio's board. He wants to help people. He's always in the background, but you always know what he thinks. He's one of the pioneers."

His father died shortly after Luis graduated from high school, and for a time he was occupied with selling family farms, reinvesting the income, and building a house for his mother and grandmother in San José. Soon thereafter he left for the United States where he spent some years as a member of one of the most contemplative and strict monastic orders in the world, during which time he also did course work for a PhD in fine arts and music at a nearby university. After his request to transfer to a more service-oriented order was denied, he was locked into his room by his superior, to whom he had once vowed absolute obedience. Ultimately Luis managed to escape to a pay phone from which he called the Costa Rican ambassador. Soon thereafter he left for Mexico, where he met philosopher-psychologist Eric Fromm. It was Fromm who helped Luis realize natural history was his first love.

In 1967, at the age of twenty-five, Luis returned to Costa Rica. He wrote leading botanists around the world and asked if he could "work as your assistant if you will tutor me. I want to learn your field to my satisfaction." Several agreed, and he started a world trek. The training he received during these years coupled with a lifetime of personal observation has made him one of the best-known tropical botanists of his generation. Self-taught and without a formal degree in botany, he nevertheless has nine books and more than three hundred scientific papers to his credit. Named to Costa Rica's College of Biologists in 1982, he is also a founding member of its National Academy of Science, the plans for which he himself drafted ten years ago.

"I admire him enormously for his personal work and his depth of knowledge," Rodrigo Gámez tells me, "but you know, there is jealousy from his own colleagues. In a way he's a protest against the system. Some of his former employees try to be like him, but it's no good being a third-rate oddball. It's only okay if you're first-rate, like Luis."

Still wondering if a contemplative life was what he wanted, Luis marooned himself on the tiny offshore island of Cocos in 1970. All of fifteen square miles, it became his home for four months. The only human contact was an occasional mail boat. "I never wore clothes. I lived off the land. I studied plants. There was no one within 500 miles. What a wonderful feeling!" Wonderful, until the day he woke up in excruciating pain and diagnosed appendicitis. He steeled himself to perform his own appendectomy and was lying in his tent with surgical instruments spread on a cloth beside him when, unannounced, a boatload of friends arrived to check up on him.

Recovered, and armed with comprehensive knowledge of the island's unique biota, Luis campaigned successfully to have Cocos added to Costa Rica's national park system. Soon after his return to the mainland an invitation came to head the natural-history section of Costa Rica's National Museum. He married and had a son, but the marriage was not a happy one and did not last. Appointed director of the entire museum, he buried himself in work, encouraging high-quality research and creating a scientific journal that is of international renown today. By 1981, however, he was exhausted and frustrated by a lack of official support. An invitation to the United States to draw biogeographic maps of Central and South America for The Nature Conservancy was welcome. The purpose of the project was to identify those areas of highest biological diversity toward which conservation dollars should be directed. "It was a great idea. I made maps of endemic organisms from Mexico to Patagonia. We called them treasure maps." With time Luis found himself doing more and more fundraising for the Conservancy, a new and public role he did not relish.

Meanwhile, OTS had asked Luis to write a job description for the director of the Wilson Botanical Garden, a private facility founded by an American couple, Robert and Catherine Wilson. In 1973 the Wilsons had sold the land and buildings to OTS, but as yet there was "no program, no outreach locally, no environmental education." Catherine Wilson died in 1984. Robert Wilson was elderly and ill and had already tried to recruit Luis for the job. Exhausted from his years at the museum and tired of fundraising, Luis "asked Bob Wilson if he would still have me as director. He said yes. I took over in 1986. I needed a break. I needed to get away.

"Five years ago when I arrived, the garden was like a retreat for me. My son was growing up and going his own way. Except for my mother, I had no other responsibilities. I became just another peon working in the garden, and I loved that. I decided not to bring my piano. I gave up my music. I was drinking too much. I am ironic and sarcastic when I drink. I can be morose, a pain in the neck. All my frustrations with the system and its people came to the surface. Then Gail came."

Gail Hewson, an American, came to Costa Rica on holiday, fell in love with it, and got a job doing publicity work and fundraising for OTS. She and Luis met by computer modem when Gail, then in the California OTS office, responded to a request from Luis for books. They were married in 1989.

"Gail," says Luis, "has given my life new purpose."

THE MANY FACES OF CONSERVATION EDUCATION

We meet the OTS students at lunch, served cafeteria style at the Hotel Georgina, a way station for buses halfway between San José and the Panamanian border. We eat in stockinged feet, our muddy boots lined up at the door. After gulping generous helpings of bean soup and hunks of sweet bread we head out, twenty-five of us packed into two vans.

Where we stop, huge oaks—a number of species that hybridize easily and are therefore difficult to identify—reach twisted limbs 150 feet into the air like tortured Modigliani sculptures. There are mushrooms everywhere, and orchids, giant carrots, bamboo, magnolias, tree ferns. The birdwatchers among us spot a black-billed nightingale thrush, a fire-throated hummingbird, a long-tailed silky flycatcher, and numerous "lbb's," unidentifiable *l*ittle *b*rown *b*irds. We are at 9,800 feet. Climbing over and around decaying deadfalls and scrabbling up steep slopes leaves some of us gasping, but we follow Luis like so many lemmings. He shows us a roadside cut where the tectonic rock below a narrow strip of topsoil is clearly visible. "This rock is very porous," he says. Although there is a lot of rain (it is sprinkling as he talks, and umbrellas suddenly unfurl from daypacks) the moisture quickly drains away. "Look here! You can see how shallow the root systems are and therefore how dependent the trees are on certain fungi for breaking down toxins and recycling nutrients. Some fungi take nutrients from the soil and literally feed the roots. You could call fungi an intermediate digestive system."

Later he explains: "Fungi are more like animals than plants. They break up heavy molecules of highly mineralized soils into substances more readily available to higher plant systems. This is called a 'mycorrhizal' association. When the fungus/plant association is limited to a single life condition or relationship, as with these oaks, it is called 'obligate.' " The oak trees cannot take up nutrients or break down toxic aluminum without fungi, which remove the noxious chemicals. Others break down litter and "feed" the roots. "Without the fungi, the trees could not survive on this narrow layer of soil. Once the trees are cut, the soil erodes to the rock very quickly."

The students are a mixed bag of talent and curiosity. Their interests range from birds to snakes, to plants, systematics, ecology, and mammals. As they fan out through the forest they call to one another, "Come see this!" "What's the name of that plant?" "This insect?" A golden beetle shaped like a miniature Volkswagen captures our attention. There are cougar, brocket deer, porcupines, squirrels, anteaters, and cottontail rabbits here, but we are making too much noise to see them. We do spot some tracks and other signs, for example scratched places on the forest floor where some small cat may have marked its territory.

I wake at six in the morning. Mine is the Hotel Georgina's only working shower, so a line of students has formed outside my door. Luis has gone back to San José to collect his mother and Gail. By the time I have breakfasted on *huevos* (eggs) and *café con leche* (coffee with milk) the OTS group has left and the Gómez family is back. I climb into the car. The road soon begins to twist and turn like a disturbed snake as it drops from 9,000 to 1,000 feet in forty minutes. The slopes are steep and high to our right, precipitous to our left. We cross San Isidro Valley, a panorama of large prosperous pineapple plantations, and two and a half hours later leave the Inter-American Highway to cross the Río Terraba on a three-car ferry.

Within half an hour we are at San Vito, a town of about 1,500 people not far from the Wilson Botanical Garden. Perched high on a 4,000-foot ridge, San Vito was founded by Italian immigrants after World War II at a time when Costa Rica was encouraging homesteading in the Panama border zone. Its buildings are for the most part sparkling white, its streets clean. It boasts a small hospital, schools, two or three good restaurants, a tiny urban park. The park was created by Aprenabrus (Association for the Protection of Natural Resources of Coto Brus), a local conservation group, from an area that was once an unsightly dump. Today a footpath winds past trickling clear waterfalls and shaded pools. In the valleys beyond the town coffee, corn, and beans are planted as far as the eye can see.

When Luis arrived in 1986, the townspeople hardly knew the garden existed just a few miles up the road. One of the first things he did was to put up a welcome sign at the front gate and to open the grounds to picnickers. "San Vito is a community in a setting that has not yet gone beyond the point of no return," he wrote at the time. "A place that is the last agricultural (perhaps even agro-ecological, too) frontier of Costa Rica." Soon after, Aprenabrus leaders came to call. Luis helped them write their legal charter and develop their program, stressing local environmental education to promote conservation and sustainable development.

Conservation International gave $2,000 to create the little park in San Vito and later gave an additional $10,000. Aprenabrus has used this money to begin a nursery of local trees for future reforestation projects and to distribute books to schools about conservation. Another project involves building boardwalks and renting birdwatching blinds in a local marsh. With coffee prices depressed, this is arguably a better use for the marsh than draining it to plant more coffee. Still another project, presently stalled because of lack of funds, was begun investigating the economic feasibility of making coffee-harvesting baskets from local natural materials to replace the ubiquitous, expensive, and nonbiodegradable plastic containers in current use.

Eliecer Rojas Salazar, a dentist, is the president of Aprenabrus. "We try to tell the people about natural resources," he informs me. "Every week I give a talk and show slides at a community or school somewhere in Coto Brus. Others do the same. We never really got going until Luis came along. We owe much to him."

Luis tells me he found the garden neglected and overgrown. Trees were down helter-skelter throughout the property and trash was everywhere. There were no phones, no fire extinguishers, and screening was broken. This is hard to believe as we turn at last into the gravel drive. Among the trees on either side painted markers guide visitors along carefully mowed and raked trails: "Bromeliad Walk," "Fern Gully," "Hummingbird Garden." There are picnic tables, a vegetable garden, and greenhouses below the brow of a hill. In addition to exotic plants from all over the world that the Wilsons collected and planted here, the 30-acre garden and adjacent 300 protected acres contain about 2,000 species of native plants, 300 birds, 80 mammals, 71 reptiles and amphibians, and more than 3,000 moths and butterflies. This is the second largest private botanical collection in the world.

Often founded to provide aesthetic pleasure to their owners or to the public, botanical gardens today play an increasingly important scientific role in propagating and protecting plants threatened with habitat loss and extinction. More recently they have become centers for studying ways of preserving habitat and species diversity and of mitigating biological damage from inappropriate development. This is especially true of the few botanical gardens like this one located in tropical latitudes.

Modernized and expanded since Luis came, the research station can house fifty visitors at one time. There is a large dining room, a lounge, a lab, a computer room, hot water, washing machines, phones, even a facsimile machine. Families and school groups wander through the grounds and tourists are welcome for a voluntary fee. Concerts and lectures are held in the lounge.

I move gratefully into a vacant room. When the OTS group catches up to us in a few days the place will be crowded, but for now I am alone. Later over a dinner of beans, rice, beef, pineapple, and melon, I meet Martha Rosemeyer, an American living in a small apartment off the laundry room. An agroecologist, Martha was recruited by Luis to help local farmers find ways to work their land sustainably. She is studying and applying pre-Columbian bean-growing techniques on experimental plots at a nearby coffee plantation. In pre-Columbian times, she tells me, the people left their fields fallow for two to three years. They would broadcast seed into the growing brush, then cut the brush down, leaving a drying mulch that prevented erosion, provided nutrients, and reduced the growth of fungal diseases. She has been able to show local farmers that with this method they will not need to use herbicides and they will get the highest return per unit of labor.

"I spend most of my time developing agroecology courses for OTS,"

Martha tells me. "Agroecology is narrowly defined as the ecology of agricultural systems, but you really have to look at socioeconomic aspects and issues as well." The courses Martha has designed attract economists, sociologists, agriculture specialists, and ecologists from throughout North and South America. Feeling somewhat isolated, she seeks kindred souls to talk to. "If you come across anyone back in the States trying to do this kind of thing, please put them in touch with me. I *know* we could benefit from each other's experience. We can't goof around any more. There isn't time."

LA AMISTAD BIOSPHERE RESERVE: CHALLENGES AND BENEFITS

I wake to the sound of birds. Outside, fog has turned the nearby forest into a sculpture garden of indistinct shapes and textures, feathery, curled, and sharp. Bright-red flowers hang disembodied in the mist. I can hear in the distance the low of a cow, a dog's halfhearted bark, a diesel truck rumbling past the gate.

In 1983 the Wilson Botanical Garden was declared a part of La Amistad Biosphere Reserve by the United Nations Educational, Scientific and Cultural Organization (UNESCO). La Amistad is an international park of more than 2 million acres some twenty-five miles from the garden. Over half the park is on the Costa Rican side of the Panamanian border, the rest in Panama. UNESCO's biosphere-reserve designation is given to important, unique, and sometimes disappearing ecosystem types deserving of international recognition, ongoing protection, and wise management. It can, and usually does, include human-occupied as well as so-called pristine areas. Unfortunately, designation is relatively easy, protection often less so. "The government of Panama is still defining La Amistad's boundaries," Luis tells me. "They have taken so long that a very important part of the Pacific slope has already been lost to agriculture."

Tomorrow we will go to Las Tablas, a range of hills at the edge of the park, and from there hike into the park itself. Meanwhile I am put to work weeding the organic vegetable garden, a 30- by 50-foot fenced plot not unlike my own back home except that many of the plants are local and traditional: cilantro, arugula, chiles, and yams are planted among more familiar brussels sprouts, mustard greens, carrots, lettuce, and beans. There are also insect-repelling herbs and antibiotic gentians. At the station we eat produce from this garden daily, but it is also used to show the *ticos* how they can grow their own vegetables instead of only a cash crop such as coffee. The idea is to help them save money they now spend on vegetables shipped from elsewhere in the country.

As I work, I spot Luis in the distance leading a school group. Gail follows a short time later with some foreign tourists. Gail is designated publicist and fundraiser for the garden, but like Luis she wears many hats: "With a budget of only $195,000 a year, we all do a bit of everything." Foreign birdwatchers come to the garden in significant numbers, she says. Tourism is the garden's biggest source of income.

Some of the children, renegades from Luis's tour, stop to watch me work. They giggle at my inept attempt at Spanish and eventually run off. After a while I quit and climb uphill to the station, hoping my work hasn't destroyed some unfamiliar seedlings, to meet Luis for coffee on the balcony.

He gazes out over the trees toward the mountains. "In 1985 former President Oduber's wife tried to get the garden expropriated by the government, but we Costa Ricans are having a difficult time maintaining our protected areas as it is. It's absurd to expect any government would pay the money needed to maintain this place, much less to expand it. Bob Wilson asked me to step in. I got the local community to take out a big ad in *La Naçion*, our biggest newspaper, and we succeeded in stopping the move. Now Oduber is dead, but if the Liberation Party wins in 1994 his widow may try again. The garden is better off in private hands, but it is not yet self-supporting."

Is privatization of other such protected areas the way to go in Costa Rica?

"Our law to create protected areas is a 1972 translation of U.S. Park Service laws, but it is not really applicable everywhere in this poor country. It would take a majority of the legislature to change the law to allow for privatization. I'm not sure that will ever happen, but I firmly believe the future is not in the hands of structured government efforts. It will be in the hands of the people. Government support is necessary, but conservation should be apolitical. Government should be a coordinator and funder, but conservation policy is always influenced by the administration of the moment. That's not good. I think many areas should be run by private groups even if this involves foreigners. For example, privatization for ecotourism would mean areas contiguous to parks would be profit-making. Even if foreign investment in ecotourism appears to be a kind of imperialism, so are Del Monte and Dole, foreign companies which are the major investors in pineapple production in Costa Rica. These companies provide many jobs. We should modify our laws if need be to allow for such concessions. How income is distributed is simply a matter of how we allow the contracts to be written.'' Luis is certain Costa Rica can control this process.

A chainsaw is buzzing somewhere off to our left. Our silence is companionable. After a while Luis speaks about La Amistad. ''Planning for the reserve is taking much too long. There are too many people trying to tackle too many problems, protecting their own salaries. They only make use of me when they need someone who knows the park and the biota. Then I do a show and tell.'' Sometimes foreign experts come with theories that won't work in Costa Rica, he says. They seldom stay long enough to see the results of their advice. This is a not-so-subtle criticism of some foreign-aid programs. ''For many places, we are past the point of no return. That embitters me. Maybe that's why I sometimes appear negative and unsupportive of, for example, more meetings just to discuss deforestation. We've had enough meetings. Now it's a hands-on thing.''

That night a storm moves in. Thunder, lightning, and rain pound on the corrugated roof above my bunk, but the next morning is sparkling, sunlit, cool. We leave early for Las Tablas. Five miles from our destination we stop to engage the four-wheel drive and to put on chains. After fording a small river, the road quickly becomes a minimal track of deeply rutted mud. Dangerously steep cliffs drop off to the left. What looks to me like virgin forest surrounds us. In fact, humans have lived here off and on for thousands of years, and this is secondary forest, cleared perhaps more than once in the distant past. Indicators of this disturbance include cecropia, fig, and banana trees that mingle with towering ancient oaks. We stop at some pre-Columbian grave sites and easily spot a number of ancient pottery shards where road construction has disturbed the ground.

Later we drive to the house of Miguel Sandí, on whose land we will camp for the next two nights. Miguel came to Las Tablas twenty-five years ago, cutting through the forest with a machete and shaping the road with pick and shovel. Today his sixty-one acres of terraced orchards and pastures hug the edge of La Amistad National Park. Close to the equator and at 6,000 feet, the weather here is often crisp and cool, similar to more temperate zones except for the excessive rainfall, which adds humidity and accounts for the lush vegetation. Miguel is proud of what he has done. Luis says his farm is a fine example of "buffer zone" use. Buffer zones are areas adjacent to protected areas where under official management plans local people are allowed, even encouraged, to farm or otherwise inhabit and make use of the land. Some people have suggested the Sandí property may actually be within park boundaries and therefore could be expropriated by the government, but plans for the Las Amistad Biosphere Reserve are still so inexact that no one really knows. I get the impression that if their tenure is threatened Luis will go instantly to bat for the Sandís among the powers that be in San José.

In the hallway of Mr. Sandí's small house several men and boys are polishing and sorting apples. Apples in the tropics? Luis met Miguel in 1982 when he was on a botanical survey. Later he introduced Miguel to an agronomist at the Israeli embassy who taught the Sandí family about apple growing, suggesting ways to adjust to local conditions. The work is labor intensive: Every tree must be pollinated by hand as bees here do not seem to do the job, preferring native plants. Last year the orchard produced ten thousand pounds of apples. They are delicious (I can attest) and sell well in markets as far away as San Vito and beyond.

A stream runs through the property and black and white cows graze on slopeside meadows, including the one where we pitch our tents. We do this hastily, as rain threatens. While I work a yearling moves in to watch me but shies off when I reach out. The OTS van pulls in shortly after we arrive and the students set their tents nearby. Señora Sandí has prepared lunch for thirty and we eat in three shifts in the family dining room: soup, beans, rice, cabbage, homemade cheese, a bottomless thermos of coffee, pitchers of fruit juice. OTS is paying for this service. Although prosperous by local standards, the Sandís welcome the additional income. Walking out with Miguel, Luis discusses building a few amenities for future OTS visitors, a screened dining and meeting hall, showers, toilets. The location is ideal for scientists wanting to investigate the park. Miguel thinks this is a good idea. Permanent facilities might help if his right to the land is ever questioned.

In the afternoon Luis and I set off along the stream where it enters the forest below the farm. Ferns and other understory plants we push aside spring back so quickly that when I look behind I cannot easily see the path we have just taken. Dappled light filters through the leaves, but not enough to do away with the damp, clean, earthy smell of compost. Warned about snakes, I tread lightly and check before touching a vine or branch. There is a sudden crashing noise to our right, then silence, but we see no animal. Luis begins to clip and collect: hibiscus, philodendron, begonia, ferns, orchids, fungi. To reach one specimen he scales a tree to a height of fifteen feet, clinging monkeylike to its crumbling bark. I hand him a long stick and after he pokes at the plant high above his head a tiny orchid falls into my hand. Luis jumps to the ground, flushed with success, grinning. This is *his* kind of fun. Later we will discover that the orchid is a rare one.

Luis stops to fish while I go sit on a rock and spot three resplendent quetzals flashing through the treetops on the other side of the stream. Quetzals nest in holes found in large, old trees. With more and more tree cutting quetzals have become increasingly threatened. On our way back to the Sandí property we surprise a troop of white-faced capuchin monkeys feeding in fig trees. A big male sends the others away and leads us in the opposite direction with a series of come-hither grunts and noisy movements. Back at camp I change into dry clothes. A sudden mountain wind careens down from the forest and across the meadow, its roar like a blizzard in the Rockies, only it brings sluicing rain rather than snow. My dome tent twists and bucks and I fetch rocks from the streambed to weight it down, not trusting tent pegs in the spongy pasture soil.

The next day Luis, six students, and I leave shortly after breakfast to climb to 6,500 feet, into the cloud forest and deep into the park. Although we slept in down bags last night, today is hot and humid. I soon peel off my jacket and stuff it in my daypack. The trail's steep switchbacks ooze black mud, sucking at our boots. It is a quagmire churned in part by people and horses crossing into Panama. Political borders mean little to the people here; half of the Sandí family lives on the other side and members go back and forth at will. The same holds true for park boundaries. Luis tells me there are only six or eight rangers for Costa Rica's 1.2-million-acre portion of the park; it is virtually impossible for them to patrol its borders well. There is another problem: only last week one of these men was seen escorting an illegal hunting party deep inside the park. Here as in many countries where wardens' pay is low, money made guiding sports hunters is too tempting to resist. Furthermore, hunting for the cooking pot is almost impossible to control. The rangers are mostly local men. Who wants to arrest one's uncle or cousin, after all?

Luis sends the students off into the forest at regularly spaced intervals on straight-line transects to sample fungi. "Observe, don't just look!" Luis calls after them. "Smell the plants! Every plant has its own smell! Use *all* your senses!"

I sit on a log holding cameras and notepads, waiting. Giant trees with buttress roots taller than a man surround me. There are strangler figs coiling around trunks; lianas, or vines, cascade from upper branches. Everywhere ferns, palms, bamboo, philodendron are a symphony of form and texture, light and dark. Each ancient tree is a microenvironment of lichen, ferns, orchids, and other epiphytes. When a tree falls it opens a space in the forest for sunlight and succession, for new generations of plants to emerge. I sense my presence is unimportant, perhaps even alien, in this endless cycle of life and death—a humbling yet somehow uplifting thought that evokes the memory of Murchison Falls, Uganda.

On our way home some of the students swing Tarzanlike from vines. We stop to eat wonderfully tart raspberries. One of the students dives after a snake and comes up triumphant. In her hand its red-and-black body flattens suddenly, appearing to double in size. Perhaps this is a defensive response to threat. The snake is tucked into a plastic bag for identification back at camp. It will be released later.

That evening the students meet in a large open shed to share the results of their various daily explorations. The portable generator we have brought with us doesn't work so we shine flashlights on the speakers and the hand-drawn graphs. Don Wilson, one of the OTS instructors, has led two groups on nighttime bat-netting expeditions, one back at the garden, one here. At the garden they caught and released twelve species of bats, while last night they caught and released eleven species in the park not far from the Sandí farm; only five were the same species as those found in the garden. However, they caught four times as many animals here than in the garden, perhaps indicative of how much more wild this setting is. Bats disperse seed and pollen and keep insect populations down. Much like Pat Wright's lemurs a half a world away, they are an important asset to the forest and in turn could not survive without it.

I ask a number of the students what they think about the future of forests and of conservation in general. They say they are concerned about rain-forest loss, but most have little time to focus on conservation now for they are in the business of getting an education. There will only be island fragments of relatively rich biodiversity left in their time, they believe, and nowhere on earth will there be truly pristine forestland. They hope that what they're learning now will be useful to the management of what is left.

Phil Keating, a University of Colorado graduate student, says, "We've got to do two things. We've got to control population growth and we've got to change the consumption habits of the developed world. All the easy things have been done." Several others nod.

Later as we walk back to our tents Luis tells me, "My happiest times have been in nature. That is now disappearing. I don't need any other motive for what I do. I have deep feelings for my people, too. They must be fed. Have roads. Electricity." We sit on a fallen log with our backs to the wind. "Every day I wake up with a conflict. Shall I keep trying or go about my business and forget conservation? The first usually wins, but I'm afraid it's too late. I despair that none of our government officials or scientists have ever thought of human populations as part of the environment. They don't equate human ecology with conservation. To me, conservation is the quality of life of the people around these parks. There is not much point in saving a place like La Amistad if the people nearby are sick and ill-fed."

A NATIONAL BIOLOGICAL INVENTORY AND ITS USES

I have a day and a half left in Costa Rica and hope to call on several people in San José before I leave. My timing is off. On July 11, 1991, there will be a rare solar eclipse in Costa Rica as predicted by Mayan priests several hundred years earlier. The government has declared a holiday and many people have gone to the beaches to watch the dramatic event. I do manage to arrange a meeting with Rodrigo Gámez, the director of INBio. INBio is headquartered in a converted warehouse about fifteen minutes outside town.

In 1987 Luis learned that the natural history wing at the National Museum was to be torn down to make way for a park in central San José. The naturalists employed there, many of them Luis's former students, came to him for help. Where could they house their collections? Where could they continue their research? Seeing the possible loss of data and of valued scientists to other pursuits, Luis phoned Rodrigo, who was then serving as advisor on biodiversity to President Oscar Arias. He asked Rodrigo to suggest that a private institution be established with presidential blessing to make the collection and inventory of biodiversity a part of national policy. Together Rodrigo and Luis convened a distinguished group of experts to discuss how this might be brought about.

Rodrigo tells me, "We decided to create a nongovernmental institution because the magnitude and complexity of the task of inventorying Costa Rica's biodiversity was such that we did not think a government agency, weighed down by budget constraints and bureaucratic controls, could do the job." Luis wrote the draft recommendation and it was accepted. Foreign foundations and other sources quickly raised the money necessary to purchase a building, and INBio was born. Rodrigo is its first director.

His office is small and cluttered. A large blackboard is mounted on a wall. Suddenly he grabs a piece of chalk and scrawls three words:

SAVED KNOWN USED

"You know, when I was advisor to President Arias the concept of protected areas being part of a rural agroecosystem was just being developed. When you do agriculture around here you are expected to know what the farmer needs to know. In agriculture you are *practical.* In agriculture you are dealing with humans *and* nature. In biology you are liable to forget the human side. We realized there would be no future if we didn't know what we were protecting. But we also discovered 'saving' was not enough.

"Biodiversity has to be saved, known, and *used* in order to survive," he says, stabbing alternately at each word. "Saving involves creating and maintaining parks and protected areas. . . . Knowing involves the acquisition of data—that's where Luis comes in. And INBio. Users are the businessmen, farmers, educators, and government officials who can take the information and make it serve their interests. Biodiversity has to be useful to society. INBio serves as a broker between the wildlands"—his finger moves to the word *Saved*—"And the users. Use it or lose it, they say. But to use it you have to know what it is. Saving is not enough.

"Long ago Luis began pushing for development of a library of biological knowledge. The work of his pupils and many of the people who worked for him at the Natural History Museum has provided the seed of the biodiversity database we now have at INBio. Luis probably knows the botany of Costa Rica better than anyone else, but that kind of knowledge has been concentrated in him and perhaps a handful of others until now. We're now saying a national biodiversity inventory must be multiparticipatory, a team effort. We have very few Luis Diegos and nearly half a million organisms."

The solution? In January 1990 INBio began training a group of thirty-one "parataxonomists," *ticos* from throughout the country. Selected on the basis of their interest in local biology and their motivation, "they already know more about biodiversity than most biology students." Among them are a bartender, a housewife, a farmer, and a schoolteacher. A six-month course at INBio headquarters has prepared them for jobs collecting biological specimens where they live. Working out of eighteen regional field stations and receiving $5,000 a year for their work—an excellent salary by Costa Rican standards—they periodically ship their collections to INBio headquarters where trained taxonomists doublecheck and catalog their finds. A second group is being trained in 1992.

"Suddenly biodiversity is being done by *ticos* named Carlos and Jorge and Rosa. Their communities are intrigued. Whole families are getting involved. With their help we will complete the entire inventory of Costa Rica's biological resources by the year 2000."

From the outset INBio received tremendous international financial support. The MacArthur, Pew, and Alton Jones Foundations, AID, and the Swedish government have all kicked in. WWF is paying for the parataxonomists' training. And with Costa Rica's Central Bank Rodrigo has negotiated an agreement whereby a $1.2 million investment will net about $4.6 million for the program. What has attracted all this money is not only the inventory, it is how the inventory will be put to work for society, perhaps by helping scientists identify new crops, pesticides, and drugs. "Chemical prospecting is a major component of INBio, and we will be collaborating with other institutions both here and abroad. If we can come up with just five good products derived from natural Costa Rican sources, it will bring money into the country. This is biotechnology, but we need the data first."

Costa Rica is looking for equitable partnerships. In late 1991 INBio and the giant drug company Merck signed just such an agreement, the details of which remain confidential. INBio will receive royalties of unstated percentage on the sales of any products developed from the institute's samples. Costa Rica's entire annual budget is $3 to $4 billion dollars. According to the World Resources Institute, "at a royalty rate of 2 percent, just 20 new drugs would generate more income for Costa Rica than it currently earns from exports of bananas and coffee."[8] The dream of future national financial gain is the carrot that keeps INBio hard at work and private money flowing to it. If useful products can be found, long-term protection of Costa Rica's forests and vast biological riches will be justified.

Many developing countries fear pirating and exploitation by outside industrial giants. Genetic thievery has been going on for a long time—the removal of rubber plants from Brazil a century ago is one example. In Costa Rica neither INBio nor Merck has a monopoly on product search; other companies or entities may start looking at any time. To whom does intangible biogenetic information derived from Costa Rica belong? Answers are still murky, although a biological diversity convention, signed by 150 nations including Costa Rica but not the United States at the 1992 Earth Summit in Rio de Janeiro, is an attempt to solve just such biotechnology transfer questions.

Costa Rica's intent is to establish a national fund to be administered openly by eminent citizens and the Central Bank. Any profits from the INBio-Merck association are supposed to be funneled through this fund to pay for conservation, releasing government money for much-needed social services. Supporters of the INBio-Merck agreement assure me that great stands of trees will not be leveled if a pricey compound is discovered in them because today biotechnology can synthesize almost anything. In fact, forests may be better protected from large-scale destruction as long as public and private entities continue to look for lucrative surprises. Will benefits from money earned as a result of the INBio-Merck association filter down to Costa Rica's *ticos*, to Luis's hungry voters who hover at the edge of their country's parks? While the increasing involvement of *ticos* in the inventory process is creating understanding and jobs, INBio and Costa Rica will have to be careful that gains do not end up in the hands of a very few.

Rodrigo takes me back into the converted warehouse where curators are pouring over large wooden cases of insect and botanical specimens shipped here by the parataxonomists. On a mezzanine others are entering data into an impressive computer bank. "When the Natural History Museum moved its collection of insects here in early 1990," Rodrigo says, opening one box where hundreds of tiny beetles are lined up on pins and carefully labeled, "they delivered just 50,000 specimens. That 50,000 took 110 years to collect. In just one and a half years we've already added 1.5 million to that inventory.

"These collections are just the beginning. The users will tell us what they need. Ours will be a very pragmatic approach. We have to be pragmatic if we want biodiversity to survive. We have to sensitize the decision-makers to all this. At the same time, we can't forget ethics and aesthetics. The new concept is conservation areas, not just parks. I don't like to call the land surrounding parks buffer zones any more. That implies conflict. I prefer 'areas of influence or input.'

"When I see all this," Rodrigo waves his hand around the room, "I can't be pessimistic. When you see what education can do for people. Our former bartender is our best parataxonomist! There's no limit to what we can do! We're standing on the shoulders of giants like Luis. . . . They've set the stage without even realizing it. I don't share Luis's negative perspective about the future because I think we're still on time. As a society, we Costa Ricans have been able to make major adjustments in the past. We got rid of our army in 1948. We nationalized services without turning into communists. With proper leadership and with an educated people—95 percent of our society is literate—ours is a can-do country."

Rodrigo's enthusiasm does not wane on the drive back to my hotel. "INBio has become a model for the world, but there's no perfect recipe. I regret Luis has not always been recognized for his contributions. I feel sad that such a pioneer does not enjoy the fruition of his dreams. Yet INBio *is* that fruition. For me, he's an idea man. He has contributed many basic ideas to the development of INBio. Even though he never comes to meetings we talk a lot by phone.

"And I always know he's watching."

CHAPTER 5

Rick Steiner: Community Activist

THE *EXXON VALDEZ* OIL SPILL

There is a steady drizzle falling when my plane lands in Cordova, a town of some two thousand residents on Prince William Sound 200 miles southeast of Anchorage, Alaska. It is September 1991, two and a half years since the huge oil tanker *Exxon Valdez* hit Bligh Reef and began seeping oil, and a month before federal and state governments and Exxon finally agree to a multimillion-dollar settlement for damages. Ultimately 11 million gallons of heavy crude were spilled into the sound, coating 1,200 miles of beach, a distance about equal to that from Cape Cod to North Carolina's Outer Banks. The spreading oil killed more than 300,000 seabirds. At least 1,000 sea otter bodies were retrieved within the three weeks following the spill and 144 dead bald eagles.[1] The next year a disproportionate number of bald eagles' nests failed in the affected areas, and it is perhaps because parent birds ate oily carrion. Ecosystem

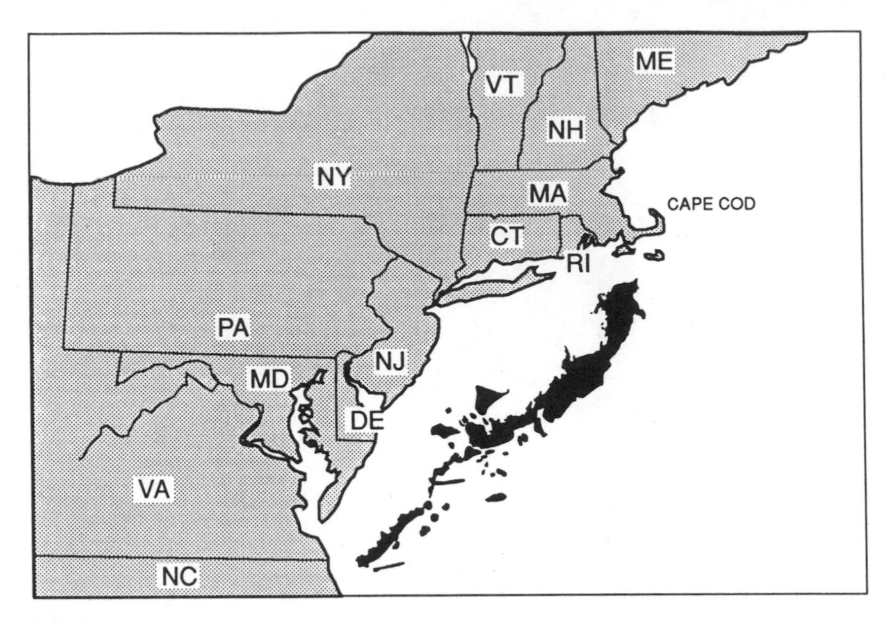

Extent of the Exxon Valdez *oil spill if it had occurred off the East Coast of the United States*
(Adapted from a map by the Alaska Department of Environmental Conservation)

damage is still being reported. It is doubtful the full story will ever be known.

Cordova's fishing fleet is the largest in Prince William Sound. From April to September herring, halibut, salmon, bottom fish, and crab are pursued by Cordova's commercial fishermen and women. The town more than doubles in size at these times, as "seasonals" (called snowbirds locally) arrive from elsewhere to take short-term jobs processing the catch or to crew on board the six hundred or so fishing vessels that choke the harbor, sometimes rafted three deep at the floats. Not a family was untouched by the events that began on March 24, 1989, when the spill occurred, for nearly all are connected to the fishing industry in some way. Herring fishing was canceled in the sound that year and the market for Alaskan salmon bottomed out with consumer fears that the product might have been contaminated by oil. As I will learn, however, more than just economic reversal has transformed the town. For the first time that day in 1989 many people saw their *own* habitat violated by human error. The experience has catapulted many into new ways of thinking about their relationship to nature.

Today visibility is poor, but through a blowing, drifting mist I glimpse mountains rising steeply to 4,000 feet alongside the river meandering through a 700,000-acre wetland known as the Copper River Delta. Not far from the airport sport fishermen are casting spinners and wet flies into turbid streams. Offshore there are killer whales, sea otters, sea lions, and seals. Thousands of seabirds bob among the waves. This early autumn a few trumpeter swans and Canada geese are still about, their young not quite ready to fly south. Huge twiggy beaver houses are humped in the shallows, and nearby blue herons stand one-legged on alert. I am told wolves, bears, moose, mink, and countless other life forms are here too, in abundance, and that their tracks and scat are not too hard to find.

Following the oil spill native hunters worried that deer, seals, shellfish, and other wildlife they normally killed or collected to feed their families were riddled with contaminants that might affect human health. Although their fears were to prove largely unfounded, some stopped hunting and years later haven't started again. Many natives and nonnatives found temporary employment with Exxon during the cleanup as boat operators and members of beach and maintenance crews. So, too, did people on shore who housed and fed an unprecedented influx of experts and volunteers. "Spillionaires" made as much as half a million dollars that spring operating cleanup boats. When compensation for the lost 1989 fishing season was doled out (fairly promptly) by Exxon, others made downpayments on new boats. Now two years later, partly because the price of salmon is still low with overproductive hatcheries and huge catches elsewhere in Alaska, boat owners are having trouble meeting payments.[2]

I had heard much of this before coming to Cordova. I had also read that scientists still do not know how badly compromised the biological integrity of the sound really is. For more than two years researchers studying the spill's effects under government contract or for the oil companies were under a gag order. This was imposed because of possible future court cases against Exxon, owner of the stranded vessel, and Alyeska, the consortium of oil companies that operates the Alaska oil pipeline and the port of Valdez where oil is siphoned onto waiting tankers. Now that some of these restrictions have been lifted, a discouraging picture is emerging. It seems attempts to blast the oil from rocks with high-pressure hot water may have killed far more life than if natural tides had been allowed to cleanse them in good time. Fertilizers sprayed to enhance oil-eating bacteria in other affected areas seem only to have cleaned a thin top layer off of sand and rocks. Thousands of nesting murres, an arctic diving bird, have failed to reproduce since the spill, it is reported, perhaps because there remain too few mature birds to defend nests against predators. The sound's sea otter population, genetically distinct from other populations in Alaska and from those farther south, was devastated by the spill and is still declining. Oil hydrocarbons have shown up in pollock 600 miles away, indicating that oil may have entered the food chain, and oil contamination has been found deep on the ocean floor.[3,4]

Certain components of the damaged ecosystem, notably murres, might not fully recover for up to seventy-five years. Some scientists speculate full return to the precise function and composition of this ecosystem as it existed before the spill may never occur. Steep oceanfront slopes bearing narrow bands of temperate rain forest, short and clear spawning streams, high annual precipitation, glaciers, and wide intertidal wetlands give Prince William Sound and the Copper River Delta their unique quality among the world's ecosystems. These characteristics also make them particularly vulnerable to degradation.

The spill is still topic A in Cordova. "It was like a gang rape," says Claudia Bain within minutes of our meeting. She has come to pick me up at the airport, as Rick Steiner, the man I have come to Cordova to meet, is out fishing. Rick calls Claudia his mate, a term he uses warmly to reflect their mutual commitment. She is a masseuse and self-described healer by profession, a gentle woman. "Cordova is an incredibly close place," she says as we turn out of the parking lot. "Those weeks right after the spill were very intense. The spill transformed just about everyone."

Within the next few hours other Cordovans are telling me, "You wouldn't believe the animosity here during the spill. It was like Nazi collaborators. Some people made $5,000 a day for months, paid by Exxon. People were toasting Exxon in the bars! Others were volunteering, just trying to save the sound and its wildlife." And, "People here never recovered from the stress of the spill. Now they're generally more suspicious of each other. It's like an infected wound. The wound was the spill. The infection is the ongoing confusion and disagreement about how to deal with the aftermath, and with new issues." And, "There's a me-first attitude here now that the sociologists are calling 'the ongoing disaster.' "

While I'm listening to them, the *Valiant Maid*, a diesel-powered 58-footer whose crew Rick is a member of, is after halibut. Rick is a fisheries biologist who works for the University of Alaska as an associate professor, but he is also a commercial fisherman. When the International Pacific Halibut Commission (IPHC) declares an "opening" for commercial fishing, that is, that fishing for this species will be legal for a certain number of hours or days, nearly everyone in Cordova drops whatever he or she is doing on shore and heads to sea. Together with the National Marine Fisheries Service (NMFS), the IPHC bases its decisions about when and for how long a species can be fished on available data about populations. The purpose of time limits and quotas is to maintain a sustainable yield, in other words, to ensure that a species will endure in adequate numbers to reproduce successfully even while being harvested. Two days before I arrive the halibut fishery was opened for just twenty-four hours. Whether or not halibut fishing is reopened again this year will depend on catch reports from returning vessels. Because this year's salmon prices are so low, nearly all Cordova's boats have gone out after halibut this time in spite of a brewing storm. Had they made more money during the summer they would not be under such pressure to make up the difference now.

"Fishing is their nature," Claudia says about Cordovans. "They are fish predators. They cannot do without it." Because of this they understand the need for regulation lest they overfish and destroy the very resource upon which their livelihoods depend.

The day I arrive the wind at sea is blowing forty knots and waves are running twenty-five feet. Fishermen I talk to tell me they overheard nineteen vessel distress calls during the three or four days they were just out. The grocery checkout clerk describes what happened to her boyfriend: Alone when his boat capsized, he spent five hours clinging to the hull before being found. Fortunately, he was wearing a "survival suit," an insulated flotation coverall which is standard foul-weather garb for most seamen in these arctic waters.

Later at Rick's house I throw my duffel into the room Claudia has prepared for me. Claudia is moving down to Juneau for the winter where her nine-year-old son has already started school. Friends are helping her pack. I try to stay out of the way, in a corner of the living room. A small dory lined with a patchwork quilt and pillows dominates the room. Drums from Southeast Asia, a lute, a lyre, a banjo, and an ancient violin hang on the walls. There is a seat made of whale vertebra, an Eskimo mask, pine cones, skulls of sealion, bear, and wolf. A snowshoe and a handsaw lean in one corner. Recycled salmon-roe crates hold a hundred cassette tapes. Houseplant vines twine around the windowframe. There are books on chess and navigation and Tibetan philosophy, McPhee's *Encounters with the Archdruid*, James Gleick's *Chaos, The Last Rainforests, The Best of Robert Service*, David Bohm's *Wholeness and the Implicate Order*.

I take a walk. Cordova is perched on the southeastern edge of Orca Inlet, a long protected fjord of Prince William Sound. It is connected to nowhere else by road, a circumstance many Cordovans hope will last. Self-contained, it is a town of several bars, two or three churches, two groceries, a drugstore, hardware and sporting goods stores, a bakery, a small hotel, a bookstore. The harbor dominates the landscape, a huge complex of wharves and floats behind a giant protective stone mole rebuilt after the 1964 earthquake. Seagulls hunker down like rows of identical paper cutouts on the roof ridges of marine-supply warehouses. A marker light winks steadily at the harbor entrance. People nod in greeting, only slightly curious. I am a stranger in a small town that two years ago was overwhelmed by strangers.

That night Rick appears. Sleepily I greet him, a tall, broad-shouldered Nordic apparition. He too is tired and he smells of fish, but a wan smile lights up his face half buried in a wild red beard. The fishing was quite good, he says. He checks his phone messages, then heads out with friends to a wood-fired sauna the community built some years ago beside a creek at Shelter Cove, not far from town. I am dead to the world when he returns.

THE TURNING POINT

Rick grew up outside Washington, D.C. His father was an education specialist with the U.S. Health, Education and Welfare Agency; his

Rick Steiner at home in Cordova Harbor

mother was on the White House staff, spanning several administrations. The setting seemed artificial, he says, an environment in which his father, a farm boy from Tennessee, seemed out of place, although "he cared enough about his professional mission to hang in there. I think some of his discomfort rubbed off on me. Where we lived, everything was the product of the human mind—shopping malls, highways, apartment buildings. I wasn't very happy. I wanted a more natural life. The East Coast megalopolis was not exactly what I had in mind." As a youth Rick occasionally went deep-sea fishing with his father. Perhaps because of this he majored in marine ecology at the University of Tennessee. "By the time I graduated, I knew I wanted to go to Alaska."

In 1975 he got a job on a hydrographic research ship, the *Fairweather*, operated by the National Oceanic and Atmospheric Administration off the Alaskan coast. "It immediately felt right," he says. Although he was paid as a deckhand, not a scientist, part of his job was to "ground truth" aerial and satellite photos by walking the beaches at high and low tides with a ship's officer. This was Katmai, the wild and remote elbow of the Alaska peninsula some 300 miles west of Prince William Sound. There were bears everywhere. He also spent several vacations as a commercial fisherman and one autumn as a fisheries biologist with the NMFS foreign observer program, sailing in the Bering Sea aboard a huge Japanese ship.

By 1979 Rick had a masters degree in fisheries science and oceanography. That year his leg was crushed while he was hauling crab pots during a storm. The memory of the accident is still vivid. "The ocean is the last true wilderness on earth. There is a mix of machismo and humility in every fisherman." As Rick points out, "Fishing is statistically seven times more dangerous than any other industry in the United States, but the reason we are out there is much more than just a dollar. If you've ever had a near-death experience as nearly everyone who goes regularly to sea has, you have a bond with the ocean that never leaves you."

Since 1980 he has worked with University of Alaska's marine advisory program, an extension service provided by the university under the federal-state sea grant program, which brought him to Cordova in 1983. His job involves interpreting federal and state regulations for fishermen, "bridging the gap between the fishing industry, conservation groups, and the government." Marine safety, fisheries development, aquaculture, and seafood processing and marketing are among the nuts-and-bolts topics he deals with. He also helps research the interaction of *orca*, or killer whales, with fishermen's "long lines," 1,800-foot hooked and baited fishing lines. "The *orca* strip black cod from the long lines during in-haul," he tells me. "They hear the winches and come running. We tried acoustical preventatives but failed to follow up with negative reinforcement, so they keep coming back." He also directs a long-term study to estimate the "incidental take" of marine mammals caught in fishing nets at sea. This is to help fishermen better understand and comply with the federal Marine Mammal Protection Act.

Until March 24, 1989, the rhythm of Rick's daily life was defined by these activities, fishing openings, the weather, and the seasons. There was time for backpacking and canoe trips in springtime, cross-country skiing in the winter, long soaks in the community sauna, potluck suppers, singing, and amateur puppet shows on dark winter evenings. Then the spill occurred. Rick was among the first to organize emergency-response teams the day after. He went out to the oiled areas and helped lay the flotation booms that kept oil from seeping into the Sawmill Bay hatchery not far from Cordova. He helped man a command post and personally provided a link among media, government officials, local fishing and environmental groups, and Exxon during those critical early days. He had no sleep and he seldom ate.

Overnight Rick became a spokesman for the sound. He was not the only one, but he was one of the most articulate. His friends say he appeared completely at ease before camera crews and handled interviews well. He is diffident about this and cannot quite understand why he was in the limelight. His friends can. "He may not be a people person in the public sense, but he has enormous charisma," says one. "He's never at a loss for words. Especially when he cares." More than two years later such demands on his time are still evident. Rick's answering machine, just outside my bedroom door, records dozens of phone messages daily from the press, congressional staffers, and environmental groups.

When nothing more could be done to clean black goo from the beaches and to save oil-covered animals, most volunteers resumed their former lives. Not Rick. In the ensuing months, together with a friend, David Grimes, he jetted from one end of the United States to the other to speak to coastal townspeople about how such disasters could be avoided. To build credibility, they have since formed an organization of local constituents called the Coastal Coalition. "Prevention is the only cure," Rick would say to coastal townspeople. "If an oil spill is not contained quickly, little can be done." He would argue for improved piloting procedures for tankers, for higher personnel standards and safety inspections, for double hulls to reduce the chances of a spill in the event a hull is torn, for planned-response readiness at ports, including adequate equipment. But he would always end with, "The best way to prevent oil spills is to reduce oil consumption." In Rick's opinion, a national energy policy based on a nonrenewable resource like oil is folly. Fishermen who understand the importance of resource sustainability know what he means, yet they are torn. Oil fuels their boats.

Dave and Rick flew to Scotland's Shetland Islands in May 1989 to talk with a citizens' group there that seemed to be having some success exercising limited oversight of the North Sea oil industry. The result in Alaska is the first Regional Citizens Advisory Council (RCAC), patterned after its Scottish prototype and now funded by the U.S. oil industry to the tune of $2 million a year. (Rick had proposed just such a mechanism prior to the spill, but it wasn't until afterwards that Alyeska agreed to it.) Members of RCAC include representatives from local communities, native villages and corporations, commercial fishermen, conservationists, regional fishery associations, and the Alaska chamber of commerce. In cooperation with industry RCAC promotes safe transport of oil, works to improve oil-spill prevention and response mechanisms, and monitors terminal operations for potential environmental problems. "The whole idea is to increase communication between the industry, government, and the public," says Rick. "No substitute exists for local knowledge, experience and commitment."

Soon Rick was also helping develop federal oil-spill legislation, writing articles, telephoning, flying to Juneau and to Washington. While government officials wrangled with Exxon over the dollar amount of claims against the oil company, Rick began lobbying for a quick settlement. "A settlement would sidestep years of costly litigation," he said at the time. "It would provide for environmental restoration and allow all of us to get on with life."[5] He began peddling a settlement plan of his own, the chief component of which was the purchase of timber rights in the affected region to remove them from the threat of clearcutting and thus aid in the sound's overall recovery. Clearcuts are once-forested areas where timber companies have cleared the land of all standing trees whether they are commercially useful or not. Wildlife accustomed to deep cover are exposed and must adapt or seek alternatives. Erosion and downstream silting, which create an oxygen-poor habitat for fish, are also the result. Regeneration of a natural forest on these sites can take generations, and the original stands will probably never be replicated precisely, as soil temperatures and structures will have changed. Rick argued then and still believes that the chief threats to biological recovery of the sound are timber harvesting, road construction in sensitive habitats, mineral development, and large-scale development for tourism and recreation. He would like to see about 80 percent of the settlement money used to buy threatened coastal forests.

The sound would eventually cleanse itself of most oil. Heavy logging along the coast begun a year or two before the spill created another set of ecological problems. Prince William Sound is at the northernmost edge of an ancient temperate rain forest stretching from Oregon north. Receiv-

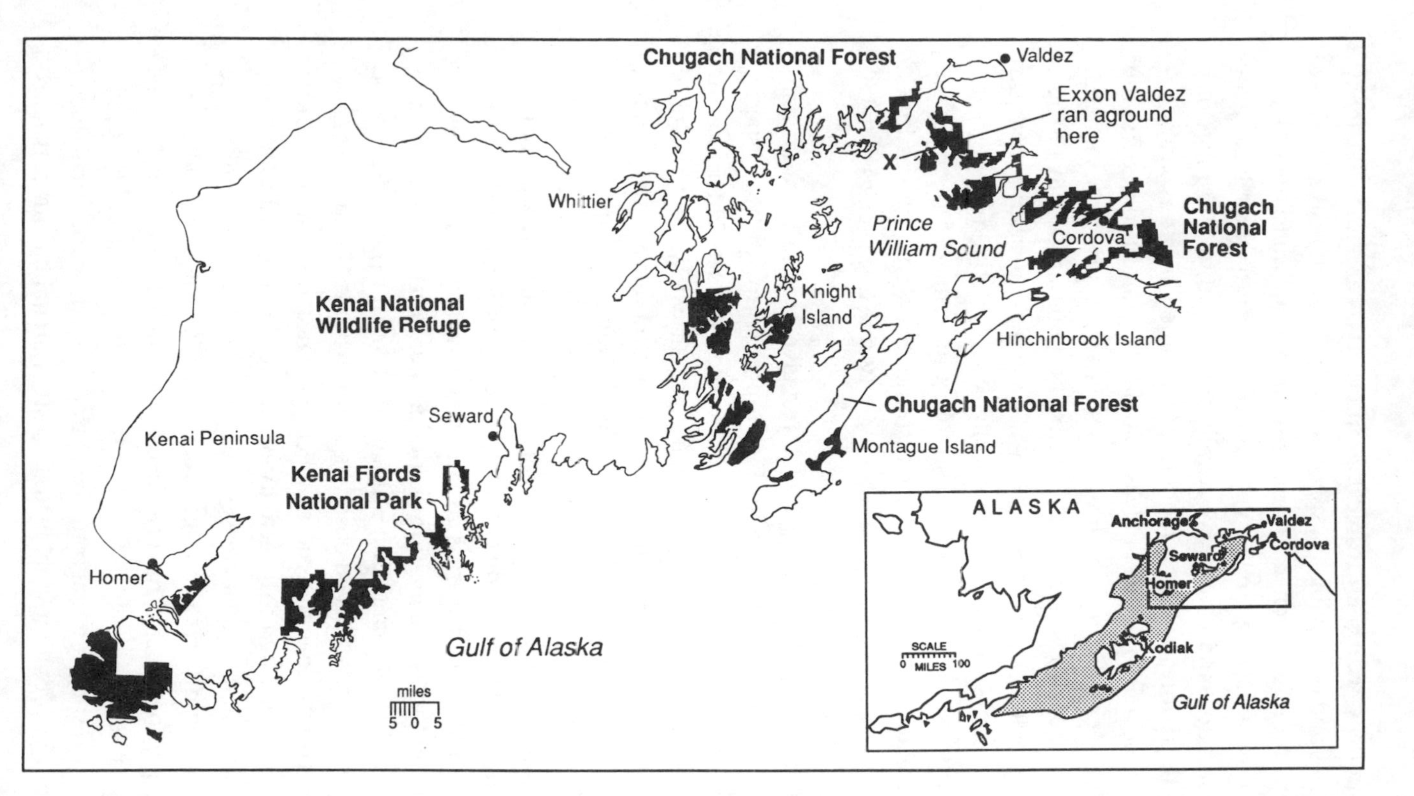

Map showing timber acquisitions (black) *proposed by Rick Steiner and others to protect the Prince William Sound ecosystem from further insult. It has been suggested that these acquisitions—approximately 500,000 acres of coastal upland habitat—be purchased with spill settlement funds. The shaded area in the inserted map indicates the approximate spread of oil residues five months after the* Exxon Valdez *spill.*
(Oil-spill details adapted from maps by the Alaska Department of Environmental Conservation. Timber-acquisition details are from the Coastal Coalition.)

ing less publicity than their tropical counterparts, containing relatively fewer species and occupying less space, temperate rain forests as a biome are perhaps more threatened. Biomes are broadscale divisions of landscape into areas having similar vegetation because of their local geographic condition and climate. Generally found within 100 miles of a coastline, these forests have a moderate maritime climate typically receiving 180 inches of rain over at least 100 days a year. In addition to the Pacific Northwest, they can be found in southern Chile, New Zealand, Australia, and Japan (a small one). Virtually none are left in Europe. Between 50 and 70 percent of the world's temperate rain forest has already been cut. Restricted geographically, such forestland is now being more heavily logged than tropical rain forest in terms of percent of the remaining whole. One half of the forestland lies along the northwest coast of North America, home to some twenty-five tree species and 350 birds and mammals.

As clearcutting spreads, old-growth forest gives way to a mosaic landscape of older fragments surrounded by younger regrowth. Many species dependent on old growth habitat will become extinct. Then too, the structure of the older fragments will change: Blowdowns—trees felled by wind—will occur around the edges, then more blowdowns around the new edges, and so on until the old-growth fragment is no more. This is very different from what happens in an unmanaged, uncut setting, where "wind, fire and other forces combine to create a mosaic of trees and openings vital to forest diversity," where the process is much slower and more random. Logged areas are connected by roads; natural ones are not. Roads add to fragmentation, allow greater access to hunters, and permit the influx of plants and animals that would otherwise not be found there, "often at the expense of species living in the interior."[6]

Every step of the logging process affects biological diversity far beyond the immediate vicinity of the activity. Clearing the forest canopy overhanging a stream not only increases water temperature in the immediate area but also eliminates the large woody debris that might otherwise have fallen into the stream. Fish need oxygen-rich riffles and pools formed by large fallen logs to travel to their spawning grounds. Recent research is also showing that some large trees float downstream to lodge at river mouths, providing stability to the estuarian habitat and sanctuary for many intertidal organisms. Other logs float out to sea, become waterlogged, and sink to the ocean bottom where they become an important food source for benthic (sea-bottom-dwelling) species in an otherwise dark and nutritionally barren environment. Biologists now recommend a minimum of 100-foot no-cut buffers along streams to "maintain optimum natural fish habitat."[7]

Replanting clearcut sites artificially, usually with a single fast-growing species—a forestry practice common to some commercial and federal programs—creates a "monoculture," a landscape lacking species variety. Food choices for birds and mammals, lichen and fungi are greatly diminished. There are no dead trees, no fallen trees where wildlife can hide, no breaks in the canopy for sunlight to reach the forest floor. "The net effect of commercial logging is to increase populations of more common and less threatened species at the expense of rarer or more sensitive species."[8] Such stands are particularly vulnerable to insect pests.

Being of somewhat lesser quality than those growing farther south, the trees harvested in the Prince William Sound region were largely overlooked by lumber companies until the mid-1980s. Then, as finer timber became more scarce in the Pacific Northwest, timber operators moved north to cut these ancient stands for the first time. A tax break in the 1986 U.S. Tax Reform Act made the move attractive to investors. This involved an amendment designed to help Alaskan native corporations recoup bad investments by selling their debts to other entities. As part of these deals, many turned over their timber rights (but not the land on which timber stands) to outsiders.

It worked like this: In 1982, when the land was originally transferred to native corporations, timber prices were high. At the time of the Tax Reform Act they were low. Native corporations therefore began selling off their timber rights to create a loss, often to joint-venture timber companies in which they remained partners. These losses (but not the timber) were then resold to large profitable corporations such as Nabisco and Hilton Hotels, which paid an agreed sum, usually about fifty cents on the dollar. The latter then claimed the losses against profits on their tax returns, while the native groups, having already received good money for their "losses," could now afford to sell the standing trees to the joint-venture timber companies at rock-bottom prices. This amendment to the tax law was eliminated in 1988, but the damage had already been done.

During Wallace J. Hickel's 1990 campaign for governor of Alaska he and his staff seemed supportive of Rick's suggestion that oil-settlement money be used to buy some of these timber rights, to conserve rather than log them. But in January 1991 when Rick met the newly elected governor in Washington he sensed a backing off. This was confirmed at a public hearing in Cordova in April 1991 at which state officials indicated they might support the purchase of a few islands and coastal and stream buffer timber tracts, but nowhere near the kind of acreage Rick had in mind. "They'd bowed to political pressure from the timber people," Rick now says. His friends say he was used by the politicians. He felt betrayed. "Hickel had strung us along and I'd helped him win public support on that basis. Now he was backing off."

Rick grins to soften a barely discernible bitterness. This is our first morning together and we are sharing a large platter of pancakes and sausage at a downtown hangout. "I'd spent a full year trying to get the feds and the state to settle. Following the April meeting I just left. I'd been so into this oil thing. Suddenly I thought maybe it was too late to make a difference. I'd ignored my physical, spiritual sides, and my relationships. It took me getting to the other side of the world to find my balance." Rick took a leave of absence from his sea grant program job and left Cordova.

Seeking an environment as different from Prince William Sound as possible, he headed for the tropics and hiked throughout much of Indonesia. In Jakarta he asked for and obtained an appointment with Emil Salim, Indonesia's environmental minister. Nothing Salim said during their hour-long conversation made him any more sanguine. Publicly optimistic about the state of the world environment, Salim admitted privately that he was not. "We agreed that environmental change from bad to worse is occurring *so* fast," Rick says, mopping syrup from his plate with a final, folded pancake. "Can we accomplish *anything* in time?" As I listen I wonder if perhaps he should have stayed away a little longer. The discouragement he felt in April is still there, barely repressed.

A friend has cautioned, "There are still so many demands on him. People suck him dry. He never says no. Rick used to play. Now he just works. He's only been back a short time. He's already gray with fatigue."

She begs me to go easy. Her warning makes me rather nervous at first. But Rick has come home from Indonesia determined to pick up where he left off. With regard to the final settlement about how much Exxon should pay in damages and how it should be spent, he says, "It's like an auto accident. If your son or daughter lies bleeding on the street, do you argue with the guy over who'll pay or take the kid to the hospital? We've got to move on, but not everyone understands or accepts that. If we don't do the right thing now, the wrong precedents will have been set for a long time to come."

THE CHUGACH CORPORATION

After breakfast we walk along Main Street. There are several sidewalk greetings, most warm. Rick admits that some Cordovans, especially professional loggers and some natives who own timber shares, are suspicious of his motives. To a few he is the ultimate anathema, a Greenie activist. Sensing this, he has removed himself from the board of a local research center he helped create because critics suspect the center will use data acquired through research to "lock up" land. This facility, the Prince William Sound Science Center (PWSSC), is housed in a converted ice house at the end of a long wharf marking Cordova's narrow harbor entrance. There Rick introduces me to Nancy Bird, its administrator. As we talk, fishing boats glide out of the slanting rain and into safe haven, the slickered men at their helms sipping coffee from steaming metal mugs, oblivious to our scrutiny. For at least fifteen years Cordova-based scientists have talked about a centralized institute where research needs could be identified and information shared about the complex biological, chemical, and physical processes of the sound and the delta. The oil spill was catalytic, pointing up the urgent need for basic and applied ecological research, both non-oil and oil related. PWSSC was opened with a $50,000 loan from the City of Cordova one month after the spill. Today it provides laboratory space, equipment, logistical and administrative support to scientists and students, and is helping accumulate baseline biological data about the region, including badly needed biological inventories of the forests. Because it is badly strapped for funds, a good deal of research as well as community outreach and environmental education activities is on hold. Nancy hopes some Federal and/or oil-spill settlement money will come this way soon.

"Some people have tagged the science center as an environmental group trying to stop development rather than to do good science for sustainable-resource management." Nothing could be further from the truth, Nancy assures me, but indicates this is why Rick has taken a back seat. Rick says the center's main objective is to address local issues, to "do conservation biology in an ecosystem context," to improve local resource management, not hinder it. I can see his decision to resign hurts. This undeniably likeable fellow does not like being disliked for the wrong reasons. He's a scientist, after all. The way he sees it, conservation biology should serve human needs as well as the environment.

Later as we stroll along the street Rick describes a small sea bird, the marbled murrelet, which nests in old-growth forest near the steep shoreline of Prince William Sound. Scientists believe this bird could be endangered by loss of its nesting habitat. Alaskans with an interest in continued logging have closely followed the spotted-owl controversy in the lower forty-eight, where thousands of acres of old-growth forests have been closed to loggers to protect this endangered bird. They do not want the murrelet to become their spotted owl. Rick worries that not everyone here sees the larger picture yet—that prospects for the murrelet, like those for the spotted owl farther south, measure an ecosystem's general stress. (Never mind that this bird may be worth saving for its own sake. Such considerations are not a part of local debate.)

In front of the bank Rick introduces me to Sylvia Lange, a member of the board of directors of Chugach Corporation, one of thirteen native regional corporations created under the 1971 Alaska Native Claims Settlement Act (ANCSA). ANCSA was an attempt by the U.S. government to settle Alaskan aboriginal land claims. Considered by some to be high-minded landmark legislation at the time, critics charge that ANCSA replaced existing Alaskan native social and economic structures with an "alien corporate form."[9] Under the act, "Alaska Natives would receive $962.5 million and, still more important to them, title to forty-four million acres of land."[10] But, instead of conveying the land to existing tribal entities, which would have left land ownership directly in the hands of the people who use it, the act set up thirteen regional and dozens of village corporations to receive title and to manage the land as a corporate asset. "Congress wanted Alaska Natives to become shareholders and businessmen, to become part of the commercial and corporate mainstream of America."[11]

Critics point out that U.S. ownership of Alaska was based on its purchase (in 1867 for $7.2 million) from Russia, whose fur trappers never had more than a toehold along the coast, whereas aboriginal people had settled throughout the land, albeit thinly, four thousand and more years earlier. Furthermore, critics claim, the 44 million acres the natives received under ANCSA is only 10 percent of Alaska's land mass. The other 90 percent was divided between state and federal ownership. In effect, the natives did not gain 10 percent, they lost 90. In hindsight, ANCSA has turned out to be a simplistic solution to a complex land and cultural problem. Rick believes the issue of native lands is perhaps the single biggest conservation challenge facing the United States today.

The holdings of Chugach Corporation encompass much of the Prince William Sound coastline. Inside its boundaries are five independent village corporations with land holdings of their own over which Chugach has no jurisdiction. The Eyak Corporation is the local village entity. Some parcels of land around Cordova are owned by Eyak, some by Chugach.

Many natives now see their traditional claim to the land threatened by corporate problems beyond their control, by possible corporate failures or takeovers. Not the least of their worries is that native corporate stock can now be sold on the open market to anyone, native or non-native. Recent amendments to the law require approval of 50 percent of the shareholders before such sales, "thus making the transfer to non-natives still possible, but more difficult."[12] Financially strapped corporations are already turning to outsiders.

When I mention this to Sylvia, she says, "ANCSA may not have helped natives socially, but that is not to say we should throw it entirely out." Sylvia is part Aleut, part Tlingit, about one-quarter native by definition, enough to qualify her to take part in native corporate ownership and management. She is a college graduate, the mother of two toddlers, a fisherwoman since childhood, and she also represents the business interests of native Chugach stockholders. Rick and I stand with her under a shop-front overhang, avoiding a pervasive drizzle, our hands bunched in jean pockets. The digital thermometer over at the bank blinks 47° Fahrenheit. My down vest feels just right.

Rick complains that so far too much money has been spent on research to determine the extent of oil-spill damage and not enough on relieving pressures to the coastal and marine environment. We talk about Rick's idea to buy back some of Chugach Corporation forests.

"Can't we think of a better phrase than 'buy-back'?" Sylvia says. "Native people are afraid. So many have heartfelt feelings about the land. After spending ten years [from the 1971 passage of ANCSA to 1982] determining what land was theirs, the people are now saying, 'We just got it, and now they want it back.' They feel nonnatives are being paternalistic, sticking it to the natives once again. There's not a whole lot of trust."

To placate critics of the buy-back idea Sylvia is careful to tell stockholders, "It's trees, not the land, we're talking about." We search momentarily for a less threatening phrase. Cordova's mayor, bookstore owner Kelley Weaverling, who has joined us, suggests "resource retention." I suggest "tree keeping." But buy-back is already part of the vernacular, it seems, and is probably destined to prevail.

Later I meet Sylvia for lunch at the Killer Whale, the cafe in Kelley's bookstore. It serves homemade soups, salads, and baked goods. We take our trays and climb to a balcony, one of two where tables and benches are available.

Sylvia tells me the Chugach Corporation has recently filed for bankruptcy. Two risky enterprises contributed to this development. A $30 million sawmill at Seward that was supposed to bring jobs and prosperity to the region had higher costs than anticipated and has recently closed. And the corporation's three fish-processing plants failed after two years of low prices and management problems. Unemployment has hit a new high, bringing hardship to many families.

The corporation might entertain a buy-back offer for its coastal forests, Sylvia says, but the offer would have to match the value they would otherwise get if they cut and sell the timber. She talks about jobs that would be lost if there were no longer logging operations on Chugach lands. "Any buy-back agreement has to include some sort of value added, a sustainable fund to replace all that auxiliary income."

Chugach has not yet cut any timber on the sound, although it has plans to do so. "We were immediately all personally involved and devastated by the oil spill. Logging plans had already been drawn up. Now there's more pressure to move faster, because of the toll the spill took. We live here. We really don't want to cut those trees. At the same time we need the cash flow. Eleven of the twelve members on the Chugach board are connected in some way to fishing and are very tuned to the meaning inappropriate timber development has for fishing in the sound. At the same time we are a corporation, and as a corporate board it's the bottom line that counts. It puts you in a tough position.

"We natives often disagree among ourselves. Some seek political power, some want dividend checks. The great majority have sincere cultural and family ties to the land and want to see it protected and preserved for our children and our children's children. But the bottom line is the ANCSA structure we live with. If a buy-back is going to work, it has to be as a workable competing economic proposal. I'd love to see it happen. I can't imagine anything more ideal . . .

"What we have is ANCSA," Sylvia says as we part at the curb an hour later, "promising economic development and diversity and assimilation into a capitalistic society. We're doing just that." She pauses, seeking words. "Therein lies the rub."

When I report this conversation to Rick, he nods ruefully. "The natives won't admit they want to save their timber until the money is in hand. The government won't give the money unless there's an indication from the natives that they want to protect their trees. It's Catch-22."

Meanwhile, it occurs to me Cordova might learn something from Costa Rica's INBio experience. There is a lot of traditional ecological knowledge here that could be tapped, then wedded to contemporary science so that the best answers could be found for managing the remaining unspoiled terrain and for restoring that which has been degraded—a tailor-made opportunity for PWSSC, involving local people and thus gaining their support.

FISHERMEN AND LOGGERS

The next morning I gaze past the misted window in Rick's living room. Rain slashes across the clearing, spruce limbs bow to 35-mile-an-hour gusts. Bruised, scudding clouds hang low over the pass, obliterating peaks. From time to time a small seaplane roars overhead as it feels its way toward a landing at nearby Eyak Lake. Rick's diesel-fired baseboard heaters are working overtime.

Cordova has seventy miles of roads, but they connect to nowhere else. The town is as isolated as I'm beginning to feel. Like everyone else in Cordova my life is tuned to the weather, only there is a difference: I'm here to listen and take notes, but I'll be leaving soon. Their lives center on what is going on outside. Their fishing, their recreation, their safety, all depend on how well they interact with the vagaries of nature, especially the sea. I'm humbled by such outsized human challenges and frustrated that I cannot meet them head on. For the time being, a scheduled boat trip to join an orca researcher vessel out in the sound has been scrubbed. So has a flight along the coast to search for marine mammals.

About ten o'clock the rain lets up. I spend part of the morning in the harbor on Ed Bilderbach's *Valiant Maid*, "unbaiting" the 1,800-foot fishing lines that he, Rick, and the rest of the crew used to catch halibut earlier in the week. Two of the crew are women, one from Germany, the other from Massachusetts. They exchange easy banter with Ed and Rick and the other crew member as they heave 100-pound plastic tubs of coiled wet line around the deck. The crew seems as intensely companionable as comrades in battle sometimes become. In this setting Rick is no longer Mr. Public Defender of the sound. Off camera he's just another fisherman.

Each tub holds a "skate" of gear. It takes fifteen skates to make up a five-mile "set" or line on the sea bed. For the halibut opener earlier this week Ed's boat put out three sets. Now we must clean fifteen miles of line, removing rotting, unused bait, straightening or replacing bent hooks, using a short piece of line to replace or retie "gangions" (sounds like *canyons*)—tough, slightly longer lines that secure the hooks. This is smelly, dirty work that requires frequent pauses for coffee or an occasional beer.

Rick has been fishing with Ed since 1985. "I've learned so much from him and the other fishermen. Their attitudes toward natural-resource conservation are so wise. Fishing has to be regulated, to make it fair for everyone. The fishermen all know and respect that." We leave the others to finish unbaiting and head uptown to the school gym where the

Cordova District Fisherman's Union (CDFU) is holding an open meeting. There are three hundred members; about thirty show up, many in plaid lumberjack shirts, truckers caps, and shin-high rubber boots rolled back at the tops. There is a faint smell of damp wool. The men and women collect handouts at a card table at the door, sign their names to a yellow legal pad, then slide into three rows of folding metal chairs. At the table facing them are CDFU's president and its executive director.

A fisherman, Karl Becker, stands up. Like many of his colleagues he sports a short, trim beard. Of indeterminate age—he could be thirty-five or ten years older—his face is weathered by the sun and there are crinkle lines around his eyes. Karl is worried about a recent Alaska Department of Natural Resources (DNR) proposal that may allow logging closer to salmon spawning streams. In the autumn of 1991 steep coastal slopes throughout Prince William Sound are being denuded with little regard for these streams, or for wetlands, and with no thought given to dispossessed wildlife or aesthetics.

No logging on state or federal lands is allowed within 100 feet of any salmon stream, Karl explains. On private lands, however, this restriction is only sixty-six feet, and automatic variations can be granted for small streams five feet wide or less, allowing logging as close as twenty-five feet from such small streams. The protected strips are called buffer zones. Sounding like a lawyer, which he isn't, Karl warns, "Now the DNR is suggesting this variance option be made available to streams ten feet wide or less. This would mean logging could be allowed within twenty-five feet of 89 percent of the streams in Prince William Sound. The timber industry wants it to apply to streams twenty feet wide or less." National Marine Fisheries Service and Alaska Department of Fish and Game research has shown that nearly all these streams, including those narrower than ten feet, are important habitat for salmon. "The intent of the law should be to protect streams five feet wide or wider. Now Hickel's DNR wants to change this, saying their proposal is a compromise between the timber industry request and the Fish and Game report, whereas in fact the Fish and Game position is the law."

There is an uneasy shifting in the seats around me. The governor's name has been invoked, and these are voters. Karl pauses. "This pits the streams' fishery value versus the dollar value of timber."

Another member speaks up. "How do you put a value on a stream you have surveyed only once, when it produces salmon every other year?" Another: "Is the only value of a stream its dollar value?" Another: "Are the Eyak natives split on this?"

Gerry McCune, CDFU's president, says, "One problem is that the native corporations and the tribal councils are fighting over jurisdiction." Another pause. There don't seem to be any native fishermen present.

Many local natives are not convinced that selective logging and streamside buffer zones are important to the health of their forests and fisheries. Yet, says Karl, continuing present practices can only degrade the ecosystem further, destroy watersheds and fisheries, preclude tourism, and close future options for economic stability. He describes a local group calling themselves the Citizens Alliance that began meeting earlier in the week to consider their options. Natives and nonnatives, fishermen and loggers attended. He says a logger's wife described how Cordova schoolchildren are ostracizing and sometimes fighting each other over land use issues such as these, their opinions clearly colored by adult vitriol. Neighbors, white and native as well as within the native community, are not talking to each other. Cordova doesn't need this.

A fisherman: "The bears are moving. We've all seen them. That's the result of clearcutting."

Karl: "It takes 100 years here for trees to regrow full cycle. If you clearcut, that's all you get. If you log wisely, you keep your tourism value, your wildlife value, *and* your fisheries value."

"What is logging wisely?" I scribble in the margin of my notebook. If a sustained salmon-fishing industry *and* a timber supply are the goal, then managing for biological diversity seems to make sense. These are sound commercial reasons for conservation, showing a clear link between jobs and the need for a healthy environment. The good news is that these fishermen recognize this. The bad news is that not everyone does.

Kate Wynne speaks next. A wildlife manager with an MA from the University of Maine in marine population dynamics, Kate is thirty-something, a no-nonsense brunette with an engaging smile. She handled Rick's marine advisory program work while he was gone, but her main job is studying the interaction of local drift-net salmon fishing with marine mammals for FWS in cooperation with the sea grant program. She spends about half of her time on research, half informing and advising fishermen about the results of this study as well as about the federal Marine Mammal Protection Act (MMPA). In 1988 the Prince William Sound fishery was designated as one of several in the United States to be studied for its impact on marine mammals. Data collected about the "incidental take" of marine mammals in salmon gill nets since 1988 will determine how future regulations will be written. Incidental take in this case refers to the number of species inadvertently killed when they become entangled in nets. The information is collected by analyzing dead animals washed ashore and by observing fishing operations on board fishing boats themselves or from ships nearby.

Kate began the observer program in 1988. Rick whispers in an aside that the fishermen were initially suspicious, fearing liability for the volunteer observers assigned to their boats. They were also afraid her figures might go against them. A 1978 study had shown a high rate of incidental take. "They knew their record was not so bad as that of ships fishing with much larger drift nets on the high seas," Kate will tell me later, "but they had no proof. Now I can tell them their initial instincts have been borne out by scientific observations."

Kate reports that the incidental take of marine mammals in and near Prince William Sound in 1990 was roughly the same as in 1989, and far less than a dozen years earlier when fishermen were still shooting many of the animals to keep them from their nets. For example, only two harbor seals were inadvertently killed in the entire sound in 1990, whereas California recorded twenty-two harbor seal kills during the same period, with only 10 percent of California net sets observed. In 1978, thirty harbor seals had been killed in Prince William Sound, several shot or killed by explosives. "Unfortunately, the media continues to quote those early figures," Kate says. "Mortality in all species is way down since 1988, the last year shooting was legal." This year (1991), after 5,700 observer hours, Prince William Sound preliminary data show a total of only seven mortalities from incidental take: two steller's sea lions, two harbor seals, and three harbor porpoises. These account for less than 1 percent of all sightings of mammals seen swimming close to nets. "Lots of encounters do not necessarily mean lots of deaths. These are state fisheries. Unlike high-seas international fishing, this fishing is highly regulated. Boats must stay attached to the gill net, for example. You can't assume there are deaths just because a drift net is being used."

Picking up on the California figures, Gerry McCune speaks up. He says the regulations should be responsive to regional differences, "otherwise national quotas can be eaten up by one fishery." The consensus is that the union should make this point publicly prior to reauthorization of the MMPA for 1993. A public comment period is a legal part of the federal reauthorization process, a means whereby constituents may register their response to newly drafted legislation. Kate urges them to speak up while there is still time. Their comments, to be heard by politicians, will be based on science.

Rick whispers again behind his hand, "Not only are there now legal penalties for shooting marine mammals under MMPA, but the fishermen fear boycotts from activist organizations like the Fund for Animals and Greenpeace. They are very aware of the power some of those groups wield. There also seems to be a growing understanding that the occasional entangled sea lion is just a part of doing business."

A few days later Kate phones me. "Let's go beach walking!" As we drive out to the airport I see the vast reach of the Copper River Delta and its mountain backdrop clearly for the first time. In the distance, Sheridan Glacier shines blue and dirt-streaked. Our pilot is Steve Rainey, a young and experienced bush pilot. As we strap in he says we are lucky to be flying today, because the weather will be bad again tomorrow. The single-engine Cessna 180 lifts off over wetlands and braided channels from which rise curls of evaporating mist. Below, the tundra is tinged yellow by autumn frost, its surface cracked into uneven geometric shapes like some giant jigsaw puzzle. Pairs of trumpeter swans stand in isolated pools, bright white dots against the water sheen. Soon long sweeping sand beaches appear and beyond, a slate-gray Pacific Ocean pulses rythmically. Foraging eagles are everywhere, perched on driftwood or sandy hummocks, tearing flesh from dead fish. Well fed, they rise ponderously and curve away on low-lying thermals as we pass closely overhead. Kate points out a whale carcass that has been here for some days, now almost entirely buried in the shifting sand. We land nearby.

"There are some gray areas in the proposed MMPA regulations," Kate says as we trudge a quarter of a mile to a sea-otter carcass she has spotted from the air. The Cessna is left behind on the hardpan, disproportionately small and mothlike against the endless stretch of beach. "The subsistence use of marine mammals is one." Subsistence use is the traditional exploitation of natural resources by native peoples for their own consumption. The U.S. government has complex laws designed to ensure that these native rights are not abridged, but the laws are not perfect. "The NMFS (which administers the MMPA) can control some marine-mammal population problems—by regulating commercial fisheries, scientific uses, and public display uses, for example. But they can't control the effect of oil spills, or of animal-vessel collisions, or of native rights. The mortality of seals or otters or whatever killed for subsistence use is not monitored. If the FWS sets an overall quota for a species and then finds that quota has been matched or exceeded by subsistence take, then they can legally control the take by others, even going so far as to close a fishing season." Kate thinks the fishermen will speak up about this in the public-comment period preceding MMPA reauthorization.

"As of now, it is not in the interest of the natives to find out the facts," because they fear the facts will show they are taking too many marine mammals. "They'd rather hide their heads, but I think I can help by responding as a biologist. Once they have population numbers, ages, and sexes of, say, sea otters, we can determine reproduction rates. Based on that, we can devise a management plan that will allow for a sustainable subsistence take of otters." She is working on this with some native groups and they are beginning to listen.

It seems to me that Kate—by providing data about marine mammals to fishermen and helping develop a sea otter management plan for natives—is doing what conservation biology is all about, at least as it relates to users' needs. Hers is a hands-on, real-world kind of science, a role she clearly enjoys. We reach the dead otter, a big elderly curmudgeon with ground-down teeth and distinctive blue-webbed feet. Kate measures it, checks its teeth, looks for a radio transmitter (there is none, though some otters in the sound have been collared by researchers), then with the toe of her boot rolls the otter over to see if there are any wounds on its body. A skull fracture from a blow? A bullet hole? None. This animal probably died naturally.

Back in the Cessna Steve watches the clouds warily. The ceiling is closing in at about five hundred feet and we must head back. Our route takes us over the brown hillside scar where Eyak Corporation is clearcutting just beyond the airport. From horizon to horizon the view is of rolling hills of green, mud flats, and watery shine, broken only below by corrugated, pockmarked roads. Big yellow tractors lie next to logging roads like slumbering prehistoric behemoths, their engines idling. Here and there one crawls slowly up a grade; it almost seems as if we can hear the roar of its straining diesel engine over ours. Large trucks wait, motors panting, to load up, to rumble later through downtown Cordova to the Eyak log boom just north of town. Timber of inadequate value lies piled like abandoned jackstraws.

What is the value now, I ask myself, of this residual moonscape?

GENETIC DIVERSITY, PANCAKES, AND THE DEMOCRATIC PROCESS

Rick's hands are badly swollen and red. Angry red lines creep up his forearm. He has been unbaiting lines of decomposing fish without using gloves. A fellow crew member of the *Valiant Maid* persuades him to soak his hands in a solution of clorox and hot water, which he does all one evening at Ed's, where we share a potluck supper with the crew after the unbaiting is done and the boat has been hosed down. Rick also has a headache and chills, which we speculate may be related to his Southeast Asia trip. After a while he goes off to the clinic to get a blood test.

The next day it is raining again. Rick sits at his desk, nursing his headache and sipping tea. Suddenly he jumps up. He's going to ignore his illness and take me hiking. As we don rain gear and boots I tell him about my day with Kate. This triggers some thoughts that Rick shares with me on our drive out toward the lake.

"I hope within the next decade we'll develop much more sensitivity and balance with regard to how we use nature," he begins. "We'll always find a need for food, but the intrinsic worth of an ecosystem is not an idea that has reached Alaska yet. It's all user management, and usually management by single species." He cites as examples the shrimp and the Tanner and King Crab fisheries, all three closely managed by the federal government and by Alaska in the early 1980s. By management he means government-imposed catch quotas, seasonal controls, gear limits, and size limits. Even so, shrimp and crab populations have collapsed. Why? Rick thinks, first, that their size and productivity may have been overestimated, and that perhaps ecosystem data such as water temperature and food availability were overlooked. More detailed, accurate, and timely science, applied sensibly by regulators, would have conserved these species better. Who is to say if the science was flawed or if the application of it was primarily at fault?

As for Alaska's salmon, millions of five different species ply the rivers of its coastline periodically to spawn and die. Right now the Coho or silver salmon are running, that is, returning to the streams of their birth after three years at sea, the females to lay their eggs in shallow depressions called *redds* they have swept clear of debris, the males to fertilize the eggs with sperm before they die. The female may lay as many as ten thousand eggs; water level, turbidity, and temperature will influence how many hatch. For several months the progeny lie hidden in the streambed, nourished by a yolklike sac. Sometime the following spring those that survive the winter turn into tiny swimming fish called fry to head downstream and out to sea. En route they face many hazards, among them larger fish, terns, eagles, fishermen. An adult salmon's unerring homing instinct can be its undoing, for years after it has swum downstream it will return to the headwaters of the specific river of its birth, although that stream may no longer be healthy. In the lower forty-eight states some salmon populations are on the verge of extinction. This has led the federal government to limit regional catches at sea drastically in 1992, although the cause of the Pacific salmon's decline is not just overfishing. Hydroelectric dams, which greatly alter rates of water flow, and agricultural and industrial pollution, including from logging operations, have badly affected both adult and juvenile salmon runs. Prince William Sound fishermen are watching these developments warily.

Some salmon species return from the high seas to fresh water to spawn only once every three or four years. If they were fry heading out to sea when the spill occurred, how were they affected? In the summer of 1991, pink salmon that spawned the year of the spill in streams feeding into Prince William Sound are the first generation of their species to return. It turns out most of the returnees are hatchery spawned, not wild. Through Herculean efforts on the part of volunteers, including Rick, hatchery sites in Prince William Sound were protected from the spreading oil. In 1991 these hatchery fish are crowding back in such large numbers that most cannot be processed—frozen, smoked, or canned—before they die and rot, clogging hatchery entrances. Meanwhile, locals are asking why the wild ones have not returned in their usual numbers; they are inclined to blame the spill, although increasingly there may be land-based causes, too. Prices are depressed to no more than fifteen cents a pound, less than half the 1990 price, almost one-fifth the prespill price. As a result, fewer boats went seining for pink salmon in the sound this year, and no one made money.

"Now the wild pink salmon runs in our part of Alaska are down," Rick says. "There is speculation that this might be caused by competition from the millions of hatchery 'pinks' which may be outcompeting the wild fish for food, and/or by high-seas interception. The wild pink salmon runs in southeast Alaska are still huge but there are no hatcheries there. Is there a message in this? I don't know. People always look for *the* reason. It often isn't that simple."

What is at stake are the yet unknown consequences of genetic diversity loss among wild salmon from remote streams. When hatchery-bred pink salmon head for sea they come from holding pens in bays at the edge of Prince William Sound. They have not had to navigate the hazards of a stream to reach open sea, and they have been well but artificially fed with nutrition-laden pellets. Therefore these fish are probably larger and in better condition than their wild counterparts to begin with. For whatever reason, they are returning from the ocean two years later in greater numbers than the wild fish. If through clearcutting, pollution, or erosion a source stream becomes inhospitable, that stream's returning subpopulation may disappear. By favoring hatchery fish over wild fish, manipulators may thus be substituting a semidomestic strain for a wild one, a strain that does well in crowded pens when fed pellets, that fertilizes its eggs only when "milked" by hand, and so forth. Yet most scientists, including many who deal with captive breeding, believe it is important to ensure the survival of different subspecies in order to provide a wide genetic base, a genetic system more responsive to unknown and unpredictable environmental change. The captive breeding of salmon and of endangered cranes faces many of the same problems, I think, recalling my visit to Baraboo. In neither case do we know enough to know what genetic traits will be important down the road.

Whitecaps whip across Eyak Lake while a wet-suited windsurfer tacks back and forth across the water. We park at a trailhead near Power Creek, the lake's inlet. Here and there the swollen current surges across the road and a few sockeye salmon have met their demise in the shallows. Contented seagulls waddle from carcass to carcass, gorging.

We climb between mountain peaks through a rain forest of hemlock and spruce, ferns and shrubs, nibbling at blue, bear, and watermelon berries as we go. There are fresh bear tracks and scat in the trail and a scraped place in a skree slide where a bear has clambered up the slope above us, but we see no wildlife. Thousand-foot falls cascade down the mountain opposite us to foam in a canyon far below. Across the valley a red-tailed hawk drops suddenly from nowhere and as suddenly disappears against the rocky landscape. Rounding a turn in the trail, we come upon the headwaters of Power Creek, a Shangri-la-like valley miles wide. Glittery ponds, marshes, and meandering water channels spread out below us in the mist like some nineteenth-century impressionistic dream. If humans have been here, they have left no trace. There is no sound but the quiet hiss of rain. No odor but the damp sweet smell of decaying vegetation and wet earth. Rick calls it Surprise Valley, his totem. This is not a place or time for talk. We return to the car slowly, each wrapped in private thoughts.

I've been in Cordova for over a week when finally the sun appears. Dan Torgensen drops by early. He came to Cordova ten years ago to run the radio station, left town briefly but returned, drawn back, he says, by its "depressurized" way of life—before the spill, that is. Now he is a fisherman. A serious car accident a year and a half ago has left him with a new appreciation for living day by day. This is a "drop-everything day," he and Rick agree.

"Hickel wants to punch a new road through the length of the Copper River Delta," Dan says, "to connect with the Anchorage Highway at Chitina, over 150 miles away. Some work has already begun. Let's go look!" Governor Hickel sees this new road as a way to open the area to recreation and tourism and other development opportunities. East of town and past the airport the road turns to gravel and runs arrow straight north into the Copper River Delta basin, a flatland miles wide through which over time the river has cut and abandoned a thousand channels. The backdrop is jagged upthrusted mountains 3,000 to 4,000 feet high cleaved by four great glaciers: Scott, Sherman, Sheridan, and Child. Today the volcanic peaks are dusted with new snow. The roads makes the delta interior easily accessible; it is moose season and the few people we meet on the road are out hunting. A pickup passes with a moose rack six to eight feet across filling the truckbed. In the distance I can see the brown, expanding scar of a clearcut.

The road follows an old rail line for a while, the latter built early in this century to carry copper from a now-closed mine to the saltwater port at Cordova. A newly bulldozed, graded stretch suddenly veers off through the wetland toward the northeast, while the abandoned rail line snakes along the base of the mountains a quarter mile away. Governor Hickel has pledged the road will follow the rail line all the way to Chitina, my companions tell me. Clearly, the new part we are driving on does not do so. Instead, it blocks several fish streams, some of which have backed up and pooled alongside the road. The natural flow of these Copper River tributaries has been altered forever, with yet unmeasured consequences to spawning fish and other wildlife.

The idea for this road has pitted Cordovans against each other for years. Some would like to see their town opened up to the outside, as would Hickel, for the income they believe the increased traffic will generate. Marylin Leland, executive director of the fishermen's union, is keeping a wary eye, however. She worries the road will block the movement of fish fry downriver after hatching and believes that if it is completed, it must be done in an environmentally sound manner. She also worries that increased sport fishing will compete with local commercial fishing. Then there are people like Dan who love Cordova's isolation. It is one of the reasons many of them settle here. In fact, in early 1991, 72 percent of respondents to a survey in Cordova were opposed to the road to Chitina.

The oil spill and clearcutting were the first two parts of a triple environmental blow to the area Dan loves; now there is The Road. "When, how can we say 'Enough'?" he asks rhetorically. "People feel caught. Who do they call or write?"

Getting out of the car to let Dan's dog run and to stretch our legs, we pick up the oily seeds of cottonwood trees that border the main channels of the Copper River. Their odor is camphorlike and pleasing. For a time we sit together on tumbled granite boulders opposite Child Glacier. The glacier calves two or three times, dropping huge chunks of ice into the fast-moving milky channel with hardly a ripple. We drive on, as far as the 70-mile marker, the end of the present road, where we must turn back. On the way home we pick up a mink that has just been killed on the road. It has a silky auburn body that Rick handles gently as if it were still alive and wraps carefully in newspaper. He knows an eight-year-old who collects wild animal skins and skeletons. This will be a special gift. But he is not happy about the find. Large and small mammals frequent the highway and if the road goes through this will be a more common sight.

The next morning Dan brings sourdough starter over and whips up pancakes on Rick's small gas stove. While eating, we listen to public broadcasting from Valdez. Someone describes how the highway to Chitina could cost from $600,000 to $1 million a year just to maintain, never mind construction costs. The 100-mile-an-hour winds that frequently whip across the delta in wintertime will force its closing periodically if not all season. Dan calls in to the radio station. "Politicians are supposed to listen to their constituents. Let's have a public forum here in Cordova so we can hear what's really planned. We're a democracy. We just want our old town back."

Rick says Trustees for Alaska or the Sierra Club Legal Defense Fund may try to stop the road with lawsuits. The U.S. Army Corps of Engineers is said to be mad because the project has been started without proper permits. And the natives have already filed suit against the state because ancestral sites have been violated.

Conservation *is* politics in Alaska, a regular source of front-page news. Rick wavers between pessimism and optimism when he contemplates the ability of democracy to tackle the problems of conservation. "Democracy is what we work with and it's basically good. But I don't know if our cooperative form of government with an apathetic public behind it will always work. Some people want the government to take care of them.

They're not beyond blaming it, either." He shrugs. "*That's* democracy." After a moment he seems to pull himself together. Determination replaces this apparent cynicism. "As individuals, I'm convinced we can make a difference in this state," he says, and digs into more pancakes.

NATIVE VOICES

We have been trying to find Glen "Duner" Lankard, Jr., all week, but he has been out fishing. Finally Rick and I track him down having breakfast at a restaurant near the harbor. Duner is a thick-set cheerful man with dark unruly hair and a penetrating gaze. He is an almost full-blooded Eyak Indian. Eyaks are among the earliest inhabitants of Alaska. There were about three hundred pure Eyaks living in 1897, most settled in the Cordova area. Then three canneries built by outsiders polluted and effectively blocked the mouths of important salmon streams. This "broke the Eyak spirit," Duner says. Disease, alcohol, and opium reduced their numbers to fifty within a few years. Now there is only one full-blooded Eyak left and about seventy-five mixed-blood descendants.

Duner's disarming grin as we shake hands does not prepare me for his impassioned and eloquent commitment to tribal rights. "My main motive is to revive our culture," he tells me. "I want to do away with corporate ownership of the land and return it to tribal holding. The timbering is wrong. I'm not leaving until there are no more trees cut."

With a quiet but attentive smile, Rick tips back in his chair. He has introduced me to Duner, he says, because he would never presume to speak for native attitudes himself. He well knows Duner's eloquence and wants me to hear his views firsthand.

Duner has spent the last six years in the lower forty-eight. After trying and failing to get onto the Eyak Corporation board in 1985 he moved to Arizona, determined to try again when he was forty. Four years later he heard from his sister, Pam, also a Cordovan. "There won't be anything left of the forests when you're forty," she wrote in a letter. "You had better come back soon." He joined the Eyak board the same year, hoping to change policy from within. The other members of the Eyak board are Aleuts, whose ancestors came to this part of Alaska in the late nineteenth century as fur hunters for the Russians.

"The land is now just a corporate asset," Duner says. "Timber cutting is just a phase. First they'll clearcut. Then they'll strip-mine. Then they'll sell the land for nothing—all in the name of profit. The corporations see their jobs as only creating money, to give natives money just to be natives. We don't need that.

"The sad thing is that the ANCSA was designed to protect native cultures, land, and subsistence ways. It took our land and put a price on it, turning us into shareholders of our own land. But in our culture we don't own our land, we borrow it from our children. The corporations have changed the moral values of our people. I'll try to stop the corporations from destroying our land for profit, or from selling shares to outsiders when the twenty-year moratorium on sales is up in December 1991. Make no mistake. There *will* be sales, but we don't want dollars or dividends. We want our land.

"If you can get money to watch trees grow, why cut them for $1,500 per shareholder when the other values—wildlife, fish, the sound, all disappear? We live in a very rugged environment. They are the most beautiful trees to us, but not as . . . timber. In fact, our trees are not very valuable as timber, and took four hundred years to grow. Our trees are kind of skinny. This is the north end of their range."

Duner pauses for the waitress to refill his coffee cup. I watch him stir in copious amounts of cream and sugar. "Sometimes forced change is a good thing," he continues. "The oil spill made us realize the environment was the most important thing. This year (1991) was an incredible year for return of fish, but the price is way down, and it isn't the wild fish that are returning. That's another forced change. It has humbled people. Sometimes such lessons are hard. The lesson from clearcutting is: We can't sit back and let it happen.

"Some people are saying, 'Duner has flipped out.' " His disarming grin flashes again. Duner clearly likes his growing reputation as an activist. With great effect, he speaks as if legions of supporters are standing behind him, as indeed they may be, although I have no way of telling.

"Now our goal is to eliminate the corporations and transfer power to a coalition of villages, back to the tribal councils. We could still make a profit but not lose our land. We believed in the corporations once, but they haven't worked. Tribal government structures exist. Our goal is to turn our shareholders back into people. Since ANCSA in 1971 between sixteen and twenty thousand native kids have been born. By law they cannot become shareholders in the corporations. What the corporations have become are a legal form of genocide, killing our people through dividends." The silverware jumps as he slaps his hand, palm down, on the table.

After breakfast I go with Duner to a meeting of a small group planning a protest against clearcutting when a foreign timber ship docks a few days later to pick up logs from the Eyak Corporation boom just north of town. This is a place on Orca Inlet where bad weather has twice destroyed the boom, releasing huge logs to float undetected and dangerously in the sound. "The road to Chitina may cross some important tribal lands, but nothing is more ancestral than Eyak Lake and Eyak River where the corporation plans to clearcut next," Duner says. The group talks about blocking the road, dumping piles of sand in the way of the huge transport trucks, marching, painting posters, attracting media attention. Someone agrees to look into how to behave if they are arrested or jailed. They are deadly serious. Duner expects to be arrested. He doesn't particularly want to serve time, but he will not mind doing so if he can make a difference for his people. Rick will probably not march in the protest. As with the Cordova research center, Rick has to tread lightly. He must beware of being tainted too "green," too one-sided, lest he lose the confidence of many factions.

FINAL DAYS

Shortly before I am due to leave Cordova David Grimes phones. He is returning to a research vessel in the sound where he has been accompanying a television crew filming killer whales. I jump at the chance to fly over the scene of the oil spill to deliver David to his boat.

We take off from a wind-tossed Eyak Lake in a pontooned Cessna 185. We fly over Two Moon Bay, where a raw new clearcut violates the green. Siltation spreads a brown stain a mile or more out into the Sound. Behind Hawkins Island, the coastline is a wall of green, scheduled, I am told, to be cut next year. I cannot visualize these slopes brown-scarred and naked.

The pilot circles over Bligh Reef for me, the same flight path Rick and Dave and others must have flown that fateful day a little over two years ago when the *Exxon Valdez* struck. "We'd be looking at oiled water now and for another hour if we were flying over here that day," Dave says. "Even at 500 feet the fumes were terrible. It shook us to the core of our being and woke us up to what we're doing chronically to the earth. When something like that happens, you reprioritize."

In my mind's eye I try to see the spread of black crude into the sound, the bays, the fjords below. There is absolutely nothing visible today in the water or on shore that indicates any damage remains from that disaster. But, Dave points out, this is not to say it is not there, unrecognized as yet.

We land in the lee of an island, having spotted the boat, *Orca II*, in mounting swells off to the north. A rubber Zodiac pulls away and comes toward us. David climbs down onto a pontoon and is gone, exchanging places in the plane with a somewhat odiferous crewman who is coming ashore to visit family. The seas are beginning to kick up and it is raining again. The pilot takes off quickly, Dave waves from the Zodiac, a diminishing speck. For a moment I think of his apparent insignificance in this enormous seascape, recalling my own sense of puniness beside Murchison Falls so many years ago.

I am alone, packing. Rick phones from somewhere downtown. "Go outside," he says quickly and hangs up. It is late afternoon. Clouds threaten more rain but a struggling sun throws an alpenglow across the upper portion of nearby slopes. A sustained call not unlike French horns only more strident turns my eye skyward. Overhead a hundred sandhill crane silhouettes circle the town in spiraling formation. Two, three times they circle before turning and disappearing eastward to settle for the night somewhere on the Copper River Delta. These same birds which have summered in the Arctic are on their way to the lower forty-eight, where perhaps they will pass not far from Baraboo as they fly to their final destination in Texas. Will George Archibald look up later in the month, as I have just done, and greet these same birds?

In October 1991, shortly after I leave Cordova, the federal and Alaskan governments and Exxon finally agree to a settlement of oil-spill damages. Exxon will pay $125 million in criminal fines and restitution immediately, and $900 million over ten years for restoration of Prince William Sound. Now a group of trustees, three from Alaska and three from the federal government, will decide how the money will be spent. The day of the announcement Rick told the *Anchorage Daily News*, "First there was the oil spill, then the division of people who got Exxon money and those who didn't, then the collapse of salmon prices, and now there's logging all around town, one problem after the next. The one solution is to settle this and use the money to protect the habitat that hasn't been damaged."[13] Timber owners, native corporations and groups, fishermen, and environmental groups have begun to work together on this, although, ironically, the federal and state trustees appointed to oversee how the money will be spent seem somewhat reluctant.

"I'm not entirely pessimistic," says Rick over the phone to me in May 1992. "The public is leading the way. Now there is a bill before the Alaskan Senate to use 80 percent of the money the state got in criminal restitution to acquire threatened habitat, and there is a proposed section in the U.S. energy bill before Congress recommending similar usage."

It's a start, but there may be another controversy brewing. Under the settlement the money can be spent for "enhancement" as well as restoration. "Enhancement means construction projects," Sierra Club's associate Alaska representative is quoted as saying in the *Anchorage Daily News*. Some proponents of enhancement envision Prince William Sound as a huge playground with marinas and camp sites dotting the coastline, with easy access by road from Chitina.

Rick says, "The sound will recover, but not if clearcutting continues and the road and outfitters begin an accumulative attack on it. We may be at a boiling point again." It looks as if Rick's crusades have only just begun.

EPILOGUE

Reflections

ETHICS

Just before we said goodbye and he rowed away on the heaving surface of a recovering Prince William Sound, Rick Steiner's friend David Grimes asked rhetorically, "If I sneeze in Cordova, would it have any effect in Washington, D.C.?" We had been talking about the oil-spill settlement and he was wondering if he might influence the direction of U.S. policy from so far away. The subject of the butterfly effect came up, an aspect of "chaos" theory propounded by some physicists who hold that the world is interconnected in infinitely subtle, random ways. If a butterfly wing-flutter—presumably a random motion—can influence faraway events, what about conscious human acts? Assuming that humans are unique in their ability to perceive past, present, and future and to grasp the meaning of right and wrong, one can argue that David and I and every other individual on earth bear responsibility for the consequences of our actions. We should therefore accept, indeed, welcome, the burden of at least trying to bring about beneficent change. Over time, lesser people give up. Not so the people profiled in this book.

It is a burden Rick Steiner thought about a lot. "When the oil spill hit, all rules were off. We were instantly in a crisis-management mode and that's gone on almost two years, a window of time that now seems to be closing. Now we are into a new phase. I don't quite know what that is yet. Are we just rearranging chairs on the deck of the *Titanic* and polishing brass while the ship is sinking? Or can we repair the hull? Either a breakdown or a breakthrough is going to happen, and very soon.

"Maybe it doesn't matter if we do not last as a species. If what they say is true, that 99 percent of Earth's life has already gone extinct, maybe we are just part of that evolutionary progression."

Were Rick truly to believe this, he would not be the activist he is. He is not always so blue. He and the others have found, I think, that to realize their value as human beings, science is not enough. Almost in spite of themselves, each has become a conservation biologist.

Pat taught me how important it is to weigh and accommodate the development and societal goals of a nation and its people. Jonah showed me the ongoing relationship of humanity to nature, and how scientific knowledge along with an understanding of social change can influence management decisions and thereby benefit both human and nonhuman species. George took me from micro- to macrocosms, linking the saving of one egg to an understanding of the significance of regional and global conservation cooperation among nations that may otherwise be at odds. For me, Luis became a symbol of all thoughtful Costa Ricans working to stave off environmental apocalypse through two grand experiments, conducting a nationwide inventory of species and integrating land management with sustainability. Rick demonstrated how science can be used to influence local, state, and federal policies within an all-too-often cumbersome democratic framework.

Riki Ott, who holds a PhD in fisheries and oil pollution from the University of Washington, lives in Cordova, and owns her own 27-foot fishing boat, has thought a lot about the democratic process. She recalled the day of the oil spill as if were yesterday. "The press was everywhere [in Valdez]. Although lots of experts flew in soon afterwards, right then I was the most knowledgeable person around. The spill would impact my life. 'This is why I am a scientist,' I said to myself at the time. 'There's got to be such a thing as destiny.' " Now she lobbies for better pollution controls and fishermen's concerns generally. "Their bottom line is, 'Fix our problems with the oil companies, but don't paint us green.' " So that is what she does, as president of a group called the Oil Reform Alliance and as a board member of United Fishermen of Alaska.

Riki told me, "A professor in graduate school once said, 'Politics drives everything.' I didn't know what he meant. Now I do. Science is black and white until you try to apply it. Then it's politics. I'm an optimist about the process. I believe consumer pressure does work. It's *our* democracy. Let's *make* it work."

Her style of speaking reminded me of Pat Wright. From time to time the passion of their commitment shines through their scientific cool. I am drawn to that. They and all the others in this book are a new breed, it seems to me: scientists who are also politicians. Perhaps that is what conservation biology is all about. Theoretical science is useless to conservation unless it is applied, and often the process is political. They have all found themselves swept into "biopolitics," as it were, confronting the criticism that sometimes comes their way that they have thereby become less scientific. This is one of the risks they accept.

If their backgrounds are as varied as their places of origin, one thing they all had in common was supportive parents. Jonah's father took him hunting, and his mother tolerated his love for the bush as well as she was able, given the loss of her husband to a stampeding elephant. George's parents encouraged his interest in birds. Luis's mother let him keep tarantulas in his bedroom; his father took him exploring in the forest. Pat's parents conveyed a commitment to excellence, Rick's, a sense of public service.

Each one is something of a dreamer, certainly an impassioned advocate of his or her own cause. What they most have in common is tenacity. They say what they think and do what they believe in. They take risks, sometimes acting on incomplete data for lack of better information. This of course can also lead to criticism, but nature is not the well-ordered machine it was once thought to be. If the mechanisms ruling biological diversity are random, as ICF's wetland ecologist Jeb

Barzen and I considered, then conservationists must include randomness within their models, which no matter how carefully designed will be touched with ambiguity.

Each of these people has an extraordinary ability to befriend local people, to communicate, to generate trust. None will ever be rich. None will ever be especially famous. They are today's new breed of unsung public servant.

True public service is farsighted. The Gaia theory propounded by James Lovelock and Lynn Margulis in the late 1970s holds that the earth is a living organism, that life on earth is self-regulating and tends to find equilibrium. I believe—and this must be Lovelock and Margulis's point—that human impact on the natural world has become so potent that its capacity for self-regulation is now greatly diminished. How can we change our behavior to deal with this reality? One way is to do what Pat and Luis and the others here have—to lengthen our view of time. Corporations clock their activities from annual report to annual report. Politicians plan as far as the next election. Most parents worry about their children's future, to a much lesser extent about that of their grandchildren and their great-grandchildren. Yet if humanity hopes to be a successful, well-nourished species a hundred years or more from now, ethical attitudes and public policies must change to account for long-term consequences.

What is meant by conservation for biological diversity? Does it mean arranging future options so that the maximum number of species survives, or merely the most desirable species? Choices involve the degree of intervention permissible and require judgment calls about the value of certain species over others. A narrow view may lead to managing a wetland for cranes, not crawfish, to worrying about numbers of haddock, not about the benthic community on which they feed, to helping elephants but ignoring acacia trees. Playing God in a shrinking natural world is no easy task.

Reductionist ecology assumes natural systems are inherently stable and that all you have to do to maintain balance is manage individual species. "This is opposed to holism," Jonah said, "which for ecology means that there are emergent properties at higher levels, important codependent linkages, so that the individual species becomes less important than the role it plays. Instead of asking which species are missing, we should ask what roles are missing and, if they are missing, how we can recreate them."

Faced with wildlife-management choices in a world of increasingly fragmented natural landscapes, users and conservators are sometimes at odds over the meaning of the value of wildlife and wild places. There are two basic camps here, those who believe in species' intrinsic worth and those who consider their utilitarian worth. Intrinsic worth means that species are valuable in themselves, without human interpretation of their value. Utilitarian worth means species have value only insofar as they serve humankind (there being benign and not so benign forms of utilization—tourism versus harvesting or hunting, for example). These opposing views sometimes pit loggers against back-country campers, hungry farmers against preservationists. Sometimes they pit North against South—developed nations, many of whose well-off citizens view wild species, especially charismatic ones like elephants and lemurs, as having intrinsic worth, versus their developing-nation neighbors, whose people have few choices but to kill wild animals for food and to cut down forests for farmland and fuel.

"This is the real world," said Elinor Savage, biodiversity-treaty negotiator for the U.S. Department of State. Elinor was about to set off for the Earth Summit in Rio de Janeiro in June 1992 when I caught up with her. As the Earth Summit's principal product, a document called Agenda 21, affirms, in the real world most humans are users. The challenge is to find ways of not using up natural resources important to human well-being. As Jonah argued as far back as 1979, natural-area management requires "comprehensive planning to ensure the sustained profitability of the resource, which depends ultimately on reconciling the dilemma of use and preservation—a universal challenge that applies to all parks, whatever their objectives."[1]

Visiting Jonah, Pat, and later, Luis, I learned how wildlife and wild places in East Africa, Madagascar, and Costa Rica may have a future if they can be found to serve humanity directly by providing income (through products and tourism, for example), thus releasing money perhaps previously earmarked for conservation to other much-needed social amenities like schools and health care. This seems to me a practical response. While we are dealing with a multigenerational problem that spans all nature, such an approach addresses immediate economic needs and thus may delay deleterious human behavior long enough for new basic values about nature to emerge. People in poverty simply will not support conservation unless they see tangible returns. Who are we to tell them otherwise?

On the other hand, the intrinsic-worth-of-species view, while it may be a luxury of the well-to-do, is a good model for the management of biologically critical areas. If some degree of intrinsic value is not assigned to species other than humans, then the vast majority is at risk. Who is willing to defend algae or fungi? Luis, but he knows their functions and can explain how their roles are of instrumental value to the survival of species more obviously useful to humankind.

In *Rights of Nature* Roderick Nash discusses the possibility of an expansion of the human mind to achieve some sort of transcendent, cooperative environmental ethic.[2] There is no right or wrong in nature, some ecological ethicists believe, but given that the earth's carrying capacity for our own species is gravely threatened by our behavior and growing numbers, this view does not give us license to adopt a laissez-faire attitude as the earth theater plays out its scenes. As Nash suggests, what separates us from all other species is that we know our own behavior is altering the natural world. Self-awareness calls for responsible intervention.

How much intervention, and where and when, are the abiding questions. Elephant researcher Cynthia Moss would argue that fencing elephants out of Amboseli's swamp as Jonah has proposed smacks of too much interference. Changes occurring in the swamps and surrounding savannah "are not necessarily bad or good," she told me in Nairobi. "You can get caught up playing God. Who has the right to decide if there is a problem and what to do about it?" Jonah would say, to the contrary, that the consequences of doing nothing may be much worse. Sometimes radical attempts at timely conservation should be tried bravely, even if one's approach needs to be altered later as new facts emerge. Albeit with feet of clay, and cautiously, we humans can only try to do our best.

HARD QUESTIONS

Beside the Namorona River in Madagascar, while we laid our laundry out on sunny rocks to dry, researcher Adina Merenlender said, "What we do now will shape the biological diversity of the future. We are running out of time." Those who make decisions about how the natural world is to be treated in the coming decades may have to do so quickly. We laymen are going to have to trust these people, but we too have a responsibility—to become as informed as possible and thereby ensure that our trust is well placed.

Limited time is not the only problem. Limited space is another. Deforestation, whether in the tropics or along the coast of Alaska, creates mosaic landscapes, changes soil, raises temperatures, affects water flow in unpredictable ways. Whatever new ecological systems evolve as we continue to fragment the earth and limit spatial options available to wild species, scientists say they will probably be less diverse. What does this mean, I wonder, for economics, especially food production? For the fishermen of Cordova, the Amboseli Masai, the householders of Costa Rica and Madagascar, indeed, for the farmers of George Archibald's bountiful Wisconsin?

A third problem is the sheer weight of human numbers. Madagascar has a fledgling family-planning program, but has it come in time? Costa Rica has one too, but Costa Rica is mostly Catholic and the Vatican is opposed to even the simplest forms of mechanical or chemical birth control. In looking for consensus among competing national, religious, and ethnic interests, world leaders tend to avoid or water down references to human population governance.

Rick Steiner talked about another problem for conservation, human transience. "What that causes [in Western societies] is an abandonment of connection with place." Paraphrasing philosopher Edward Abbey, he said people who do not love the land do not guard it well. In non-Western countries, on the other hand, mobility (except for environmental and political refugees) is usually not an option. The people of Madagascar or Costa Rica and in many of the places where George's cranes may land during their migrations must learn to live sustainably where they are.

Conservationists and developers are in constant tension despite more than a decade of trying to define phrases like "wise use" and "sustainable development" to satisfy both sides. Not the least of the problem is that these phrases have different meanings for different folks living close together, fishermen and loggers, for example.

"Wise use" was first coined by conservationists to describe how natural resources can be managed sustainably to benefit the health of natural systems and the people in them. It has more recently also become a rallying cry for those who would use resources less benignly. In fact, today there is the so-called Wise Use Movement abroad in our land, a "network of at least 250 groups whose stated goals are to eliminate any governmental limitation on the exploitation of natural resources found on public land and to resist constraints on the use of private property."[3] These people would say wise use means draining a wetland to plant crops or clearcutting a forest regardless of the effect on the riparian habitat of fish, and that zoning and other regulations preventing such freedom of action are wrong. Conservation biologists do not agree, of course.

"Conservation has to meet basic human needs," George told me one day in his Baraboo office. "I have confidence the human race can meet that objective. Our key word around here is wise use. Population control and wise-use development. Beautiful birds don't fill bellies." By wise use, George means the sharing of renewable natural resources by wildlife and humans so that the well-being of both is assured. He and the others in this book are morally unable to deny fellow human beings such fundamental rights as freedom from want and hunger, yet they remain hopeful that through good science they can also continue to save wild species and ecosystems from overwhelming human predation. Indeed, pristine nature may sometimes have to be compromised for local human acquiescence to their cause. Humanity, after all, has its place in the natural equation.

If we fail to manage nature in an ecologically and economically balanced way, there is only one winner—the current generation. Even this generation may suffer later when it discovers future opportunities closed because the deforested watershed, the overfished ocean, and the drained wetland no longer produce the products on which their livelihoods depend. Finding livable solutions for people while ensuring that natural systems function healthily around them is the goal of the men and women in this book. Their hands-on field experiences have inevitably led them in this direction.

The tradeoffs are basically pragmatic and have to do with scale and time—how much and for how long, what constitutes inappropriate use and what does not. If maintaining functioning natural systems is a goal of conservation biology, then the humans who are undeniably a part of those systems must not overwhelm or misuse them. Their activities must somehow be integrated smoothly. How far conservationists should go to accommodate shorter- rather than longer-term human needs is the stuff of endless debate. Again, the issues are political. And in the end so are the solutions.

Isn't it provocative that the words *economics* and *ecology* have the same root, *eco-*, meaning "household" in Greek? I recall a conversation I had with Martha Rosemeyer as we talked about her work with Costa Rica's *ticos*. She longed for interdisciplinary cooperation among academics. "Biology only measures environmental problems, while social forces influence them," she said. More interdisciplinary thinking, for example between economics and human ecology, is needed if we are to achieve a holistic approach to solving problems. The edges of these disciplines and activities are inevitably blurred.

The people I interviewed, scientists first, have each learned how to be consummate politicians, like it or not. Jonah's intercession with the Kenya Wildlife Service on behalf of Amboseli's Masai, Pat's dealings with the Malagasy Ministry of Water and Forests and with U.S. funding sources to build her park, George's globetrotting rendezvous with heads of state and foreign scientists, Luis's networking, Rick's grassroots activism—all are forms of political involvement.

The political process we call democracy mandates public debate, presuming that the voices of the Masai tribesman, the Malagasy villager, the Vietnamese rice farmer, the Costa Rican *tico*, and the Cordovan fisherman, logger, and native will be heard. I worry about democracy's imperfections, however. Politicians more interested in votes than in good science often misuse, suppress, or ignore data. Competing constituencies compromise management decisions to the point of ineffectiveness. A hungry populace may someday vote to invade a protected park.

Does democracy only work well in situations where natural resources are abundant and economies strong? The democratic process requires an involved and educated citizenry, people with the luxury of time to organize, the capacity to express themselves, and the will to do so. This is much easier for people with full bellies. Whatever its shortcomings, the democratic format is the best we humans have devised. But it requires in addition to an informed and articulate citizenry the passage of adequate regulations and provisions for their enforcement by legislators of high purpose mindful of their constituents' long-term needs. For the environment, "national resolve is what matters," Jonah said once, and I agree. Democracy, prosperity, and the careful husbanding of nature's capital go hand in hand. None can exist without the others. Thus I fear for democracy as I fear for prosperity if our natural-resource base continues to be so heavily taxed.

SOME ANSWERS

Luis and Rick are not very sanguine about the future. They are willing to be more optimistic, however, *if* ethical attitudes can be changed, *if* human populations can be controlled so that they do not outstrip resources, and *if* we can devise ways to alleviate poverty while defending the natural-resource base. I spent many a late night with Pat, Jonah, George, Luis, and Rick considering ways to improve the chances for a longer-lasting, healthy planet. They gave me much to think about.

How do we instill in others a conservation ethic? Lacking time, we must initially be practical. To convince people it is in their immediate self-interest to protect a park, for example, they must be involved in its design and maintenance and see benefits accrue from it. The Masai are now meeting periodically with researchers and managers from the Kenya Wildlife Service to make decisions about Amboseli. This is a start. INBio is also a beginning, possibly a model for other nations to follow, at the very least a holding action to influence human behavior until a wider understanding of nature and our part in it evolves.

Aprenabrus in San Vito, the Science Center in Cordova, the Wildlife Clubs of Kenya, the International Crane Foundation, the Wilson Botanical Garden, and Ranomafana's tiny museum are all examples of local conservation-education efforts highlighting why and how natural areas or resources should be conserved. In these settings "ambassador" species—the elephant, the crane, the lemur—are helping influence attitudes even while utilitarianism remains the primary focus of the local people. Humans often respond sympathetically to the beauty of animals in natural settings. Indeed, direct-mail gurus in the United States have developed a sophisticated art of playing on such sympathies to raise money. Whatever one thinks of this form of fund-raising, it is effective and at the same time has helped inform the public about important conservation issues. Who has not heard of the plight of China's pandas, or of the shrinking world of Rwanda's few remaining mountain gorillas?

While conservation education in schools is vital to the future, so urgent is our need for immediate solutions that it must also reach adults, now. In Madagascar adults may be more interested in schools and health than in biodiversity, but the two are linked. Programs like those of OTS that bring decision-makers of numerous persuasions together, including corporate leaders, to consider such connections should be replicated elsewhere.

In a democracy conservation activists can and should organize and communicate from the bottom up, using existing infrastructures and creating new ones. This takes political will, which conservation education can encourage. And keeping a regional or even global perspective while acting locally helps one identify one's place in the "grander scheme." Friends of mine who attended the vast meeting of nongovernmental organizations in Rio, held while the Earth Summit was under way in June 1992, report that an almost overwhelming sense of community was generated there, regardless of differences in approach to solutions. Representatives of nascent conservation movements in developing countries were especially moved by this. Can the momentum be maintained? We must listen to them, as well as to indigenous people everywhere whose traditional relationship to land and wildlife is so different from our own. They can help us redefine our attitudes toward consumption.

How can we improve the scientific effort? A commitment to training and to encouraging a new generation of biologists to meet the demands of an increasingly complex science is essential to the future of conservation biology. Nowhere is mentoring more widely practiced than in science, as I saw during my stay with these people here, listening to their stories about how they got their start and how they continue the tradition. It is as if each has a placard on the refrigerator door proclaiming, "Teach by example! Teach by *being* an example." But it is not enough that INBio reaches down to train parataxonomists and coequals work to design and manage parks in Madagascar; the scientific constituency must be greatly expanded elsewhere. And as Martha Rosemeyer pointed out, "We must create interdisciplinary thinking, but there are not many models. Until now academia has functioned along disciplinary lines, but the problems don't behave that way."

One evening at Las Tablas I overheard Luis exhort some graduate students, "There is no distinction in my mind between conservation and science. They are complementary attitudes toward nature. . . . Pure science is a thing of the past—to just describe and inventory. We can't afford that any more. A scientist who doesn't commit time to conservation is doing science a disservice. We as scientists must change the ways of today into more sustainable ways by tomorrow. We cannot remain forever halfway committed, sort of doing it on the back seat." What I was hearing was this: Share data; combine disciplines; communicate; trust each other—the collective scientific voice is as wise as it is possible to be at this time and place. Playing God—making live-or-die choices between competing species, for example—cannot be fun, yet playing God is what much conservation biology is about. Don't worry that the distinction between pure and applied research is blurred. Conservation biology is a synthesis of many forms. As problems in the environment grow more acute, biology will inevitably link with other disciplines, then link again, through politics, with all the actors from powerful decision-makers down to peasants.

In the future, protected-area management should be based on these new principles in order to conserve biological diversity *and* to meet society's needs, in order to preserve as many viable fragments of habitats and ecosystems as we can. As we have seen, Costa Rica recently established seven national conservation areas, each with a core composed of established parks and wilderness areas and a surrounding "zone of influence." The cores will be managed for ecosystem perpetuity and biodiversity; the zones of influence will be managed for the sustainable use of natural resources. Local communities will participate in decisions affecting their own area, scientific research will be integrated as part of management decisions, and private-sector funding will be sought. A single government entity will manage all the protected areas, eliminating considerable bureaucratic confusion and divisiveness.

This innovative plan involves broad vision on the part of Costa Rica's leaders, what Jonah referred to as national resolve. It involves understanding bioregional roles more clearly—how careful logging or even denial of a logging permit upstream may improve fishing far out at sea, for example, although the benefits do not necessarily accrue directly to those practicing or directly affected by the conservation measures.

I came home from my trips with a new appreciation for the importance, finally, of national population strategies. One obstacle is that some developing nations see suggested limits to population growth as a new form of imperialism imposed by the haves on the have-nots. Such concerns must somehow be dispelled. Perhaps the new sense of community generated at Rio will help.

CREDO

It is all very well to talk about transforming ethics and improving science and implementing better land-use planning and population strategies, but how do we get these jobs done? There are many paths. Money is at issue, of course, and will always limit what can be done. But in the end it is people who will make the difference. Are my five friends having an impact? I would say unequivocably yes, each in his or her own way, on his or her own turf. But for every Pat, Jonah, George, Luis, and Rick, we need thousands more like them. We others, perhaps less trained or skilled, must learn to listen to and apply their knowledge well, for they are our experts, among the best there are. And we must remember that each of us can do more than we have been.

Years ago I used to read my children a favorite Dr. Seuss book, *Horton Hears a Who,* the story of an elephant named Horton who discovers quite by accident that on a tiny speck of dust lives a teeming population of "Whos." Horton's battle to convince the other animals that microscopic life exists on that speck and that it should be saved is told in delightful rhyme and with tremendous urgency. The Whos try to save themselves by crying out, "We are here! We are here! We are here!" at the top of their lungs, to no avail.

Then at the very last moment, when the smallest member of their species adds his minute voice to their desperate cry, they are heard. Apocalypse is avoided and the Whos are saved. A fairy tale? I hope not.

Notes

PROLOGUE

1. U.S. National Research Council report, National Academy of Sciences, quoted in *Earth Summit Times* (March 5, 1992).
2. John Ryan, "Conserving Biological Diversity," in *State of the World 1992*, Worldwatch Institute (New York: Norton, 1992).
3. Global biodiversity strategy fact sheet, World Resources Institute, World Conservation Union, United Nations Environment Program, February 1992.
4. J. Joseph Speidel, president of the Population Crisis Committee, letter to author, October 26, 1990.
5. Peter Berle, "How Do We Define Nature?" reprinted from *Audubon* (May–June 1991).
6. Aldo Leopold, *Game Management* (New York: Charles Scribner's Sons, 1933), 21.
7. Michael E. Soulé and Kathryn A. Kohm, eds., *Research Priorities for Conservation Biology* (Washington, D.C.: Island Press, 1989), 1.

CHAPTER 1

1. Alison Jolly, "The Madagascar Challenge: Human Needs and Fragile Ecosystems," M. Jeffrey Leonard et al., *Development Strategies for a Common Agenda* (New Brunswick, N.J.: Transaction Books, 1989), 193.
2. Ibid.
3. Russell Mittermeier, "Strange and Wonderful Madagascar," *International Wildlife* 18, no. 4 (July–August 1988): 6.
4. Roderic Mast, director Madagascar program, Conservation International, personal comment, April 1991.
5. "Lemurs of Madagascar and the Comoros," IUCN Red Data Book, 1990.
6. Jolly, "Madagascar Challenge," 199.
7. Alison Jolly, "Madagascar: A World Apart," *National Geographic* 171, no. 2 (February 1987): 148.
8. "World Conservation Strategy: Living Resource Conservation for Sustainable Development," IUCN, WWF, UNEP, 1980, section 3.
9. Bernhard Meier, Patricia Wright, et al., "A New Species of Hapalemur (Primates) from South East Madagascar," *Folio Primatological Separatum* 48 (1987): 211.
10. Bob Wilson, "Promoting a Preserve for Primates," *Duke*, Duke University, (January–February 1989): 8.
11. Adina Merenlender, University of Rochester, personal comment.
12. Department of State telegram SHB 3228, 21 May 1991.

CHAPTER 2

1. David Western, "Amboseli," *Swara*, East African Society, 5, no. 4 (July–August 1982): 13.
2. David Western, "Dynamic Approach to Amboseli Ecology," *African Wildlife News* 6, no. 2 (December 1971): 1.
3. W. K. Lindsay, "Integrating Parks and Pastoralists," eds. David Anderson and Richard Grove, *Conservation in Africa: People, Policies and Practice* (Cambridge, England: Cambridge University Press, 1987), 153.
4. Ibid, 150.
5. David Western, "The Ecology of Tourists," *Animal Kingdom* (December–January 1977–78): 30.
6. Western, "Dynamic Approach to Amboseli Ecology," 6.
7. David Western, "Proposals for an Amboseli Game Park," Institute for Development Studies, University College, Nairobi, staff paper, no. 53, 1969.
8. David Western and Wesley Henry, "Economics and Conservation in Third World National Parks," *BioScience* (July 1979): 417.
9. Lindsay, "Integrating Parks," 157.

10. David Western, "Africa's Elephants and Rhinos: Flagships in Crisis," *Tree* 2 no. 11 (November 1987): 346.
11. Janet Bohlen, "Africa's Ivory Wars," *Defenders* (March–April 1989): 13.
12. David Western, "An African Odyssey to Save the Elephants," *Discover* 7, no. 10 (October 1986): 68.
13. Nicholas Georgiadis, John Patton, and David Western, "DNA and the Ivory Trade: How Genetics Can Help Conserve Elephants," Elephant Ivory Information Service, no. 12 (1990): 6.
14. "Ivory Poached? Moi?" The *Economist* (October 13, 1990).
15. David Western and Helen Gichohi, Kitengela Conservation Project synopsis, January 1991.

CHAPTER 3

1. Jon R. Luoma, "Born to be Wild," *Audubon* (January–February 1992): 54.
2. Aldo Leopold, *A Sand Country Almanac* (London: Oxford University Press, 1949), 96.
3. Gretchen Holstein Schoff, *Reflections: The Story of Cranes* (Baraboo, Wis.: ICF, 1991), 36–37.
4. Ibid.
5. Ibid.
6. William K. Stevens, "Efforts to Halt Wetland Loss," the *New York Times*, March 1, 1990.
7. EPA wetlands protection hotline, quoting an FWS 1990 report to Congress, "Wetlands Losses in the U.S., 1780s–1980s."

CHAPTER 4

1. Ree Strange Sheck, *Costa Rica: A Natural Destination* (Santa Fe: John Muir Publications, 1990), 6.
2. Luis Diego Gómez, "The Conservation of Biological Diversity: The Case of Costa Rica in the Year 2000," eds. Frank Almeda and Catherine M. Pringle, *Tropical Rain Forests, Diversity and Conservation* (San Francisco: California Academy of Sciences and Pacific Division, AAAS, 1988).
3. Rodrigo Gámez and Alvaro Ugalde, "Costa Rica's National Park System and the Preservation of Biological Diversity: Linking Conservation with Socio-Economic Development," in Almeda and Pringle, *Tropical Rain Forests.*
4. Gómez, "Conservation of Biological Diversity."
5. Sheck, *Costa Rica*, 25.
6. Bruce A. Wilcox, "Insular Ecology and Conservation," eds. Michael E. Soulé and Bruce A. Wilcox, *Conservation Biology: An Evolutionary-Ecological Perspective* (Sunderland, Mass.: Sinauer Associates, Inc., 1980), 95–117.
7. Ibid.

8. World Resources Institute, "Executive Summary," *The Global Biodiversity Strategy* (Baltimore: World Resources Institute Publications, 1992), 3.

CHAPTER 5

1. Lisa Drew, "Truth and Consequences Along Oiled Shores," *National Wildlife*, June–July 1990.
2. *Bangor Daily News* (AP), July 23, 1991.
3. The *Washington Post*, February 21, 1991.
4. Ibid., June 27, 1991.
5. The *Anchorage Daily News*, August 22, 1990.
6. Richard E. Rice, *The Uncounted Costs of Logging*, volume 5 of *National Forests Policies for the Future* (Washington, D.C.: The Wilderness Society, 1989), viii.
7. Joseph R. Mehrkens, "The Proposed California Forest Practices Act and Streamside Buffers" (Juneau: The Southeast Alaska Natural Resources Center, 15 April 1991).
8. David S. Wilcove, *Protecting Biological Diversity*, volume 2 of *National Forests Policies for the Future* (1988), v.
9. Jerry Mander, *In the Absence of the Sacred* (San Francisco: Sierra Club Books, 1991), 287.
10. Thomas R. Berger, *Village Journey: The Report of the Alaska Native Review Commission* (New York: Hill and Wang, 1985), 20.
11. Berger, *Village Journey*, 7.
12. Mander, *Absence of the Sacred*, 292.
13. The *Anchorage Daily News*, October 1, 1991.

EPILOGUE

1. David Western and Wesley Henry, "Economics and Conservation in Third World National Parks," *BioScience* 29, no. 7 (July 1979): 418.
2. Roderick Frasier Nash, *Rights of Nature: A History of Environmental Ethics* (Madison, Wis.: University of Wisconsin Press, 1989).
3. *Alaska Conservation Foundation Dispatch* (Summer 1992), 2.

Glossary

Agroecology. The biology of relationships among organisms in a farmed environment. Helpful in determining how to manage farmland sustainably.

Austral. Southern. Among biologists and botanists in the western hemisphere, it refers to species of South American origin. "Boreal" refers to species of North American origin.

Benthic. Adjective derived from the noun, *benthos*, meaning sea-bottom-dwelling flora and fauna.

Biological diversity, or biodiversity. The entire array of animal and plant life that makes up interactive communities of species within ecosystems. Biodiversity can also be measured in terms of multiple habitats or ecosystem types.

Biomass. A dry-weight measure of living and sometimes dead biologic tissue.

Biome. A broadscale division of landscape into areas having similar vegetation because of their local geographic condition and climate.

Bioregion. An area greater than an ecosystem or a landscape and involving processes such as water currents and weather patterns.

Biosphere reserve. Land or water areas selected by UNESCO as being representative of important biomes, thus deserving ongoing protection and wise management. Can and usually does include human-occupied as well as pristine areas.

Buffer zone. Specified land adjacent to protected areas where, under park-management plans, limited or full human exploitation of the land is allowed provided resource use is sustainable.

Clearcut. A particular stand or area where all the trees are cut.

Conservation biology. Research directed toward solving conservation problems in order to slow the loss of biological diversity. Conservation biologists hope to anticipate, prevent, minimize, and/or repair ecological damage.

Dispersion. The process whereby species spread from one location to another. "Random dispersion" refers to the unpredictable ways in which these movements are likely to occur, and the consequences.

Disturbance regime. Foreign factors introduced into and changing a given landscape.

Ecology. The study of how organisms interact with each other and with their surroundings.

Ecosystem. A broad geographic area sometimes given artificial boundaries for scientific clarity, for example, a forest, lake, desert, river, swamp, ocean, or part thereof.

Endemic. Describing species unique to a location.

Gaia. From the Greek word for Earth goddess. Modern theory holding that the planet is a living organism.

Holism. In ecology, the study of links among species and conditions. See Reductionism.

Human ecology. The science of humanity's relationship to nature.

Imprinting. The process of identifying with one's own species or, on occasion, with a substitute species.

Incidental take. The usually inadvertent killing of nontarget species in the pursuit of a target species. Marine mammals that become entangled in fishing nets are one example.

Indigenous. Describing species native to a specific location but also existing elsewhere.

Instrumentalism. See Utilitarianism.

Intrinsic worth. The notion that a species has value solely because it exists.

Island biogeography. The biology of isolated ecosystems. Also called insular ecology.

Keystone species. A species whose presence or absence in an ecosystem affects many other species in important ways.

Landscape. A broader area than an ecosystem, for example, a watershed whose components are rainfall, hillside, lake, river, and ocean.

Malagasy. The people and language of Madagascar.

Maximum sustainable yield. The limits beyond which a species should not be harvested lest the resulting reduction in its numbers threaten its healthy participation in its environment.

Megadiversity. The biological condition of certain areas of the world believed to contain the richest mix and highest number of species.

Minimum viable population. The lowest total number of a species beyond which extinction becomes a real possibility.

Modeling. In science, the attempt to reduce the complexity of the real world to a mathematical or computer formula. Models help scientists analyze the consequences of certain actions and sometimes help predict the future. Ecological models are usually based on data relating to the controlling mechanisms in a defined time and space.

Monoculture. Cultivation of a single species (of tree, for example) to the exclusion of others.

Primary forest. A forest that has never been altered by humans. A secondary forest is one that grows after an area has been cut or otherwise cleared and then either replanted or left to its own devices to regenerate.

Prosimian. A primitive form of primate that evolved before monkeys and apes and whose remaining members are lemurs, bush babies, pottos, and lorises.

Reductionism. Theory that all material can be reduced to a sum of its parts, hence analyzed part by part. In ecology, this can lead to a species-by-species approach to conservation.

Reintroduction. The placement of captive-bred animals in wild habitats of which their ancestors were once a part, or in wild habitats similar to the original ones. Sometimes a species will have been entirely extirpated from a location; sometimes a few wild members of their kind will still be present.

Restoration ecology. A technique used by ecosystem site managers to guide ecological processes in desired directions based on the best scientific knowledge of their time. Restoration of an ecosystem is often undertaken in the hopes of reviving its historic biological diversity, but usually at best ecological restoration can only simulate historic "nature."

Speciation. Evolutionary process by which species are formed or by which variations in a species become fixed.

Succession. Ecological events (such as species replacement) following one after another, many of which occur randomly and cannot be accurately predicted.

Utilitarianism. Theory that a species has value only insofar as it is useful to humans.

References

Almeda, Frank, and Catherine M. Pringle, eds. *Tropical Rain Forests, Diversity and Conservation*. San Francisco: California Academy of Sciences and the Pacific Division, AAAS, 1988.

Anderson, David, and Richard Grove, eds. *Conservation in Africa: People, Policies and Practice*. Cambridge: Cambridge University Press, 1987.

Berger, Thomas R. *Village Journey: The Report of the Alaska Native Review Commission*. New York: Hill and Wang, 1985.

Chase, Alston. *Playing God in Yellowstone*. New York: Harcourt Brace Jovanovich, 1987.

Davidson, Art. *In the Wake of the* Exxon Valdez. San Francisco: Sierra Club Books, 1990.

DeBlieu, Jan. *Meant to Be Wild*. Golden, Colo.: Fulcrum, 1991.

Gleick, James. *Chaos: Making a New Science*. New York: Penguin, 1987.

Leonard, M. Jeffrey, et al., eds. *Development Strategies for a Common Agenda*. New Brunswick, N.J.: Transaction Books, 1989.

Leopold, Aldo. *A Sand Country Almanac*. London: Oxford University Press, 1949.

Mander, Jerry. *In the Absence of the Sacred*. San Francisco: Sierra Club Books, 1991.

McNeely, Jeffrey A. *Economics and Biological Diversity*. Gland, Switzerland: IUCN, 1988.

Nash, Roderick Frasier. *Rights of Nature: A History of Environmental Ethics*. Madison, Wis.: University of Wisconsin Press, 1989.

Ryan, John. "Conserving Biological Diversity." In Worldwatch Institute's *State of the World 1992*. New York: Norton, 1992.

Sheck, Ree Strange. *Costa Rica: A Natural Destination*. Santa Fe: John Muir, 1990.

Soulé, Michael E., and Kathryn A. Kohm, eds. *Research Priorities for Conservation Biology*. Washington, D.C.: Island Press, 1989.

Soulé, Michael E., and Bruce A. Wilcox, eds. *Conservation Biology: An Evolutionary-Ecological Perspective*. Sunderland, Mass.: Sinauer, 1980.

Western, David, and Mary Pearl. *Conservation for the Twenty-first Century*. London: Oxford University Press, 1989.

Wilderness Society. *National Forests Policies for the Future*, volumes 2 and 5. Washington, D.C.: Wilderness Society, 1988 and 1989.

Index

About the Author

Janet Trowbridge Bohlen is a travel and environmental writer who has worked as a writer-editor and communications director for the African Wildlife Foundation and World Wildlife Fund. She and her husband, E. U. Curtis Bohlen, divide their time between Washington, D.C., and the Eastern Shore of Maryland, where they have a small farm. They have three grown children with whom they have shared many backpacking, sailing, and skiing adventures. This is her first book.

ALSO AVAILABLE FROM ISLAND PRESS

Balancing on the Brink of Extinction: The Endangered Species Act and Lessons for the Future
Edited by Kathryn A. Kohm

Better Trout Habitat: A Guide to Stream Restoration and Management
By Christopher J. Hunter

The New Complete Guide to Environmental Careers
By The Environmental Careers Organization

Crossing the Next Meridian: Land, Water, and the Future of the West
By Charles F. Wilkinson

Death in the Marsh
By Tom Harris

The Energy-Environment Connection
Edited by Jack M. Hollander

Farming in Nature's Image
By Judith Soule and Jon Piper

Ghost Bears: Exploring the Biodiversity Crisis
By R. Edward Grumbine

The Global Citizen
By Donella Meadows

Green at Work: Making Your Business Career Work for the Environment
By Susan Cohn

Healthy Homes, Healthy Kids
By Joyce Schoemaker and Charity Vitale

Holistic Resource Management
By Allan Savory

The Island Press Bibliography of Environmental Literature
By The Yale School of Forestry and Environmental Studies

Last Animals at the Zoo: How Mass Extinction Can Be Stopped
By Colin Tudge

Learning to Listen to the Land
Edited by Bill Willers

The Living Ocean: Understanding and Protecting Marine Biodiversity
By Boyce Thorne-Miller and John G. Catena

Nature Tourism: Managing for the Environment
Edited by Tensie Whelan

Not by Timber Alone
By Theodore Panayotou and Peter S. Ashton

Our Country, The Planet: Forging a Partnership for Survival
By Shridath Ramphal

Overtapped Oasis: Reform or Revolution for Western Water
By Marc Reisner and Sarah Bates

Rain Forest in Your Kitchen: The Hidden Connection Between Extinction and Your Supermarket
By Martin Teitel

The Snake River: Window to the West
By Tim Palmer

Spirit of Place
By Frederick Turner

Taking Out the Trash: A No-Nonsense Guide to Recycling
By Jennifer Carless

Turning the Tide: Saving the Chesapeake Bay
By Tom Horton and William M. Eichbaum

Visions Upon the Land: Man and Nature on the Western Range
By Karl Hess, Jr.

The Wilderness Condition
Edited by Max Oelschlaeger

For a complete catalog of Island Press publications, please write:
Island Press, Box 7, Covelo, CA 95428, or call: 1-800-828-1302